D1642459

Nostalgic Angels:
Rearticulating Hypertext Writing

Johndan Johnson-Eilola
Purdue University

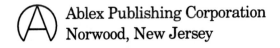
Ablex Publishing Corporation
Norwood, New Jersey

Material on page 40 reprinted from *Imperial Eyes: Travel Writing and Transculturation,* by Mary Louise Pratt (1992), with permission of the publisher, Routledge, New York.

Material on page 87 reprinted from "The Case for Hypergradesheets: A Modest Proposal" *College English 54*(1): 25–26. Copyright 1992 by the National Council of Teachers of English. Reprinted with permission.

Printed in the United States of America

Library of Congress Cataloging-in-Publication Data

Johnson-Eilola, Johndan.
    Nostalgic angels : rearticulating hypertext writing / Johndan
Johnson-Eilola.
    p.   cm. -- (New directions in computers and composition
studies)
    ISBN 1-56750-280-6. -- ISBN 1-56750-281-4 (pbk.)
    1. Hypertext systems.   I. Title.   II. Series.
QA76.76.H94J63   1996
808--dc21
                                                            96-46981
                                                                CIP

Ablex Publishing Corporation
355 Chestnut Street
Norwood, New Jersey 07648

Cover design by Anne Wysocki

Contents

Acknowledgments

I am not one in this. I thank

Cindy Selfe, for never asking simple questions;
Stuart Selber, for never offering simple answers;
Marilyn Cooper, for helping me find answers;
Kelly Johnson-Eilola and Carolyn Eilola, for listening to answers;
Dan and Aileen Eilola, for not asking questions; and
an anonymous reviewer, for asking questions without answers.

In addition, an almost innumerable number of people have read and commented on or discussed various sections or versions of this text with me:

Jim Porter,   Jennifer Slack,
Max Seel,   Stuart Moulthrop, and
Pat Sullivan,   Martin Rosenberg.
Carole Yee,

Finally (and not the least), many people have provided me with material in print or hypertext and contributed enormously to this work:

Michael Joyce,   Anne Wysocki,
John McDaid,   Mark Bernstein,
Mary Hocks,   Rex Clark,
Nancy Kaplan,   Bill Klein,
Martin Rosenberg,   Richard Bolt,
George Landow,   Ted Nelson, and
Ann Greene,   Carolyn Guyer,
Martha Petry,

Thank you.

Within our common language, in a particular country, we can be conscious of social differences, or of differences of age, but in the main we use the same words for most everyday things and activities, though with obvious variations of rhythm and accent and tone. Some of the variable words, say *lunch* and *supper* and *dinner*, may be highlighted but the differences are not particularly important. When we come to say "we just don't speak the same language," we mean something more general: that we have different immediate values or different kinds of valuation, or that we are aware, often intangibly, of different formations and distributions of energy and interest. In such a case, each group is speaking its native language, but its uses are significantly different, and especially when strong feelings or important ideas are in question. No single group is "wrong" by any linguistic criterion, though a temporarily dominant group may try to enforce its own uses as "correct." What is really happening through these critical encounters, which may be very conscious or may be felt only as a certain strangeness and unease, is a process quite central in the development of a language when, in certain words, tones and rhythms, meanings are offered, felt for, tested, confirmed, asserted, qualified, changed.

—Raymond Williams (1983, p.13)

Chapter 1

Border Times:
Writing and Being Written
in Hypertext

On the other side of our data gloves, we become creatures of colored light in motion, pulsing with golden particles. Forget about Andy Warhol's petty promise of fame for fifteen minutes. We will all become angels, and for eternity! Highly unstable, hermaphrodite angels, unforgettable in computer memory.

—Nicole Stenger (1991, p. 52)

Everything is metamorphosed into its inverse in order to be perpetuated in its purged form. Every form of power, every situation speaks of itself by denial, in order to escape, by simulation of death, its real agony. Power can stage its own murder to rediscover a glimmer of existence and legitimacy....

To seek new blood in its own death, to renew the cycle by the mirror of crisis, negativity, and anti-power: this is the only alibi of every power, of every institution attempting to break the vicious circle of its irresponsibility and its fundamental non-existence, of its deja-vu and its deja-mort.

—Jean Baudrillard (1982, p. 37)

Writing has always been about borders, about the processes of mapping and remapping the lines of separation between things. Writing constructs implicit and explicit boundaries between not only product and process and said and unsaid, but author and reader, literacy and orality, technology and nature, self and other. Although we often build these borders in order to help us assert a disciplinary identity, these same borders also threaten to marginalize us. In this book, I illustrate the difficulties of our border constructions— and the potential for change—through the primary example of hypertext, a computer-supported technology for writing and reading that has gained broad use over the last 10 years. Composition has constructed (and allowed the construction of) borders around a scant handful of specific forms of hypertext, declaring other, more culturally popular forms of hypertext out of

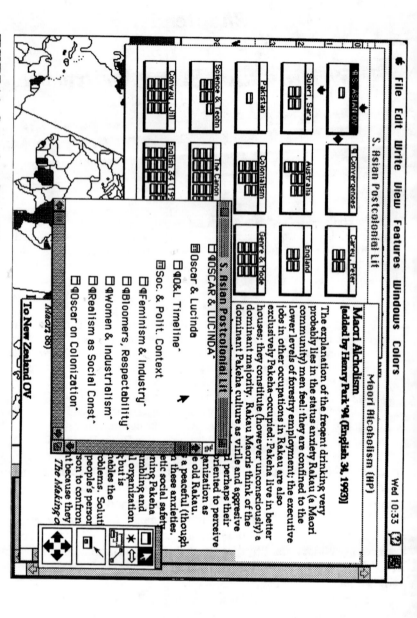

FIGURE 1.1. Screen from CONTEXT34.

4

bounds. In this mapping, compositionists think and work with "traditional" texts (first-person essays, literature and literary criticism, argumentative papers, and the like), whereas other disciplines work with "mundane" texts (online documentation, databases, and informal notes passed from person to person). English faculty and students at Brown University reconstruct historical and present contexts and relations around postcolonial literary texts (Figure 1.1). Technical communicators design a functional text that helps people navigate a large information space quickly and find information needed in order to use a word-processing program (Figure 1.2). Hypertext *is* writ-

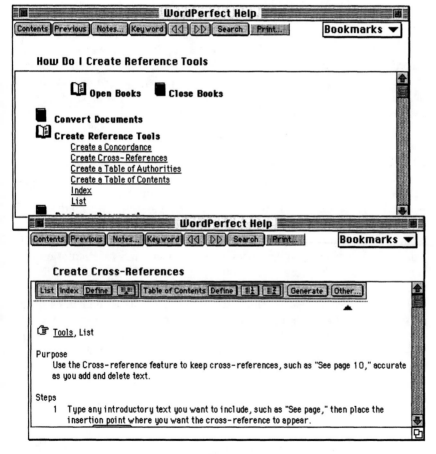

FIGURE 1.2. Functional hypertext online help in WORDPERFECT 3.0A.

ing and reading, and we should understand by now that there are many forms and functions of literacy, each involving different social positions and responsibilities (Selber, 1995b). However, we should also understand that these positions and responsibilities do not inhere in isolated texts and literacy technologies but also in social situations constructing the writing and reading of those texts. It is foolhardy to celebrate one type of text as automatically and necessarily liberatory and deride or ignore the rest, as we in composition often do. Those "other" texts, the ones we allow to pass without critical attention because we think they are purely functional or lacking in imagination, may in fact be our ways of leveraging broad social changes. Unless we are able to rearticulate our definitions of writing—both to ourselves and to the world at large—we risk increased marginalization in a world already moving beyond conventional, print-based textuality.

Furthermore, we must reject hierarchical structures that place creative writing (fiction or nonfiction) in high status and functional writing (instructions, databases) in low status. At the same time, we must avoid the common inversion of this hierarchy in the way of those who value texts only according to technical efficiency and simple usability, divorced from broader contexts. If we want our work to gain broader cultural relevancy, we must question and remake the currently existing borders separating composition studies from these other productions and uses of text.

Compositionists are beginning to take seriously items such as journals, drafts, and collaboratively authored works, but we need to greatly expand on this start, to include topics and contexts such as online documentation and databases—these things we think of as *tools*, a term that unfortunately downplays their deep implications for our ways of living in the world. These tools are actually texts—maps that suggest and validate ways of thinking and acting; they are not isolated artifacts. The invisibility of tools, in fact, sometimes constitutes important aspects of their power. In this book, I examine the processes of articulation and rearticulation concerning one specific literacy technology, hypertext. This particular discussion can also suggest similar operations in relation to other technologies.

In my concern for border construction and deconstruction runs a parallel theme, a concern about postmodernist tendencies in contemporary society. In particular, this theme is important to the idea of questioning existing disciplinary borders because of the ways in which postmodernist approaches call into question ideas about artistic creativity and distinctions between high culture (essays, literature) and low culture (users manuals, databases). But as many compositionists are discovering, although postmodernist perspectives can help us contest hierarchy and oppression, the same movements sometimes become ways of dismissing agency and reason (see, among others, Downing, Harkin, & Sosnoski, 1994; Ebert, 1991; Faigley, 1992). Whatever other cultural functions they served (hegemonies of racism, sexism, and elitism, to name but three), universal truths provided apparent anchors for locating ourselves and directing our actions. Postmodernism denies the foundational truths on which many of us learned to stand. In its most extreme manifestations, postmodernism does not appear to provide even contingent sites from which we might enact positive social change. So along with other theorists and teachers of writing, my own history has moved through postmodernism and into cultural studies and critical pedagogy. These approaches can help us to understand the complex and often contradictory process by which borders are constructed, to deconstruct those borders, and—perhaps most importantly—to rearticulate new, positive mappings. In this process, composition can become truly interdisciplinary and productively intertextual, working across and within the multiple discourses in which we all write and are written.

In this book, then, I take *composition* to mean something much broader than it currently does to many of us: not only traditional argumentation and prose style, but also the writing and reading of online documentation, the construction and use of vast online databases, and the electronic messages sent back and forth between participants in electronic discussions on bulletin boards, local area networks, and the Internet. The growth of these technologies requires us to rethink what we mean by composition. We cannot merely add these technologies to our classrooms and theories as tools with which our students arrive at their primary task (a common stance); we must take these forms of communication to be at least as important (and often more culturally relevant) than singly authored papers arguing a single, clear point forcefully over the course of five, neatly typed, double-spaced pages. This narrow focus was helpful historically for composition in defining itself against a range of other disciplines and academic departments; today, however, we must expand our definitions to gain broader influence and relevance.

The focus on redefining composition motivates the selection of hypertext as the topic of my study. Here we have (and have constructed) a literacy technology of both relatively recent origin and rapid acceptance and reconstruction. The depth, breadth, and speed at which the technology has been rearticulated by differing groups makes it an important analytical topic. Hypertext provides vivid examples of the ways in which the activities of writing and reading are transformed and appropriated by widely divergent communities, each of which reconstructs general characteristics of hypertext in relationship to that community's goals. Hypertext, like every other text and technology, is a *social* technology. However, rather than acknowledging the partial, overlapping, and contingent nature of these social histories, each community naturalizes and mystifies the technology, making invisible the ways in which every hypertext is constructed in a web of institutional forces acting as a form of nostalgia. Those features of the technology that are most alien encourage us to think happily back to our old lives, to rearticulate new technologies to function like old ones. Bolter, interested in the historical and present spaces engendered by literacy technologies, enacts a type of hypertext that straddles print and electronic cultures, showing how each technology influences and interferes with the other (as well as how he, as writer, and we, as readers, both affect and are affected by the text; Figure 1.3). Reform-minded writing teachers Guyer and Petry (1991b) used hypertext as a feminist method that can help them "deconstruct priority," to speak of complex and partial visions, and to prevent closure (Figure 1.4). Librarians, quickly embracing online access, articulate

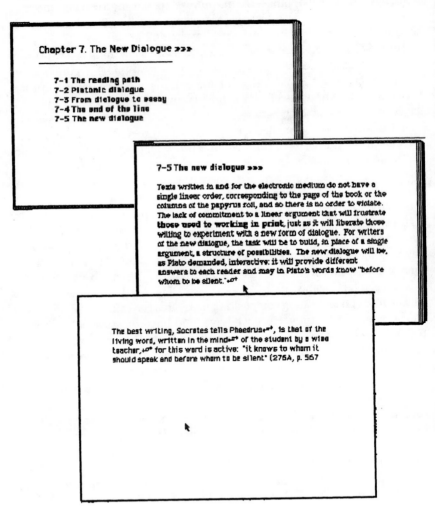

FIGURE 1.3. Screens from Bolter's (1991a) Hypertext version of WRITING SPACE.

hypertext as a card catalog (Figure 1.5). By necessity, we must negotiate a technology in relationship to our histories.

But isolated communities do not completely determine the form and operations of any technology because communities are rarely, if ever, isolated in a strict sense. In the first place, technological systems—considered broadly to include not only a discrete object but also the sprawling systems of design, manufacturing, distribution, and marketing—are too complex to be described by simple cause–effect relationships. In the second place, every technology user operates (constructs and is constructed) across numerous discourses. No single person is ever written by or writes only

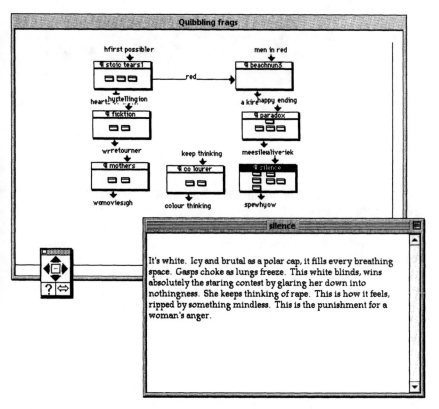

FIGURE 1.4. Screens from Guyer and Petry's IZME PASS.

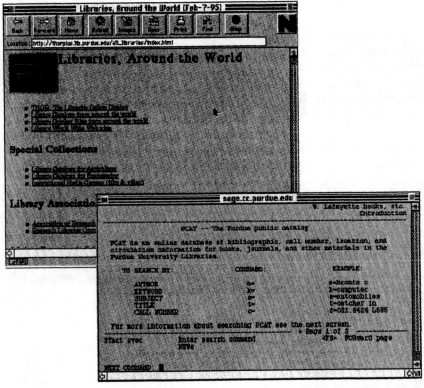

FIGURE 1.5. Online library resources available through Purdue University's Web page.

one, isolated context. The different discourses of hypertext I discuss here are not all-or-nothing affairs, but weighted aspects and tendencies. So although I argue in Chapter 3 that most existing functional hypertext validates a mechanistic, reductive approach to communication, these same texts still always potentially allow users spaces in which to act against the interests of the mechanical model—learning the system in order to work against it, for example. Conversely, in Chapter 5, I show that although collaborative hypertext environments can encourage ideas of intertextuality and revised notions of authority, such systems sometimes also reinforce conventional ideas about authorial identity and creativity by automatically attributing specific nodes to specific, discrete individuals. So whereas each specific articulation (both concretely and socially) tends to encourage some uses over others, we can also productively examine and rearticulate the technology along lines of weaker (often unacknowledged) forces. Hints about the multiple nature of any hypertext can be seen in Joyce's (1990)

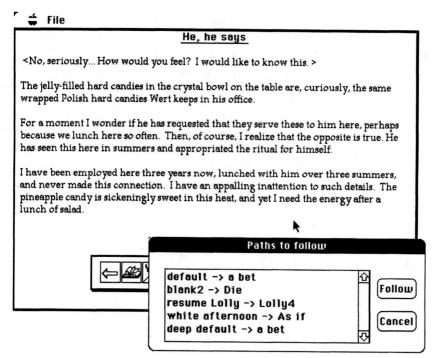

FIGURE 1.6. Joyce's hypertext novel, AFTERNOON, A STORY.

famous postmodern hypertext, AFTERNOON, A STORY. AFTERNOON pointedly questions authorial intention, unified meaning, and the conventional idea of what constitutes a novel (Figure 1.6). At the same time, this hypertext is articulated in some ways as functional text, speaking to readers in the simple, apparently unambiguous, single-voiced phrases of online documentation (Figure 1.7).

The differences among each of these multiple discourses of hypertext I discuss in this book—functional documentation, databases, literature, composition—represent both opportunity and danger. When any discourse is successful in naturalizing its own operations (i.e., of hiding its interests), the discourse operates in a repressive manner. At the same time, the always-present overlaps and contradictions implicit in the operations of these discourses open the opportunity for demystification, collaboration, resistance, and rearticulation.

By considering hypertexts of *all* types as specific constructions of the general instance of composition,[1] we can increase our critical understand-

---

[1] "General" should not be confused here with "essence": There is no single true type of hypertext, but only multiple constructions (which is the point of this book).

---

a hypertext

This story is created with STORYSPACE, a hypertext program which is both an author's tool and a reader's medium.

• You move through the text by pressing the Return key to go from one section to another
(i.e., "turn pages"); and you click the Back arrow (on the bar below) to go back ("page back");

or

• You double-click on certain words to follow other lines of the story. Window titles often confirm words which yield.

The story exists at several levels and changes according to decisions you make. A text you have seen previously may be followed by something new, according to a choice you make or already have made during any given reading.

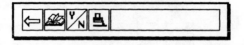

FIGURE 1.7. Functional instructions from AFTERNOON, A STORY.

ing of the ways in which technological systems are constructed from place to place and across time (including not only the concrete mechanics but also ways of acting and thinking in the world). The hypertext currently popular in online documentation shares basic features with the hypertext in vogue for writers of experimental fiction. Structurally, each is composed of nodes of text connected by multiple links. But the potentials, epistemologies, and specific uses of these two specific articulations of hypertext vary in wild and interesting ways. Usually, however, the existence of these variations does not translate into questions about divisions in and between discourses except at the most concrete level. Perhaps this unconsidered divergent history provides a partial reason for the contradictory nature of claims for hypertext, which is portrayed as both the freedom from single contexts and as the ultimate tool for recontextualization.

Sometimes these positions overlap within single texts. For example, in Landow's (1992c) generally important and insightful *Hypertext: The Convergence of Critical Theory and Technology*, hypertext offers:

1. A forum for enacting a Derridean and Barthesean rupture of context (pp. 8–9).
2. A self-controlled space in which "anyone who uses hypertext makes his or her own investigations the de facto organizing principle (or center) for the investigation at the moment" (p. 12).

3. A more truthful medium in which an individual text "would now be woven more tightly into its context than would a printed counterpart" (p. 5).

Landow articulated three contradictory (but potentially radical) forms of hypertext—environments stressing loss of control of context, assertion of individuality, and social construction, respectively. However, the disjunctions between these constructions remain below the level of commentary, let alone action.

In a sense, we can think of borders as deconstructive "hinges," the sites at which a single text can be forced to contradict its own position. In the famous argument between Derrida (1977) and Searle (1977) on authorial meanings, for example, Derrida playfully interrogated the tension between Searle's signature—his proclaimed authorial identity—and Searle's acknowledgments of the help of others in his work. In effect, Derrida pointed out, Searle argued for the idea that the author of a work is a discrete, self-conscious will at the same instant he admits the presence of the Other in his own work.

So although the boundaries dividing different articulations of hypertext go largely unquestioned, the very existence of those borders—and their historical processes of construction—can illustrate their contingent nature. For technologists, hypertext represents the possibility of perfecting mechanical efficiency by including the user as a working part; for database vendors, the technology translates information into postcapitalist commodities and marketplaces; for teachers and theorists of composition and literature, hypertext realizes the contradictory dreams of romanticism and postmodernism.

As I argue in this book, the wonderful and productive contradictions inherent in hypertext development and use remain largely unconsidered, as different ways of making and remaking hypertext—ways of living—continue to be channeled into existing structures of power. As Rosello (1994) pointed out, our insistence on thinking of hypertexts as ways to map texts back into their contexts prevents us from undertaking the important task of *rethinking* context. We allow our nostalgia to channel new possibilities into old pathways (while continuing to proclaim radical revolution). As Tuman (1992) observed, "There are many old uses for a new technology" (p. 57). In hypertext, we are like angels without maps, suddenly gifted with wings discovering not only that we cannot find heaven, but also that walking made us less dizzy, that our new wings snag telephone wires and catch in door frames. We recognize the apparently radical enactment of nonlinearity inherent in the node–link structure of all hypertext; we proclaim in various ways that revolutionary potential; and then we immediately rearticulate those potentials in terms of our conventional, normal practices. Although I understand that it is impossible to somehow step completely outside of the discourses in which we operate, we should make critical inquiry into the ways in which we rearticulate such technologies a primary disciplinary project. At the very least, we need to recognize the exaggerations of our slogans. We catch ourselves sometimes, but not often enough. "[T]he reader's freedom can never be absolute" Bolter (in a discussion in Tuman, 1992a) cautioned, "The rhetoric of hypertext (and all of us who work in hypertext are guilty of this exaggeration) tends to be a rhetoric of liberation" (p. 60; cf. Hawisher & Selfe, 1991; Johnson-Eilola, 1991a; Moulthrop, 1989b; Raskin, 1987). Hypertext (or any technology) is never neutral or transparent to our intentions. At the same time, we are never completely written by the technology. Technological changes open at least the potential for productive change.

The contradictions motivating such forms of nostalgia are useful, but only when they are recognized. Users and developers must gain awareness of the social and political environments in which they live and work, of the ways in which literacy technologies both write us and are written by us. Juxtaposing the different discourses of hypertext can highlight some of the political, social, and technological forces constructing our lives. Like urban planner and social theorist Virilio (1993), I am "fascinated by technology and dismayed by the fact that it had not been able to transform social space in adequate ways" (p. 242). Too frequently, the variances in the forms, development, and uses of hypertext remain invisible and unquestioned. The borders between hypertext fiction and hypertext online help appear as natural features of the landscape—when in fact we construct and maintain that terrain.

SEARCHING FOR BORDERS IN POMOLAND

Some of the most intelligent and articulate preachers of the electronic gospel proclaim a New Age in which not only omniscience and omnipotence but, more important, omnipresence becomes possible. In cyberspace, the limitations of temporality and spatiality seem to be overcome in an out-of-body experience that realizes the most ancient dreams of religion. Fleeting electronic images carry the hope of immortality.
—Mark Taylor and Esa Saarinen (1994, p. 7)

Utopian visions such as those characterizing the history of hypertext are not in themselves failures. One of the most influential utopian ideals, the project of modernism, seems outdated, but its utopian hopes of emancipation provide a useful touchstone for postmodernism (Giroux, 1991; Laclau & Mouffe, 1985; Pratt, 1987). Mannheim, writing in 1936 far before postmodernism, explained that "the road of history leads from one topia over a utopia to the next topia, etc." (p. 198). Utopias tell us about possible connections, contradictions, and social forces—but such visions should not be uncritical or totalitarian.

One intriguing and powerful element of postmodernism as it is surfaced in composition and literature has been its ability to call into question "common sense" structures of authority (Cooper, 1989; Faigley, 1992; Harkin & Schilb, 1991; Lynn, 1990). Such modes of questioning can provide students and teachers with ways of deconstructing ideas of single, given, classic readings of texts. In theory (and frequently in practice), the space opened through these operations gives students room for movement and self-construction, activities of empowerment. Unfortunately, the flip side to the postmodernist coin has been the same tendencies toward incessant questioning of authority, both textual and social (the two aspects connected to each other): If the classic author does not hold sway over meaning in textual interpretation, then how can student readers think that their own constructions have any validity?

In the language of borders, the postmodernist issue can be developed along spatial and architectural lines as has been done by Jameson (1991, 1992) and Soja (1989), among others. The problem then becomes, if there is no ground zero or common Cartesian grid on which to draw a unified (true) map, how can people orient themselves; how can they move with confidence from one place to another on a map? In fact, what makes one map more truthful than another? How can we assume that some maps are good and some maps bad when we lack a ground against which to measure each?

The issues here are complex and I am oversimplifying, but frequently the difficulty of postmodernist writing and mapping is connected to the ways in which the project is defined. For those of us accustomed to dealing in terms of textual truth (and most of us still are), *questioning* authority is somehow mistakenly equated with *denying* the existence of any authority, even though all but the most radical versions of postmodernism have recognized and are attempting to work beyond such nihilism. Authority cannot be so simply done away with; we necessarily recognize and participate in its various workings every day. The relation between maps and lives remains complex. Common sense tells us not to confuse the colored lines on paper maps with reality, but maps certainly participate in the real activities, suggesting and authorizing ways of living—maps are part of reality. Illegal aliens (the term itself acting as an extremely powerful border) queued at customs posts or sliding through cut fences under the cover of night would argue (often to the death) for the reality of borders. Even the borders of discourse formations are real practices and structures: I, for example, can move across the borders separating composition from technical communication, cultural studies, literary theory, and a handful of other disciplines with some facility; I have much less success negotiating movements into the discourses of nuclear engineering, bird watching, European history, and midwifery, to name only a few. Likewise, the borders of the discourses in which I do participate frequently discriminate against others through the markers of race, age, gender, income, and so on.

The key to thinking about these situations lies in considering borders as both real and contingent. The border is currently here, but what are the reasons that the border cannot be there? This question does not *dissolve* borders, but it can at least help make evident the political nature of their construction and continued existence. In answering the question about why borders are where they are (a long and always incomplete process), we can begin to see the ways in which borders are contingent instantiations of multiple, unequal forces, the nodal points at which numerous forces can become visible. At the same time, looking at these social forces can also lead to tactics for recomposing the borders by bringing to bear different forces, by looking at and highlighting border disputes. Taken this way, postmodernism is not necessarily only about removing borders, but perhaps more about rethinking the given, naturalized nature of most borders, of asking, why not put the border here? or, what prevents me from moving from this empire to that? or, what are the effects of these borders on these people? Postmodernism then becomes less the idea of removing all borders and more the activity of questioning and remaking borders in relation to real cultural conditions (with the understood caveat that "real conditions" are complex, contradictory, and not given to us by simple social classes; see Hall, 1989; Laclau & Mouffe, 1985).

Such cultural conditions account for the divergent developments of hypertext in the areas I discuss in this text. Like language, hypertext is remarkably ambivalent, affording construction in a wide variety of ways. But—and this is crucial to my argument—hypertext does not innocently mold itself to the self-conscious intentions of any single force (person, society, or technology). At most, texts are *suggestions* not commands, and suggestions that readers may recognize in many ways. Reader or users are not passive receptors of communications but active constructors of meaning. They do not merely choose, automatically, to read a given text as simple, unquestioned instructions; they are trained to do so through practice and through insertion into institutional contexts encouraging these readings. At the same time, the simple tag *institutions* can be productively complicated by understanding that such forces can include not only large corporations but also small community groups; family life; age group; gender, political, sexual, and religious orientations; and much more. These multiple forces compete to validate and reproduce meanings consistent with particular practices and goals. Despite my critiques in Chapter 3, I would not want to encourage the idea that every (or even any) functional hypertext can be so cunningly designed that it automatically overpowers a reader or user's mind. No one can ever completely and simply recognize their self as the perfect, implied "you" of instructional documentation (even though this seems like the goal of much traditional technical communication). The ability to recognize oneself as the spoken subject of a discourse is a learned but never perfected ability. Other forces always intrude, from small but important questions about the meaning of specific words to other workers' voices, thoughts about seeing family and friends after work, or questions about the place of one's self in the company's future.[2] So at the same time that we talk about "genres" of hypertext, we can also see that they are separated by contingent boundaries, the subjects of disputes, negotiations, and transgressions. Looking closely at the ways in which these boundaries are constructed and reconstructed can also help us to understand the ways in which these many institutional forces operate, as well as ways in which we might question and remake (and reunderstand) the boundaries.

In order to undertake the general sorts of critique I have suggested, we must understand technologies as political structures and activities rather than neutral, easily demarcated, and isolated objects. We must begin looking and acting from positions of critical awareness during the development and expansion of these technologies. Technologies such as hypertext must be explicitly negotiated rather than accepted. When hypertext developers and theorists assert that the technology *necessitates* or *automates* deconstruction, they may be short-circuiting explicit efforts toward that end. Deconstruction becomes vacant when it does not enact resistance toward dominant codes. Our position should be one of social critique, resistance, and reconstruction, with teachers, theorists, and students attempting to situate writing and reading as a political and social responsibility. In the broader project of critical literacy, Berlin (1992) argued, writing and reading should be "instances of discourse analysis and, significantly, negotiation" (p. 24). As Berlin continues:

> We want students to begin to understand that language is never innocent, instead constituting a terrain of ideological battle. Language—textuality—is thus the terrain on which different conceptions of economic, social, and political conditions are contested with consequences for the formation of the subjects of history, the very consciousness of the historical agent. We are thus committed to teaching writing as an inescapably political act, the working out of contested cultural codes that affect every feature of experience. (p. 31)

This type of thinking and teaching requires unending problematization,

---

[2] See, for example, Hamper's (1992) articles about assembly-line work at General Motors in *Rivethead*.

not merely for the language of the text but for the politics of the technology in which those texts—and writers and readers—are situated. We must find a way in which to talk and think and write about writing as a complex activity involving not only writers but also readers, texts, societies, politics, economies, and technologies (as well as the complicated way each of these terms is articulated).

Exploring—and constructing—relations between these elements involves a process of self-reflective, situated mapping (in effect, composing the multiple sites of ourselves). Toward these ends, this book maps hypertext theory and practice, but not as a simple reflection of reality. Like hypertext, one of the most dangerous features of maps is their apparent no-nonsense, straightforward, ideological innocence: As geographer Wood (1992) maintained, "[T]his is what maps do: they mask the interests that bring them into being; this is to make it the easier to accept what they say as... *unsaid*... as... *in the air*" (p. 95, ellipses and emphasis in original). To the designers and users (writers and readers) in the various discourses of hypertext I discuss, the technology often seems to be constructed in a spontaneous, neutral, and natural manner that is under the complete control of the user or designer.

Wood's postmodernist objections to this naturalization of cartography parallel in useful ways the postmodernist strand running through contemporary composition theory and practice. One of the most valuable components of such postmodernist perspectives continues to be the ways in which it encourages us to question the given nature of such maps, to question their meanings and destabilize their truths. The debates raging in the pages of our journals, the rooms of our conferences, the exchanges of our e-mail lists, and the growing web of interconnected online discourse make visible—and vital—these tensions. Unfortunately, the extremes of either postmodernism or romanticism are in themselves debilitating. As I discuss in more depth in Chapter 2, the recent trend toward cultural studies in composition and rhetoric can provide us with important ways of moving beyond polarized debates over intention and meaning continually restated in critiques and celebrations of postmodernism. By closely examining the ways in which social forces combine to construct a specific manner of using and thinking about hypertext—as well as the ways in which users sometimes subvert those forces—we can open up the technology to critique and reconstruction.

SOCIALIZING TECHNOLOGY: FUNCTION AND CRITIQUE IN LITERACY

Despite (or perhaps because of) revolutionary claims for hypertext, the technology is often constructed in very familiar ways. Hypertext is frequently seen as a tool, a mechanical device for doing something else, much like other technologies that came before—the slide and overhead projectors, the typewriter, the photocopier. Each of these once seemed new tools, things to be used in a simple way. As Ong (1982) showed, print literacy is more than a simple tool or the use of a simple, controllable technology. Print is something closer to a new environment or epistemology with wide ranging and profound implications, a technology in the broadest and most sociopolitical sense of the term. (Ong, however, ended in going too far in the direction of technological determinacy.) In many contexts, print literacy itself is articulated as a tool, the mechanical skill allowing people to get basic (and often dead-end) jobs. However, the technologies with which we learn, teach, and enact literacies encourage differing practices. Kaplan (1991) demonstrated this well:

> [C]onsider the blackboard, a ubiquitous technology for teaching, perhaps as old as the clay tablet. While it has a range of utility, and every classroom has one, the blackboard limits the conceptions of writing and revising that it can serve. Many teachers use one to demonstrate revisions because nothing inscribed on it is necessarily fixed or final: as with a word-processing program, anything written on it can be changed. But the blackboard favors certain transformations and discourages others: for example, the blackboard is best at word-for-word substitutions—erase one word, write in another—worst at complete reordering that would require erasing everything and starting again. Even the amount of text the blackboard will hold conveys messages about the scope revision might or should take. As a tool for teaching revision, the blackboard subtly constructs limits of possibilities. (p. 27)

But whereas composition and English teachers have become familiar with the operations of the blackboard (even if they are unaware of the ideological operations), computers are less instructionally familiar, hypertext even less so. Such unfamiliarity and unpreparedness is a dangerous but common component in the composition curriculum.

Certainly there are benefits to looking at hypertext from the tool perspective, particularly that view's idea that we should make explicit our priorities and goals and not allow the technology to set our agendas. Too often, however, this perspective encourages teachers and scholars to forget the always-present technological forces, to assume that people construct the technology in ways that achieve their predetermined ends and nothing else. This compulsion surfaces in the frequent claim that hypertext liberates readers from the prison of print, an assertion typically without a corresponding critique of the technologies of hypertext, of institutional forces authorizing certain types of readings and writings over others, among other things. The technology is thought of in a curiously simple fashion: *all powerful* (in that the switch from linear text to hypertext automatically

rts of wonderful and empowering effects on users) and *absent*
the last analysis, the artifacts are the simple, isolated results
.ctions). The contradictions surrounding the construction and
ion of these technologies are eminently valuable as forums for
dlysis. But even though we attempt to value dissensus and contingency in text, we do not take a similar position in our relations to other
technologies of literacy.

I am not arguing here for the traditional computer literacy, which, as it
is normally taught (programming skills, file commands, printing, and e-
mail) is a useful but relatively short-sighted and functionalist approach.
Such knowledge corresponds to what Knoblauch (1990) critiqued as merely *functional* literacy—a valuable skill, but one that should be the foundation for political awareness and action. We need a *critical* literacy of
computer technology that helps us to not merely interrogate technologies
as isolated mechanical objects, but also to critique (and reform) technologies as condensations or constructions of social and political forces in and
across particular situations. I argue here not merely for a celebration or
rejection of the powers of the computer but for a reunderstanding of our
relations to and within technologies.

Looking critically at hypertext is useful not merely in our work with
hypertext, but in relation to our primary work as literacy theorists and
teachers. Hypertext reveals a great deal about literacy and technology, our
assumptions about the functions and values of literacy (including who is
authorized to be literate in what ways and situations), and assumptions
about technological progress. As Joyce (1992) observed, hypertext may offer
us "the momentary advantage of our awkwardness"; hypertext sometimes
makes old assumptions suddenly visible. At the same time—that moment
of vertigo when writing and reading feel most unnatural—we often grasp
for something familiar, some sense of order and authority. Too frequently,
we accept that structure uncritically, the dominant social forces structuring (and naturalizing) what was a potentially productive process of discor-
poration or alienation, something that might have told us a great deal
about literacy as a social and political technology. The contradictions and
struggles are still there, but are weakened and downplayed.

Admittedly, we do talk about such things in some areas of composition,
but these discussions are typically limited to our professional writings to
each other in journals and in graduate seminars; furthermore, these conversations invariably focus on traditional genres of text. However, our work
gains its widest influence not in graduate seminars but in first-year composition courses, and in upper level technical communication and business
writing classes we teach to students both in and out of our discipline.
Although specialized theoretical discourse holds power in the ways we use
it to extend some areas of social possibility, we must continually rearticu-

late that work in terms that can make a difference in the broader social sphere. We must take our critical stances and relate them convincingly to the tasks of not only first-year composition, but also to areas such as technical communication, interface design, library and information science, and others. Where Drucker (1988) and other business management theorists have been wildly successful in rearticulating the rise of postmodernism into a philosophy of networked, flexible, and sometimes inhumane business structures and practices, composition theorists and teachers dealing with postmodernism typically remain trapped in (or rebuffed by) the theoretical discourses of White French Men. I believe in the relative importance of these theorists—Derrida, Foucault, Baudrillard, and so on—but I also understand that I will have little success in convincing the general public (let alone everyone in composition and rhetoric) of that importance. So I attempt to rearticulate those theories and cross boundaries into other important discourses. Teaching to groups other than one's own graduate disciples should not be punishment, but an opportunity to help students learn to enact broad and varied forms of social critique, as Scholes (1985) recognized in *Textual Power*:

> Though I am convinced that the entire English curriculum needs drastic revision, I know too well the politics of change in academic institutions to suggest that such revision can be accomplished by fiat. The majority of college students, in any case, will not be working through an elaborate English curriculum. They may go a bit beyond the basic or required courses, in some instances, but many will not even do that. Our best chances to help them learn our lessons will come in those courses now called "Freshman Comp." and "Intro. to Lit." or some variant on those hallowed titles. (p. 19)

The pedagogies of hypertext can potentially go even further because hypertext represents the opportunity for an unparalleled blurring of discourses—a way to question not only the boundaries separating first-year students, advanced undergraduates, graduate students, and professors, but also those between academy and business, the sciences and the humanities, management and line worker. I am not, however, pronouncing the coming age of computer freedom; I am just observing and working toward the realization of possibilities, the construction of a range of movements and tactics designed to appropriate certain aspects of hypertext and foreground other aspects to work against and change.

STANDING ON THE BORDER

In turning from print to hypertext, some composition teachers look for a way to encourage more active writing and reading (Johnson-Eilola, 1992;

Kaplan & Moulthrop, 1991; Landow, 1992a, 1992b, 1992c); nonlinear, non-hierarchical, and non-patriarchal thinking strategies (Beeman et al., 1987; Guyer & Petry, 1991b; Joyce, 1988; Smith, 1994); and collaboration among writers (Landow, 1992c; Slatin, 1990). Composition instructors and theorists are now coming to understand that printed texts often speak with overriding authority and singular authorship rather than participation (in either writing or reading; Bruffee, 1973; Cooper and Selfe, 1990; Trimbur, 1989), of univocality rather than intertextuality (Bazerman, 1988; Berkenkotter, 1991; Derrida, 1977; Lynn, 1990; Ong, 1982; Welch, 1987), and of artifact rather than process (Bialostosky, 1991; Johnson-Eilola, 1992; Murray, 1984; Phelps, 1988). Hypertext here seems especially suitable for critiques of book culture because the book, as Belsey (1980) argued, works by "suppressing the processes and conditions of the production of literary texts... helping to create a world of autonomous subjects who 'work by themselves' in subjection to the existing social formation" (p. 128). The ways in which hypertext varies from print are seen by many proponents as ways of demystifying print's operations.

Potentials surely exist, but often these same proponents are guilty of participating in the simultaneous mystification of the operations of hypertext as a social, technological process. For although poking fun at print in our culture has become a relatively innocuous act, our increasing dependence on computer-supported communication makes the naturalization of hypertext a powerful ideological operation. So teachers often unwittingly reproduce what they were trying to displace. Hypertext itself is a cultural artifact and process in which the interested nature of acts of production and consumption are often rendered invisible or natural. The technology affords change but also encourages nostalgia. By appearing to accelerate writing or reading to infinite speed and depth of perception, the postmodern dispersion of the subject and text comes full circle to the perfect expressive-realist true understanding. As the traditionally separate activities of writing and reading increasingly resemble each other, the distinctions among writing, reading, and text all tend to collapse (Tompkins, 1988) and, paradoxically, result in perfectly fluid total knowledge—both the absolute impossibility of full context and the gathering of more (truer) context; nihilistic postmodern wanderings versus highly efficient online documentation.

We must be careful when we proclaim the "death of the book" (Coover, 1992, p. 1), for as Baudrillard (1983) warned, book culture writers and readers may have sacrificed the print text in ways that allow other forces to more subtly (and opposed by less resistance) assert power. Hypertext can be (and often is) articulated as a powerfully conservative technology, a way to introduce wider groups of people more quickly and effectively into traditional structures of power. Landow (1992a) made explicit (but did not adequately critique) relations between hypertextual literary study and T. S. Eliot's relatively conservative idea of canon formation and change (p. 212). And Lanham (1993) defined "democracy" in a similarly limited way in *The Electronic Word: Democracy, Technology, and the Arts*:

> Codex books limit the wisdom of the Great Books to students who are Great Readers—as, to be sure, all of us who debate curricular matters were and are. Electronic text blows that limitation wide open. It offers new ways to democratize the arts, ways of the sort society is asking us to provide.... I don't think that the Great Books, for example, the classical tradition now defended with Luddite determination, will suffer by electronic presentation. Just the opposite, in fact. (p. 105)

Democratic possibilities are articulated here as expanding access to classic versions of Western culture. By partially naming its inadequacies, an ideology can "tighten rather than loosen its grip" (Eagleton, 1991, p. 61; see also Moulthrop, 1989b).

TECHNOLOGY AND POSSIBILITY

> [P]erhaps the computer is neither good nor evil but both. By this I mean not merely that computers can be used for good or evil purposes, but that they can evolve into very different technologies in the framework of strategies of domination or democratization.
>
> —Andrew Feenberg (1991, p. 91)

Metatheory becomes vital because the computer in general and hypertext in particular are *ambivalent* technologies, objects or concepts that can be used in various ways depending in part on the social conditions in which they are constructed and reconstructed in use. Ambivalent here does not connote neutrality but multiplicity, contingency, and tendencies of varying strength. The computer can emulate a linear print book on screen, but it can also act as a web of text, a telegraph, a psychoanalyst, a postmodern theater, a classical opera house, or a battlefield, among other things. And precisely *what* the computer appears as (and is used as) depends in a large part on how that system is currently constructed. The computer is not a *tabula rasa* but an ecology: A command-line interface encourages hierarchical, top-down, verbal approaches whereas a graphical interface more readily supports visual, virtual-tactical work. There may be gendered differences between these two environments, with females succeeding less in the more common command-line interface (Turkle & Papert, 1990). Technological artifacts, as Winner (1986) said some time ago, do "have politics" (pp. 19–39).

In current articulations of hypertext, for example, the idea of "choice" is often constructed in a way that degenerates into the disappearance of broader social contexts. As I argue in the following chapters, the fragmentation afforded by some genres of hypertext may also make social activities more easily orchestrated by late capitalism even as its proponents claim the opposite. Functional hypertexts usually articulate a post-Fordist approach to labor, where workers act in the interests of the company through an internalization of efficiency-gaining techniques rather than the old, bureaucratic model of supervisor explicitly providing directions to subordinates. The workplace context provides very clear delimitations about appropriate actions. In functional hypertext, workers act more efficiently on their own than allowed by old-fashioned, hierarchical, print text. The systems of control become internalized, defeating broad notions of freedom.[3]

Along related lines, hypertextual discussion forums such as those increasingly encountered in composition and literature classrooms (as well as in Internet LISTSERV groups, USENET news groups, and MOO/MUD spaces) may act to neutralize rather than strengthen resistance. The mere fact that each person is offered the same functional opportunity to contribute to the text—to "have their voice heard"—does not put everyone on equal footing. In the first place, the sheer volume of some of these discussions makes it possible for any single person's work to be absorbed without further commentary. In the second place, all conversations take place within the context of institutional agreements about what constitutes a valid point, about whose voice "carries" the most authority, about which types of arguments are valid, to name only a few (Johnson-Eilola & Selber, 1995). The technology in which the conversation is carried out does not automatically and totally determine the conversation. For example, anyone who has attempted to raise issues related to misogynist or racist practices on "inappropriate" e-mail or USENET lists will recognize that the right to speak in these conferences is often regulated by conservative[4] agendas and disempowering rhetorics. Any single aspect of these discourses—technology, participants, agendas, and others—only involves tendencies of varying

---

[3] As I argue in Chapter 3, post-Fordist approaches to management (popularized by management expert Drucker, 1988, among others) do away with rigorous hierarchical layers in organizational structures, but are successful primarily to the degree that individual workers can provide their own management. In a Foucauldian sense, the systems of control are transferred from the panoptic eye of the manager to the epistemology of the employee.

[4] As in most other places where I use the term conservative, I intend the broader meaning of "conservation of existing dynamics and structures of power" rather than the traditional (but related) political stance. In the metadiscourse of functional hypertext (designers talking about design issues), discussions of gendered technologies, multicultural approaches, commodification, and so on are frequently labeled as "political" and (therefore) somehow invalid topics.

strength, not determinations. Discourses are defined in part by their rules and their silences. So although my approaches to a critical practice of hypertext focus in a large part on the texts themselves, I want to situate these texts in the social, economic, and political environments in which they are designed, sold, used, and rearticulated.

I am interested in ways of working through the following issues: (a) conceptualizing and roughly categorizing current hypertext theory and practice from a social/technological standpoint and (b) constructing a critique of hypertext that complicates the categorical scheme I laid out, in order to enact a critical practice of hypertext. The three basic models of hypertext I discuss include functional hypertext, online research spaces, and writing and reading spaces (such as those commonly occurring in composition and literature classes). This critique attempts, in turn, to encourage theorists, teachers, and students to cross disciplinary boundaries and politicize textual activities. Such a practice deconstructs the common binary opposition of functional versus creative uses of hypertext; this critical practice must allow hypertext writers and readers the capability for productive, purposeful, empowering action in a range of text types and social situations.

The structure of this overall project presents some awkward problems: Criticisms of each genre are separated (sometimes by a number of chapters) from suggestions about possible responses to the problems I note. This is intentional, for the most part, because the recuperations I offer in Chapter 6 depend on the critique of not a single (or even stable) articulation of hypertext, but an understanding of the range of possible articulations and the ways that those genres might be played off one another. For example, the critique of online help in Chapter 3 (about the fragmentation and decontextualization of that articulation of hypertext) can be addressed not by merely rethinking online help in isolation of other discourses, but by combining that discourse with another, that of hypertext used for collaboration and discussion, which is not discussed until Chapter 5. Furthermore, the tactics I suggest about rearticulating online help in Chapter 6 rely on not only a simplistic application of structures and mechanisms taken from hypertext affording collaboration and discussion, but those structures and mechanisms in light of a discussion of literary hypertext found in Chapter 5. So the complex structure of this book is a response to the structure of the problem.

It is customary in printed books about hypertext to mourn the fact they are not written in hypertext. The writer points out, somewhat sheepishly, that if this book were a hypertext, the reader could jump from x to y, and then call up z in a parallel window. That is certainly true of this book—and there may eventually be a hypertextual version—but that structure would not solve the awkward structure I already noted. It might, in fact, exacerbate the problem. If I were to feel sheepish about anything, it is the early publications and presentations and discussions in which I and my colleagues argued that print = repression, hypertext = liberation. It is not that simple.

In structuring the book as I have, I want readers to see point *x* before point *y*; I want to bring a number of things together before attempting to change them and their relationship to each other. As I take pains to discuss throughout this book, hypertext is not some magical technology that transforms the information within it into a free, open space. In fact, the communities in which specific forms of hypertext are taken up, appropriated, and remade typically act in a way consonant with their current structures of power, action, and knowledge. So although there would be value in rethinking the current book as a hypertext, that would not mean a dispersal of authority or control, at least not if the current book were to be recognizable in the hypertext. As with many contemporary texts, there are numerous elements here we could parallel in hypertext, in particular my use of extensive quotation and citation. I use these mechanisms less to validate my own ideas than to suggest places where an interested reader could branch off, slip from this text to another. These points are not an attempt to totalize other positions, but something closer to points of contagion, outbreaks of one text within another.

Or I could lament the immense time span involved in the writing and publication of this text, which began in its earliest forms in conference presentations at CCCC in the early 1990s and as a first draft manuscript in late 1992. In many ways, a book is an unwieldy, modernist structure, slow-moving and relatively static even when the on-screen text can be rewritten and reprinted at will. In many cases here, the specific articulations of hypertext I discuss have been "surpassed" (the term mystifies the notion of "technological progress") by newer, faster forms. The critiques and responses I construct here are a series of historical (and, I hope, historicizing) maps that situate hypertext among and within various discourses. Current and future versions of hypertext must continually be connected back against these maps in order to understand their histories (and our presents and futures).

In my first detour, I also want to discuss some of the frameworks and strategies informing my general project of constructing critical literacies of hypertext. These theoretical perspectives, developing as responses to and rehabilitations of postmodernism (both as a theory and a cultural shift) include recent work by Henry Giroux on radical and border pedagogies, by Louise Pratt on linguistic contact zones and literacy, and by Stuart Hall on articulation theory in cultural studies; they speak strongly to the expanded and politicized version of composition central to this book.

The series of critiques takes place in Chapters 3, 4, and 5, where I define aspects of what separates each category of hypertext from the others and what those separations entail for writers and readers. I also begin sketching a background for rearticulating these technologies, rethinking of the ways in which each category offers writers and readers methods for subversion and rearticulation (as mentioned earlier, the background is not foregrounded until Chapter 6). Although it is most common for computers and composition theorists to concentrate on a specific instantiation of technology (usually one occupying a highly visible place in writing, such as word-processing or style-analysis programs), I have chosen to highlight the multiple, variable nature of hypertext by working with a wide range of uses, including some that are not commonly considered as objects or actions for critique by composition theorists or teachers, environments such as online documentation and bibliographic or textual databases.

Computer use of any sort relies on the specific ways in which people learn and use (and are used by) systems. The increasing use of functional hypertext as a method for teaching these skills encouraged me to begin the analysis with this articulation, commonly seen in the online documentation designed for contemporary operating systems and computer programs. Chapter 3 explores one particularly popular and influential way in which hypertext is constructed: the little machine in which the technology assumes the place of the book in the process of mechanical transfer of information from writer to reader. This articulation itself relies on the connection of a number of other complexes, including the reductive idea of efficiency as a simple, technical attribute and the concept of communication as information transfer. The apparent conservatism of the little machines articulation of hypertext relies on a naturalized substitution of computer book for print book, where hypertext is seen as merely making communication more efficient without exerting any complicating forces.

Chapters 4 and 5 provide examples of two closely related articulations that appear to offer more visible, critical applications than functional documentation. Both the commodity space and construction space of hypertext rely on the increasingly common idea that knowledge is spatial. This articulation of knowledge is constructed at the nexus of not only concepts of land and space as a commodity but also the related issue of postmodern capitalism's use of decontextualization and fragmentation. In Chapter 4 on commodified spaces, I discuss the ways in which online information spaces such as DIALOG, computerized card catalogs in libraries, and Internet-based, World Wide Web-supported information spaces such as MOSAIC (1994) and NETSCAPE (1994)—technologies increasingly popular in academic research but as yet relatively uncriticized—work to construct information as both a space and an object. Unfortunately, these spaces and objects often tend toward making intangible and easily reproducible information into a commodity for ownership, development, colonialism, and economic circulation (even as they appear to value association).

Chapter 5 then examines the construction of a postmodern space of hypertext. This space is the project of academics influenced by postmodernism and literary theory although, as I argue later, other influences exert strong force. Here, hypertext is frequently articulated as a space in which authorial control and unified subjectivity are seen as dispersed. Specific approaches to constructing this type of space reveal two contradictory dangers: a geometrical representation in which knowledge is organized and categorized as a method of control (a project apparently contradictory to postmodernism), or a geographical, flattened terrain that succeeds so well at achieving postmodernity that writers and readers are unable to construct resistance to the broader, decentralized forces of late capitalism. I argue that the geometrical and geographical instantiations of hypertext must be combined as a way of enacting what Jameson (1991; 1992) called "cognitive mapping," a way of representing—incompletely, partially, and nondeterministically—a subject's relation to the global system.

The conclusions of Chapter 6 rehearse the implications of the previous chapters and build on these critiques by suggesting ways in which some aspects of the technology might be appropriated by both designers and users for social reform through rearticulations of hypertext. In particular, I suggest that although hypertext is currently constructed along existing (and unquestioned) lines of social power, the *potential* openness of the text—the ease with which not only "obviously" related texts can be linked, but also the ways in which discourses typically thought of as mutually exclusive can potentially be mapped against each other—might possibly be exploited as an explicitly political and social activity by writers, writing teachers, and writing theorists, who can use the technology to question the hegemonic tendencies of disciplinarity and discourse communities.

Chapter 2

From Postmodernism to Cultural Studies: Approaches to Critical Literacies of Hypertext

Cultural workers need a language of imagination, one that both insists and enables them to consider the structure, the movement, and possibilities in the contemporary order of things as well as how they might act to prevent the barbaric and develop those aspects of public life that point to its best and as yet unrealized possibilities. This is a language of democratic possibilities that rejects the enactment of cultural difference structured in hierarchy and dominance; it is a language that rejects cultural, social, and spatial borders as shorelines of violence and terrorism. In opposition to this view, the concepts of democracy, border, borderlands, and difference must be rewritten so that diverse identities and cultures can intersect as sites of creative and cultural production, multiple resources, and experimentation for expanding those human capacities and social forms for a radical democracy to emerge in this country.

—Henry Giroux (1992a, p. 248)

Before beginning a discussion of current articulations of hypertext, I want to lay out in a little more detail some of the theoretical approaches informing this book: the early postmodernism of Lyotard and the cultural studies work of theorists including Giroux, Pratt, and Hall. Tracing the trajectories of postmodernism through cultural studies can help us think critically about hypertext because hypertext theory in general seems stuck within a stage of postmodernism incapable of the self-critique and rehabilitation that cultural studies has begun working toward. Where theorists and designers of hypertext have remained relatively uncritical of the technology (with the normal exception of the problem of "getting lost in hyperspace"), cultural theorists have responded in important and constructive ways to early versions of postmodernism.

The relation between postmodernism and critical literacies of hypertext may seem odd, but hypertext and postmodernism are constructed around strikingly similar premises. As numerous literary critics writing about hypertext have argued, the value placed on nonlinearity, multiplicity, loss of authorial control, and the association of elements in complex webs characterizes both hypertext and postmodernism (see, e.g., Bolter, 1991a, 1991b; Delany & Landow, 1990; Johnson-Eilola, 1994b; Landow, 1992c; Moulthrop & Kaplan, 1994). For this reason, we might begin the search for a critical literacy of hypertext by drawing on critiques and extensions of postmodernism taking place in cultural studies. Such perspectives can be worked back against existing discourses of hypertext to help us construct a more positive response to hypertext than we are currently enacting.

The relations between hypertext and postmodernism began long before anyone used either term. Most hypertext researchers locate the articulation of current hypertext in the work of Vannevar Bush, the popular science advisor to President Roosevelt in the 1940s. Bush's (1945/1987) writings about a prototypical hypertext appeared in, among other places, *The Atlantic Monthly* and *The Saturday Evening Post*. For Bush, science was mired in the enormous growth of knowledge and the resulting specialization of science into myriad branches. In order for any person to gain in-depth knowledge of one discipline, they were required to devote their professional life to that quest, painstakingly acquiring the mass of information needed to build their expert status. In each of the branches, then, the "best" knowledge was limited to the discourses of the experts, who shared their knowledge only with others who had also achieved a similar level in that specialization. Bush criticized this situation because it made difficult (if not impossible) the task of important interdisciplinary work—a scientist could not make connections among the specialized discourses of any field because the relations between concepts had not been drawn from one branch to the next.

Bush's solution to the situation—which he saw as responsible for much of his day's cultural and political strife, including World Wars—was to construct massive, nonlinear textbases devoted to the development of interdisciplinary connections among the various specialized disciplines of the sciences. Bush's proposed system, called the *memex*, was a desk-shaped machine including microfilm projectors and cameras for viewing and annotating the interdisciplinary web of knowledge.

Although Bush's machine (like Babbage's difference engine) proved to be some years ahead of its time, the idea of the memex was later taken up by Nelson (1974/1987a, 1987b) in the 1960s. (Nelson is credited with originating the term *hypertext*.) For Nelson, as with Bush, hypertext was necessarily networked and open to both writing and reading. Nelson, however, was able to articulate hypertext to the growth of computing. In addition, Nelson envisioned something much broader than Bush's scientific text. Nelson's Project Xanadu would include any type of text, from science to literature, political opinion, and conversation. Xanadu aimed at overthrowing the distinction between "high" and "low" literature, putting all text into a global, multithreaded network available to people at McDonald's-inspired Xanadu SilverStand access sites. Widespread and open, Xanadu would (according to Nelson) functionally dissolve long-standing distinctions between authorial control and passive reading by placing both authors and readers in the same environment, allowing readers the ability to annotate texts, make connections between disparate sources, and add their own texts into the developing docuverse. Although Project Xanadu has never been constructed beyond small prototypes, Nelson's vision has remained an important inspiration for many of those developing and writing about hypertext today, in particular the World Wide Web.

For both Nelson and Bush, hypertext represented an explicit repudiation of simple hierarchies and specialized (and exclusionary) disciplines. But these antiauthoritarian gestures remain uncompleted in their work and in the work of the numerous hypertext developers who cite the work of these pioneers as inspiration. Both Bush and Nelson are incapable of considering the more problematic implications of breaking down disciplinary or literary hierarchies. That is, these breakdowns do not occur in isolation, but in a broader cultural movement toward what we now call postmodernism. Where Bush and Nelson apparently believe in a foundational human spirit that would lend coherency and consistency to a freer culture, postmodernists such as Lyotard are more willing to look critically at the disintegration of hierarchies.

Lyotard's work then offers a useful starting point in our own project because of the importance of his work to the postmodern movement and because of the central place he gives to broad social and ethical issues (as opposed to the rather more gleeful discussions of postmodernism by theorists such as Baudrillard). In his influential *The Postmodern Condition*, Lyotard (1984) argued that contemporary society is faced with a "legitimation crisis." The roots of this lay in death of the grand narratives traditionally used to legitimate science, utopian narratives such as those characterizing the Enlightenment or Marxism. Lyotard's argument here parallels Bush's lament of overspecialization, but with decidedly different goals. Although science, at the surface, values only objective, disinterested statements and normally subordinates (or completely disregards) forms of communication such as narrative (precisely because it is "unscientific"), science is also paradoxically forced to rely on narrative in order to justify its own work (the narrative of scientific progress toward human emancipation, for example, or the sterile narratives of scientific discovery published in peer journals). And whereas the discourse of science would seem, by the rules of its own construction, to be limited to purely *denotative* statements ("The temperature is 78 degrees Fahrenheit"), that discourse also includes and typically validates its own activities through *prescriptive* statements ("The minimum wage should be set at X dollars," to use one of Lyotard's examples). Prescriptive statements illustrate a fundamental problem: They cannot be verified as true with simple, easily interpreted, controlled experiments. More importantly, they do not merely describe preexisting behavior in objective terms but make value judgments about the way in which people should act. Science cannot negate the importance of prescriptive statements because the discourse of denotative statements is not, by itself, capable of supporting contemporary science, let alone contemporary society.

The loss of the legitimating power of grand narratives corresponds to a more general shift in the structure of what counts as knowledge. With the grand narratives no longer able to legitimate the activities of science, science and society develop toward operationalism and heterogeneous, localized language games. People communicating rely on provisional social contracts about permissible moves, with each utterance in a conversation counting as a move. The rules and participants in each game shift and overlap, with each subject living at the nexus of numerous (often contradictory) language games (or discourses). Furthermore, without social contracts, there are no games.

The rules of these new games, in general, tend to grant "right" to the side of the argument capable of arraying the largest quantity of information on its side. Increasingly, valid moves are not associated with the creation of new knowledge in the traditional sense, but with the possession and combinations of existing information. Descriptive statements (based on the wealth of data accumulated) can lead to the legitimation of prescriptive statements. Those descriptions, then, become the field on which people construct policies and less formal ways of acting—rules for their language games.

Linking postmodernism with the rise of communication technologies and information-processing machines, Lyotard (1984) argued that "knowledge" will only be valuable "if learning is translated into quantities of information"; thus begins "a thorough exteriorization of knowledge with respect to the 'knower'" (p. 4). Lyotard's critique comes to share crucial traits with the earlier visions of Bush, who insisted that human language would have to be recoded into a hypothetical language of scientific symbols in order to be entered into the memex for viewing and manipulation by other scientists.

We can see these very real tendencies toward externalized knowledge in Zuboff's (1988) description of workplace automation, which requires workers to translate knowledge about performance (often previously unverbalized) into discrete, stepwise actions that can be coded into computer memory. After that coding, the workers' relations to their work can no longer be the same. In addition, for Lyotard (1984) the "mercantilization of knowledge" threatens the power of the State because the State is perceived by multinational corporations as "noise" in the communication channel (p. 5). Questions in higher education move from "Is it true?" to "Is it salable?" and "Is it efficient?" (p. 51). The increasing movement of total quality management (TQM) and reengineering programs from the workplace into academia illustrate the latest (but certainly not last) developments in this trend.

In correspondence to the mercantilization of knowledge, Lyotard (1984) argued that genius and imagination are redefined away from their traditional definition as isolated, individual well-springs of creativity:

> [The] capacity to articulate what used to be separate can be called imagination. Speed is one of its properties. It is possible to conceive the world of postmodern knowledge as governed by a game of perfect information, in the sense that data is in principle accessible to any expert.... (p. 52; see also Virilio, 1986)

Lyotard here spoke in language strikingly similar to Nelson's discussions of the emancipatory potential for hypertext.

Although postmodernism has gained notoriety for its amoral tendencies, Lyotard (1984) recognized the potentially dehumanizing effects of the new language games, arguing forcefully for open access to information for all people, utopian scenarios he called "perfect language games." For Lyotard, games of perfect language can be contrasted with the present case of unequal access to information. For example, in current discussions about minimum wage levels in the United States, valid moves in the language game lean toward those involving statistical evidence: population data, class, age, gender, and head-of-household studies, computer-driven economic predictions; surveys; and so forth. Access to such information falls outside the realm of most individual citizens, particularly those actually earning minimum wage in an effort to support themselves and their families. Even in the relatively rare case of a person being called on to recount their experiences of earning minimum wage, it is difficult to think of these people as "players" in the game; they are closer to pieces of data called on from a large reserve.

Science is now, in large part, based on the use of vast arrays of experimental and data-collection apparatus. Following this critique, Lyotard (1984) argued in the final section of *The Postmodern Condition* that society as a whole must "give the public free access to the memory and data banks" (p. 67). Lyotard has been rightly criticized for this program on the grounds that it apparently validates a combination of liberalism and free-market y (see, e.g., Connor, 1989; Eagleton, 1991).

ever, despite these and other criticisms, this analysis of postmod-
_____ offers a useful starting point for the project of constructing a critical literacy of hypertext. Hypertext appears especially suitable as an
environment for the language games of postmodern society. Hypertext prioritizes not merely the content of individual nodes, but also (and sometimes
primarily) their connection. Theoretically, hypertext values association at
least as much (if not more) than individual, isolated contribution. (I take
up later the degree to which these potentials are achieved.) And, as with
Lyotard's proclamations about perfect information games, many hypertext
theorists, developers, and users also validate a grand narrative of complete
access to information. This narrative, generally referring back to Nelson's
(1982, 1974/1987a, 1987b) description of the docuverse, presents the medium as (a) containing all information, and (b) providing a greater degree of
dissent than possible in print through the association and juxtaposition of
conflicting ideas.

Although objections to Lyotard's (1984) specific arguments are many
and complex, the fact remains that his observations about the fragmentation of grand narratives is borne out by many current social conditions: the
increasing gap between informational "haves" and "have-nots," the growth
of multinational corporations, the growing use of computer-based instruction and correspondent stress on searching skills over the transmission of
what counts as knowledge. Certainly there exist associated counterobser-
vations to each of these, but the general thematic of social fragmentation
seems inarguable. In fact, much of the disagreement between the political
left and right can be generalized as opposing perspectives on the value of
these trends.

One interesting aspect of Lyotard's (1984) projection is the tension
between differing instantiations of postmodernism: liberation and oppression. On one hand, we find celebrations of the loss of single, univocal, self-
present identity that legislates against concepts of single, univocal identities
and fragments each writer or reader's image, multiply (a tendency in the
work of Derrida and a valued extreme in the writings of Baudrillard and
Deleuze and Guattari, for example). In hypertext, the optimistic version
(which is, with few exceptions, the only version offered) corresponds to the
idea that the open hypertext denies authorial control, not only allowing but
requiring the reader to rewrite the text, to become the writer (Joyce's AFTER-
NOON, A STORY, 1990, is the most popularly cited example).

On the other hand, the pessimistic version of postmodernism articulates
the situation as the loss of self, the potential paralysis of morality and
ethics, and the general decline of both classical and liberal ideals of humanity. Importantly, postmodern capitalism rewrites this pessimistic view in
optimistic terms, as low-level workers are given increasing responsibility

and relative structural freedom in order to increase the efficiency of their work. Hypertext-based instructional text is more efficient than old, linear text in solving workplace problems; online marketplaces attempt to remove physical constraints in order to maximize freedom of purchase choice and the movement of commodities. All of these complex strands are present in Lyotard's (1984) work. But although Lyotard appeared to understand the complex and dark nature of postmodern cultures, his primary response in *The Postmodern Condition* is only to call for free access to information. In addition, although access is an important concern, it will not assist in the frequent situations in which other cultural forces discourage participation or support some modes of discourse better than others (Joyce, 1995, pp. 157–158). The general right to freedom of speech in our culture remains subject to restrictions of numerous sorts, including the famous prohibition against shouting "fire" in a crowded theater, libel and slander, various codes against hate speech, and also consensual agreements involving issues of appropriate forums, speakers, and topics.

However, if information access offers a necessary condition of one strategy toward social justice, it is neither a sufficient nor required condition. Democracy may be related to equality, but the two are certainly not equal or in simple relation. Language games are founded on social contracts, sometimes as the consent to oppression of one form or another (such contracts are hegemonic to the degree that they seem to be based on natural orders and common sense). That consent can (and often does) include the idea that information is free to all but can only be used in certain ways by certain people in certain contexts.[1] Furthermore, it is extremely difficult to conceive of a society in which all information access is free: Although free access may eventually be possible, starting social reform with that point hardly seems feasible given current conditions.

The critique of hypertext I am working at accepts the idea of information access as important, but is primarily concerned at this point in thinking through, in reformist ways, the naturalization of the various discourses of hypertext. This discussion can help us to see the ways in which designers and users consent to sometimes oppressive or conservative uses.

So although Lyotard's (1984) general thematic provides us with useful descriptions of contemporary discourses of technology, science, and education (among others), working productively to change current systems requires more than informational anarchy. Lyotard's analysis remains important even if it, in the end, cannot motivate a construction of political practice because of Lyotard's perspective on information technology (which,

---

[1] The control of context is increasingly replacing control of literal content as a means of enforcing power relationships.

although not missing in these other approaches, is not discussed so clearly). In addition, Lyotard placed special importance on heterogeneity among various language games (little narratives): precisely because the grand narratives are in decline we can now think of the ensemble of language games as fundamentally heterogeneous, overlapping, and interconnected (pp. 40–41).

Lyotard responded to many of these difficulties in his subsequent works, especially *The Differend* (1988) and *Just Gaming* (Lyotard & Thébaud, 1985). Lyotard argued more forcefully here for critical, localized examinations of the connections and overlaps between genres. Because there are no longer single language games capable of orchestrating a transhistorical truth under which all discourses fall, the linkages constructed between discourses are often the site of inequality and even violence.

Based on Lyotard's ideas of the localized justice in the heterogeneous space of language games, Faigley (1992) ended *Fragments of Rationality*, his discussion of postmodernism in composition and rhetoric, with the call for critically examining composition as a space for the nontotalized intersection of discourses. Lyotard provided few recommendations for overcoming this situation; Faigley himself merely noted that looking at the ethical and moral implications inherent in the conjunction of different language games is an important project for composition. For example, although Faigley's tactic of holding composition classes in asynchronous computer conferences offers a number of important capabilities for cultural workers, Faigley oversimplified their nature by giving the chapter in which he discussed these technologies the title "Achieved Utopia." In Chapter 5, I build on Faigley's observations of the postmodernist tendencies of this technology by attempting to resocialize and problematize the online discussions in hypertext.

For the purposes of working toward critical literacies, I turn now to three related perspectives that begin to sketch out political possibilities for social reform: the cultural approaches of border pedagogy, linguistic contact zones, and articulation theory. Based on the general critique of technology and language games provided by Lyotard, the theorists I introduce in the next section can help us construct a theory and practice of hypertext that is both plausible and political. These perspectives can help us to both identify the overlap and contradictions among the various language games played in hypertext; in turn, these critiques can also specify the ways in which these overlaps and contradictions might be reconstructed in more positive ways.

TECHNOLOGY AND/AS SOCIETY: BORDER CROSSINGS, CONTACT ZONES, AND ARTICULATIONS

The ambiguity inherent in hypertext seems to be one of the most u
and one of the most troubling features of hypertext. Systems of technologies are far too complex and indeterminate to ever be fully within our
knowledge, let alone our control. "Control" of technology is itself a difficult
term to unpack; as Winner (1977) observed, "The conclusion that something is 'out of control' is interesting to us only insofar as we expect that it
ought to be in our control in the first place" (p. 19). We are neither completely free to construct hypertext according to our own whims nor completely under the sway of the technical system. There is not a simple
cause–effect relationship here, but something like a complex set of borders
that we are crossing and recrossing, or sets of dynamic, multiple, conflicting social forces. If our maps and travels are to be more than haphazard or
short-sighted accommodations to technological systems, we need a way to
interrogate and influence the formation of these borders through the maps
we write and rewrite, our theories and practices.

Vital to this approach are observations about the ways in which various
discourses of hypertext naturalize their isolation from other discourses and
where users assent to language games in which the rules validate inequality. Current articulations of instructional hypertext "clearly" differ from
articulations of online research databases; and both are "obviously" distinct
in construction and use from hypertext literature and criticism. These nat-
uralizations are dangerous, because they leave unquestioned the wildly different forms in which the node–link mechanism common to all hypertext
is constructed and used.

Struggling Over the Terrain of Postmodernism: Culture as Geography

In common usage, borders are what separate one thing from another: the
United States from Mexico and Canada, my homeland from the Other's;
print from hypertext; good from evil. The computer interface itself reifies
cultural borders. Anzaldúa (1987) situated herself in the geographical,
technological, and linguistic borderlands between Mexico and the United
States: "I sit here before my computer, *Amiguita*, my altar on top of the
monitor with the *Virgen de Coatalopueh* candle and copal incense burning"
(p. 75). The metaphors structuring the computer interface prioritize
Western, corporate cultural experiences and understandings through the
icons of watches, file folders, and hierarchies (Selfe & Selfe, 1994).

For radical pedagogue Giroux, borders not only separate but can also
point out the need to cross and remap. Borders offer a way of talking about
division as well as a way of overcoming the separation that engenders and
perpetuates inequality. Border pedagogy is founded on the project of finding

"a politics and pedagogy developed around new languages capable of acknowledging the multiple, contradictory, and complex subject positions people occupy within different social, cultural, and economic locations" (Giroux, 1992a, p. 21). By recognizing boundaries and working to overcome them, such theories attempt to help students become border-crossers, transgressors who can cross and remap boundaries in order to create new public spaces for discussion, deconstruct boundaries even when they are given as oppression, and situate and historicize students while also helping them recognize the multiple discourses in which every subject is situated.

Giroux (1991, 1992a) constructed border pedagogy from aspects of modernism, postmodernism, and feminism—three disparate (and often openly hostile) theoretical standpoints—in an effort to overcome a number of crucial problems plaguing each of them alone. Rather than choosing one of these perspectives over another, Giroux attempted to bring the three together, using the strengths of one to recuperate the weakness of another (and remaining mindful of the dangers of the inherent contradictions among each). These three stances intersect in an appropriation, deconstruction, and reconstruction of social mappings, ways of articulating a local politics that do not ignore global projects and, at the same time, refuse to be subsumed into the global. From modernism, Giroux (1992a) attempted to rescue the project of human emancipation; from postmodernism, the celebration of multiplicity, fractured identities, and deconstruction of authority; from feminism, the lived political project of speaking from the position of the Other (as well as the ability to provide a rein on the dehumanizing tendencies of postmodernism and the defeminizing aspects of modernism). Border pedagogy attempts to be sensitive to power relationships in order to open up discourse and help both teachers and students recognize their own cultural positions:

> What border pedagogy makes undeniable is the relational nature of one's own politics and personal investments. But at the same time, border pedagogy emphasizes the primacy of a politics in which teachers assert rather than retreat from the pedagogies they use in dealing with the differences represented by the students who come to their classes. For example, it is not enough for teachers to merely affirm uncritically their students' histories, experiences, and stories. To take student voices at face value is to run the risk of idealizing and romanticizing them. It is equally important for teachers to help students find a language for critically examining the historically and socially constructed forms by which they live. (pp. 140–141)

Pratt (1991) likewise noted the ease with which educational programs dissolve into systems of rules, reducing the multiple, fragmented, contradictory selves that compose various groups of people (women, Whites, Blacks, etc.) to homogeneous players in a game (p. 38; cf. Ellsworth, 1989;

Haraway, 1985). As Giroux (1983) wrote, "In the radical approach, the traditional emphasis on consensus is replaced by a radical focus on conflict, and the liberal concerns with the way teachers and students create meanings is replaced by a focus on social structures and the construction of meaning" (p. 56).

Giroux's work is useful here in answering the frequent assertion that hypertext somehow "levels the playing field" for users. Rather than allowing users to focus on the ways in which marginalization occurs in society, hypertext may just deny discussion of marginalization (with textuality here totalizing the world—"the text lacks margins, then so does the world"). In the following chapters, I examine the forces structuring both the design and use of such texts, showing how they operate by assuming that the reader or writer has already been positioned in a certain social relationship to the technology. The increased "freedom" of hypertext is, in fact, illusory because the reader's goals and tasks have already been written in part by both social and technological forces. The reader is free to choose among numerous options in the text insofar as those options satisfy the efficiency requirements the reader assumes from their position in a technological society. Neither the technology nor the reader or writer's social position(s), though, completely determine their navigations and uses of the text. These types of text present, rather, a space of possibility for *rearticulating* the significance and operations of the text—but the strength of the forces contributing the technical efficiency are difficult to work against in this articulation.

This rearticulation is not, however, limited to functional hypertext—there are also many crucial but largely unexamined and difficult aspects of other types of hypertext: the possibility for students to lose a sense of self as the communal text develops, or the chance that their writing will develop as a commodity rather than a forum for thinking and communication. These partialities, the multiple articulations possible in the margins between the differing constructions, might be seen as something more than a thin line inked between two regions on a map and something more like the interzones between regions—unofficial but real spaces opened at the margins between regions.

Such spaces are the focus of work by literacy and cultural theorist Pratt (1992), who developed at length the concept of *linguistic contact zones*: "social spaces where disparate cultures meet, clash, and grapple with each other, often in highly asymmetrical relations of domination and subordination" (p. 4). Pratt analyzed the ways European and North American cultures have "explored" and "discovered" other cultures such as Africa and South America. Although her discussions seem far removed from thinking about hypertext, they provide an important, clearly spoken example of the ways in which any cultural clash—even those seemingly "internal" to a single culture or person—are negotiated, enforced, and resisted.

One of Pratt's (1991, 1992) most intriguing discussions involves a single text constructed at the intersection of two primary discourses—Inca and Spain in the 17th century. In 1613 Guaman de Poma de Ayala, an indigenous Andean, wrote *New Chronicle and Good Government and Justice*, a 1,200-page letter with profuse illustrations, to King Philip III of Spain four decades after Spain had conquered the Incan empire. According to Pratt, Guaman Poma, who both claimed descent from Incan royalty and had adopted the Christianity of his conquerors, wrote in an attempt to "construct a new picture of the world, a picture of a Christian world with Andean rather than European peoples at the center of it" (Pratt, 1991, p. 34). Pratt refered to Poma's text as an example of autoethnographic writing, discourses of the contact zone that

> involve the selective collaboration with and appropriation of idioms of the metropolis or the conqueror. These are merged or infiltrated to varying degrees with indigenous idioms to create self-representations intended to intervene in metropolitan modes of understanding.... Such texts often constitute a marginalized group's point of entry into the dominant circuits of print culture. (p. 35)

Although the relationship between Poma and King Philip III is superficially that of conqueror and conquered, the undercurrents present in Poma's text illustrate the continually partial nature of such conquests. Poma, for example, listed the Amerindians descending ancestrally from Noah and equated the five ages of the Christian history of his conquerors to the five ages of Andean history (Pratt, 1991, p. 34). Poma's drawings use Andean spatial symbolism in order to introduce his own cultural language—his self—into the Spanish Christian narrative. As Pratt (1992) described the text:

> [T]he manuscript proposed nothing less than a new view of the world. It began by rewriting the history of Christendom to include the indigenous peoples of America, then went on to describe in great detail the history and lifeways of the Andean people and their leaders. This was followed by a revisionist account of the Spanish conquest, and hundreds of pages documenting and denouncing Spanish exploitation and abuse. The four hundred illustrations followed the European genre of the captioned line drawing but, as subsequent research revealed, they deployed specifically Andean structures of spatial symbolism. Guaman Poma's letter ends with a mock interview in which he advises the King as to his responsibilities, and proposes a new form of government through collaboration of Andean and Spanish elites. (p. 2)

Poma's resistance succeeds in many ways at appropriating a culture that was appropriating him. As Pratt observed, Poma was able to speak from a subordinate position in a way that shows clearly his own power—a power constructed discursively in this contact zone.

But in the end, Poma's resistance was localized and neutralized: The letter never reached King Philip III. The manuscript "disappeared" soon after being written, discovered in 1908 by a researcher at the Danish Royal Archive in Copenhagen (no one has ever explained how it came to be stored there). Only in the 1930s was the text printed for wider reading, and not until the late 1970s, with the rise of interpretive reading and postcolonial theories, was the manuscript discussed publicly to any extent. "The letter got there, only 350 years too late, a miracle and a terrible tragedy" (Pratt, 1991, p. 34).

As a teacher, Pratt (1991) uses her analyses of texts such as Poma's *New Chronicle*, Sir Richard Burton's narrated "discoveries" (and their place in the colonialism and imperialism of the 18th centuries and beyond), and journalistic accounts of "alien" cultures such as Joan Didion's *Salvador* to critique notions of culture as homogeneous and authoritarian. Closer to home, Pratt finds the resistance of "border" writings similar to Poma's letter in her son Manuel's fourth-grade homework:

> On several occasions my fourth grader… was given writing assignments that took the form of answering a series of questions to build up a paragraph. These questions often asked him to identify with the interests of those in power over him—parents, teachers, doctors, public authorities. He invariably sought ways to resist or subvert these assignments. One assignment, for instance, called for imagining "a helpful invention." The students were asked to write single-sentence responses to the following questions:
>
> > What kind of invention would help you?
> > How would it help you?
> > Why would you need it?
> > What would it look like?
> > Would other people be able to use it also?
> > What would be an invention to help your teacher?
> > What would be an invention to help your parents?
>
> Manuel's reply read as follows:
>
> A grate adventchin
>
> Some inventchins are GRATE!!!!!!!!!!!! My inventchin would be a shot that would put every thing you learn at school in your brain. It would help me by letting me graduate right now!! I would need it because it would let me play with my friends, go on vacachin and, do fun a lot more. It would look like a regular shot. Ather peaple would use to This inventchin would help

> my teacher parents get away from a lot of work I think a shot like this would be GRATE! (1991, p. 38)

Here, the contact zone is not between European conquerors and indigenous peoples, but between a child's subordinated place in the educational system and his perceptions of the teacher's task as one of communicating a predetermined body of knowledge (cf. Brooke, 1987; Cook, 1993). In completing the assignment, Pratt's son received the normal satisfactory credit; by completing the task in a parodic, contestatory manner, he also retained his own sense of resistance to power by appropriating the tasks of dominance for resistance.

The difficulty for students such as Manuel, who resist authority without so disrupting the order that they are removed from it, is that their efforts are officially unacknowledged, let alone encouraged: "If a classroom is analyzed as a social world unified and homogenized with respect to the teacher, whatever students do other than what the teacher specifies is invisible or anomalous to the analysis" (Pratt, 1991, p.38; here we can see how and why Poma's 17th century letter disappeared—it was invisible, outside the boundaries of officially recognized discourse). Against this, border education is the project of explicitly encouraging students to develop their own positions and to recognize the positions of others. Such resistance is only rarely successful in restructuring larger social systems, but recognizing oppression and enacting resistance are still necessary tasks if only because they hold the potential for success.

Although the concepts of borders and zones are important in helping bring about the recognition of multiple cultures so that they might be remapped, the use of maps sometimes ignores ideological issues. Certainly it is important to map the boundaries of oppression and inequality, but these mappings can also potentially exacerbate and perpetuate existing conditions—us versus them. The broader concept itself becomes problematic in the ways that it encourages this attitude—useful for analysis, but perhaps an impediment to change. "It is not enough," Anzaldúa (1987) wrote:

> [T]o stand on the opposite river bank, shouting questions, challenging patriarchal, white conventions. A counterstance locks one into a duel of oppressor and oppressed; locked in mortal combat, like the cop and the criminal, both are reduced to a common denominator of violence. (p. 78)

Borders are important acts of recognition, but recognition should lead to rethinkings, real cultural changes.

The Multiplication of Spaces: Articulation Theory

The projects of border pedagogy and contact zones explicitly attempt to rethink and remap, but it is difficult to hold in mind the concepts of multiplicity, fragmentation, and contradiction and simultaneously think in terms of the binary distinctions offered by the weighty metaphor of borders, which encourage us to think of discourses as primarily geographical and national. Border pedagogy must also be supplemented in one of its most crucial tasks—that of developing what Giroux (1992a) called a "language of possibility" that is able to speak about reform without falling into empty utopianism. Although borders are useful for describing situations of repression and/or of difference, there is little theoretical import given to the task of how, specifically, to remake both the map and the world.

Articulation theory offers a practical approach to remaking borders. In this work, meanings are not given, boundaries are not fixed, but always multiple, open to connection in more than one way (often at the same time). As Giroux (1992a) recognized, "cultural studies offers a theoretical terrain for rethinking schooling as a form of cultural politics and provides a discourse of intervention and possibility" (p. 164).

As Hall (1989) situated it, important aspects of articulation theory grow out Althusser's (1970, 1971) critiques of Marxism, especially the difficulties (now much discussed) of totalizing social critiques in terms of economic class divisions—an important observation for critiquing the metaphor of borders. The movement from geographical to ideological frameworks helps us out of the one-to-one concept of bordering regions and toward the complexity of real social life. But a rehearsal of some of the ideological theory on which Hall began his project might be useful. In classical Marxism, economic class has remained the primary determinant of society; peoples' ideologies simply reflect their class belongingness in the stratifications that characterize societies. Ideology then expresses a form of "false consciousness." Althusser began a critique of this construction of ideology by attempting to account for the ways in which ideologies are lived relations produced and reproduced in and through social structures.

One of Althusser's (1971) key conceptions is the ways in which cultures are reproduced—by visible force and by invisible, unconscious assent. Althusser distinguished between the Repressive State Apparatus (RSA), which controls activities through the institutions of police, military, courts, and so on, and the Ideological State Apparatus (ISA), which works through schools, churches, and popular media. The exercise of power by an RSA is always an explicit (and sometimes physically violent) activity. Less visible are the mechanisms of control used by ISAs, which reproduce subject positions at the level of thought. ISAs act in much more powerful ways because they do not rely on explicit coercion but arise out of apparently spontaneous free will. Although not directly related to the coercive forces, ideological forces such as schools reproduce an ideology that encourages subjects to view their oppressions as "natural" ones.

In Althusser's theories, then, the submission of subjects to rule is not an instance of orders being given from the ruler to the ruled (as when the victors in a war sit down to redraw maps), but of an *overdetermination* of invisible influences, working from multiple sites of production, that result in the workings of social and political oppression. Ideological state apparatuses and repressive state apparatuses both operate with the same general goals, but through a multitude of techniques, a relatively coherent *system*. Althusser spoke of the way in which subjects are "hailed"—being a "subject" is also being "subjected." When an ideology hails the subject, the subject recognizes that call and, thereby, assumes a place in the social system. The dominant ideology positions subjects from people by constructing (and reconstructing) a systemic place for each person, a place that each subject then recognizes as "naturally" their own. As Hall (1983) developed the idea:

> There is the discourse of "the market," the discourse of "production," the discourse of "the circuits": each produces a different definition of the system. Each also locates us differently—as worker, capitalist, wage worker, wage slave, producer, consumer, etc. Each thus *situates* us as social actors or as a member of a social group in a particular relation to the account of the process as depicted in the discourse. The worker who relates his or her condition of existence in the capitalist process as "consumer"—who enters the system, so to speak, through that gateway—participates in the process by way of a different practice from those who are inscribed in the system as "skilled labourer"—or not inscribed at all, as "housewife." All these descriptions have effects which are real. They make a material difference, since how we act in certain situations depends on what our definitions of the situations are. (p. 77)

Technologies, as objects articulating and being articulated by ideologies, are powerful methods for constructing subjects at least partially into specific positions. Consider, for example, the way in which a ringing telephone "hails" the hearer, who is instantly put into the position of accepting demands even before they know the identity of the caller (Marvin, 1988; Ronell, 1989). Even if we refuse to answer the phone, we recognize ourselves as the subject of the call. Similarly, an instructional hypertext normally offers users a large number of possible paths through the document, but the ideology of the workplace (prioritizing technological efficiency) provides for only one correct choice among the many offered; the subject hailed as worker is positioned in a mechanical way in this machine.

The primary failing of Althusser's version of ideology can be located in its apparent dismissal of the possibility of resistance. Althusserian ideologies still seem to act in the interest of the dominant class—the repressed always recognize themselves in the hailings of the dominant ideology and cannot resist that domination because the overall system works without significant contradictions. This conception of ideology seems to work automatically and without significant challenges to authority. As Hall (1985) commented on the pessimism of Althusser's work:

> If there is an ideology of the dominated classes, it seems to be one which is perfectly adapted to the functions and interests of the dominant class within the capitalist mode of production.... Ideology seems to perform the function required of it (i.e., to reproduce the dominance of the dominant ideology, to perform it effectively, and to go on performing it, without encountering any counter-tendencies). (p. 99)

Hall introduced the concept of articulation as a way of naming the struggles among these multiple and sometimes contradictory meanings. Rather than considering the operations of ideology as closed and always operating in the interests of the dominant ideology, Hall theorized a complex relationship that affords both the conservatism of ideologies and the forces that work against the conservation of power. Hall noted the ways in which terms carry weight (ideological influence) by the ways in which those terms are connected to chains of signifiers. Signifiers connect to multiple chains; dominant ideologies are constructed with and supported by the chains with the most force.

The construction (and possible analysis and reconstruction) of these social connections relies on four observations about the ways in which articulations are constructed (and deconstructed). Cultural theorist Slack (1989), defined articulations as sharing the following characteristics:

> (a) connections among elements are specific, particular, and nonnecessary— they are forged and broken in particular concrete circumstances; (b) articulations vary in their tenacity; (c) articulations vary in their relative power within different social configurations; and (d) different articulations empower different possibilities and practices. (p. 331)

For example, the articulation connecting "reading" to "technical efficiency" is particular, tenacious, and strong in functional hypertext. That articulation has much more power and tenacity than an articulation connecting functional reading to "analysis" and "critique" (two signifiers asserting greater force in the current articulation of "hypertext" in composition and literature discourses), even if these forces are present in weakened states.

The articulation commonly constructing functional hypertext depends on the naturalization of a specific type of efficiency—one that values transparent, high-speed, high-volume communication. Hypertext becomes constructed, in this articulation, a better medium than print because hypertext appears to be more transparent. The technological efficiency view of communication relies on the (often unacknowledged) acceptance of

Shannon and Weaver's (1949) model of communication, whose work on technologies of communication became a theory of human communication in which information is transferred from sender or writer to receiver or reader through a conduit or medium. In developing this line of inquiry in Chapter 3, I attempt to highlight some of the repressive articulations involved, as well as methods by which writers and readers of such texts might articulate hypertext to a broader, more explicitly social discourse. So although this articulation of hypertext certainly prioritizes a relatively stable and strong meaning for the key term *hypertext* in functional discourses, that meaning is not completely closed to change. Hall's work modulates importantly between structural determinisms and postmodernism: There is both structure and contingency. The opportunity for social action shows most clearly when one moves from one discourse to another (in the current study, the movement across the numerous discourses of hypertext). The simultaneous disjunctions and connections between the significations of the same term across two (and more) discourses shows places in which chains of signification may slip.

As I argue in later chapters, we might begin thinking productively about the mixing of discourses in relation to literacy technologies such as hypertext. Many current articulations of online research space (including databases such as DIALOG, LEXIS/NEXIS, and some areas of the World Wide Web), for example, encourage one, limited concept of literacy (the ability to move information from one point to another in the capitalist sphere). However, every act in this sphere must also, necessarily, correspond to a movement in the discourse of functional hypertext (with which users come to learn accepted place[s] in technological systems[2]) and socialized communication (determined by the situation of online research space as a tool—albeit subordinated for the moment—for communication from one person to another). Normally, the commodity articulation makes (or attempts to make) invisible the operations of the subordinated discourses. But the borders between these discourses intersect in the act of using an online research space, even if that fact is not often commented on. These intersections are, at the very least, spaces where determined users might rearticulate their uses in important ways.

INVADING THE HEARTLAND: CRITIQUE AND CHANGE

[2] As I pointed out in an earlier footnote and as I discuss at length in Chapter 3, a user's "accepted place[s] in the technological systems" is not always organized by the organizational chart's hierarchy, but in post-Fordist corporations a complex internalization of corporate identity and social functions defined by that identity and purpose.

The related projects of linguistic contact zones, border pedagogy, and articulation theory offer powerful approaches to thinking about the ideologies of hypertext and ways of rewriting the technology. Border pedagogy and linguistic contact zones recognize the propensity for pluralism and multiculturalism to develop as mere lip service, especially in a technology such as hypertext that purports to give all writers a voice and to turn readers automatically into writers.

By also taking up articulation theory and noting its strong relationships with (as well as differences from) the previous two approaches, we can begin to see the ways in which these unequal and repressive relationships might be rearticulated; they offer an additional way in which to critique the connotations of "information" as "power" and "knowledge" and "commodity," perhaps rewritten as "possibility" and "access" and "multiplicity." Articulation theory is well suited to critiques of technology such as hypertext because of the ways in which this perspective tracks multiple, contradictory influences throughout the processes of production, mediation, consumption, and redefinition (see, e.g., Hebdige's *Subculture*, 1979, and *Hiding*, 1988).

These activities begin with the recontextualization of the differing articulations of hypertext. As technology critic Feenberg (1991) argued, capitalist organization of technology and labor operates through decontextualization and a corresponding naturalization of this process: "Technology is constructed from the bits and fragments of nature that, after being abstracted from all specific contexts, appear in a technically useful form" (p. 185; see also Hirschhorn, 1984; Paradis, 1991; Zuboff, 1988). This abstraction allows the rearticulation of the worker's body into the mechanism of the assembly line as in Taylorism (as well as less visibly oppressive articulations). Roughly similar abstractions turn the processes of reading and writing into mechanisms of technological production and consumption, information ownership, transfer, and exchange. This rearticulation of the functions of reading and writing in hypertext are possible not only at the most obvious level, functional hypertext, but also the navigation of large information spaces, whether constructed as databases of information or docuverses of writing (Johnson-Eilola, 1994a) as well as interpersonal communication (Johnson-Eilola & Selber, in press; Selfe, 1992; Zuboff, 1988).

This multisite analysis constructs complex, often contradictory relationships at both local and global levels. This is how articulation theory can help, as Slack (1989) wrote, make evident articulations "we either can't see at all or that, if we do see, appear like shadowy ghosts or possibilities—dreamy and unreal" (p. 335). This project can help us think about sets of technological uses without reducing their intersecting social spaces—the spaces in which all of us write and are written—into cause-and-effect relationships. Instead, we can work toward defining critical literacies of hypertext. Hypertext can be rearticulated as neither a completely conservative replication and automation nor a postmodern dispersal of order and agency, but instead as a conscious struggle to appropriate, reinvent, and criticize structures of meaning and power.

Chapter 3
Little Machines:
Hypertext, Automation,
and the Politics of Amnesia

The ability to forget the machine is the ideal of technical perfection.
—Jacques Ellul (1964, p. 413)

Elegance is the key to good design: the machine must perform all necessary actions, and no unnecessary ones, with the fewest possible parts. Although a machine with more parts might be better able to do all the required tasks, it would cost more to build and maintain; moreover, the risk of parts slippage would increase. Generally in good mechanical design the same part or series of parts simultaneously transmits power, transforms motion, and controls the speed and direction of movement, in this way minimizing the number of parts and preventing unwanted action.
—Larry Hirschhorn (1984, p. 16)

A book itself is a little machine…. We have been criticized for overquoting literary authors. But when one writes, the only question is which other machine the literary machine can be plugged into, must be plugged into in order to work.
—Gilles Deleuze and Félix Guattari (1987, p. 4)

Although we grant much fame and funding to big technology, our cleverest machines are easily forgotten, used without thought, adapted, and made part of our lives. As Haraway (1985) analyzed the situation, technologies become intangible—"made of sunshine; they are all light and clean because they are nothing but signals… ether, quintessence" (p. 70). Although textual forms such as hypertext fiction retain the capability to surprise us (Douglas, 1992; Heim, 1987; Joyce, 1992), most hypertext escapes our critical attention. The texts that help us learn how to use computers become with hypertext so light and clean that we can no longer easily question their operations. Where consulting functional instructions in print requires

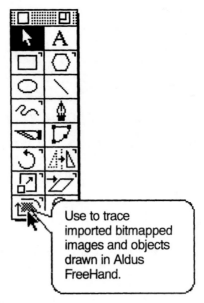

FIGURE 3.1.   Balloon help in Aldus FreeHand 4.0.

retrieving books from shelves, locating and consulting indexes, physically turning pages to locate information, functional hypertexts automate many of these physical actions (Figure 3.1). When these texts work, we are hard pressed to notice, let alone criticize, the interplay of social forces in writing and using online help.

Anyone who has used well-designed functional hypertext can recall the sensation that whatever was needed was right there (such a sensation has become, in fact, the definition of "well-designed"; see Norman, 1988; Price & Korman, 1993; Woolever & Loeb, 1994). The machine seems to anticipate the user's needs, responding like a shadow to every wish and movement. The machine is never completely absent, but it becomes increasingly diffi-cult—pointless, it seems—to reflect on the operations of the machine, like thinking about breathing. Functional hypertexts are defined, socially and politically, in this politics of amnesia.

For these reasons, research on hypertext is less likely to invoke the terms "reading" or "writing" than to name as its topic "knowledge management," "processing load," or "information flow." Through the act of naming, such research constructs a vision that is "sanitized," a general process Hall (1989) defined in the context of communication as erasing or denying the "funda-mentally dirty, semiotic, semantic, discursive character of the media in their cultural dimensions" (p. 48). In the automation of an automotive assembly line, the union's uproar can remind us of the sociopolitical ramifications of advanced mechanization; when the act of reading a text becomes automated, the strongest cries are frequently those for faster, more powerful, more efficient technologies. The relative invisibility of functional documentation—print or online—is attested to by its notable absence in the topics discussed by technical communication teachers (including the large number of those whose work also involves composition theory and practice).

Although work by academics such as Miller (1979), Sullivan (1990), Allen (1992), Ede and Lunsford (1990), and Odell and Goswami (1985) among others has begun constructing a bridge between composition and workplace writing, these works typically pay more attention to the writing and reading of memoranda (Dombrowski, 1992) and progress reports (Ede & Lunsford, 1990; Miller & Selzer, 1985; Paradis, Dobrin, & Miller, 1985)—activities that are considered somehow more constructive, creative, and demanding than the writing and reading of online help. Functional documents such as online help have been relegated to technical, efficiency-oriented analyses that, although certainly important, in isolation may contribute to a mystification and naturalization of technology (exceptions include Dobrin, 1983; Johnson-Eilola & Selber, in press; Paradis, 1991; and Selber, 1995b, among others).

The immersion of composition teachers in an increasingly technological culture has surely not gone without a growing awareness of our own complicity with this culture, but our critiques have too frequently prioritized "creative" workplace writing—memos and reports—over the less visible functional documents, which are so ingrained into the technology that they seem a technological rather than a human function, ubiquitous rather than isolated to single environments such as the office or factory. Ideological analyses of networks of memoranda such as the *Challenger* shuttle disaster can (relatively) easily be seen as cultural narratives questioning the construction of meaning (Dombrowski, 1992; Herndl, Fennell, & Miller, 1991). After all, technical reports and proposals nearly always contain some sort of situational material explicitly referencing a real-world context, a stated purpose, and a plan or request for action. Even though this contextualization does not exhaust meaning (the explicit contextualization is rarely critical in a broad social sense), it at least serves to remind both technical communicators and compositionists that there is a context that might be pried open to questioning:

> [A] purpose statement casts the content report in light of on-going social, organizational, professional, and discourse community concerns while the summary section and conclusions and recommendations section cast the raw material of the report in interpretations and applications, for example, constructions, along the line of social interests broadly defined. (Dombrowski, 1992, p. 82)

One of the difficulties of trying to think critically and politically about functional documents, either print or online, is that too much is obscured: The text denies its context in the act of functioning. The very context, in effect, denies itself in order to more fully take advantage of resources (including the designers and users). Functional documents seem to afford evaluation along only one axis: efficiency, in the strict technical sense of swift and easy operation.

Compositionists should be interested in this situation. Composition theory and practice retains the ability to help technical communicators think rhetorically—in the broad sense—about their activities. Writing about the connections between classical rhetoric and technical communication, Dale Sullivan (1990) observed:

> [T]hough technical communication shares classical rhetoric's orientation toward the professions, those of us who teach technical communication don't often think of ourselves as carrying on the rhetorical tradition. Indeed, it is rather hard to do so, since we teach thought forms and discourse forms demanded by the workplace, and we often find ourselves representing the military-industrial complex instead of the humanistic tradition. (p. 375)

Although Sullivan placed technical communication "even more in tune with [classical rhetoric's] aims than composition" (p. 375), composition may be better able to mobilize cultural analyses of functional documentation, especially in the more radical forms of composition theory and practice that I identified in the previous chapter, drawing on cultural studies and border pedagogies.

In addition, as writers in many areas begin to rely more heavily on computerized writing and research environments, ways of learning computer use also play critical roles. Although even paper-based documentation tends to make invisible numerous assumptions about the complex relations between user and technologies, online documentation holds the potential to broaden and strengthen that sense of invisibility by increasing the technical efficiency of texts. The technical environment constructs a very specific, powerful, increasingly prevalent form of hypertext. If we are to design and use such environments, we must gain some measure of critical awareness and the ability to deconstruct our uses of such text even while we write and read them.

Hypertext is appropriated in this specific technical environment as one way of increasing a limited type of technical efficiency—the speed and volume of accurate information flow. Using the text should be both fast and transparent. What becomes problematic is the (seemingly) automatic manner in which the rationalization of technical efficiency generates its own justification and provides a map of its own conquests and goals as pregiven and natural. Functional documents succeed, in part, by redefining the terms of success, by breaking down complex, hazy activities such as writing or page layout into discrete steps. Aspects of the activity not amenable to this process are replaced or simply removed. The apparently self-constituting object remains a powerful way to discourage critical reflection on the object.

Functional hypertext here is mapped as a naturally occurring act of technological progress. What is not mapped are the influences of the Shannon and Weaver (1949) model of communication; the breakdown of top-heavy (and "inefficient") hierarchical systems of overt control; the accompanying Foucauldian internalization of mechanisms of control; the evolution of the earlier, industrial movement from apprenticeship to self-paced, machine-based learning, and more. Consider, for example, the types of uses engendered by the Shannon and Weaver model, sometimes called the transmission model of communication. In accepting the transmission model of communication, the primary goal of functional communication becomes increased technical efficiency—increased speed and volume and clearer channels. Because hypertext appears to be, in these cases, an automation (and rendering transparent) of communication media, hypertext becomes disarticulated from the critiques of language, technology, education, and society that were present to at least some degree in the pioneering work of Bush and Nelson discussed in Chapter 1: Bush pointed to language as the imprecise medium impeding understanding between cultures; Nelson critiqued technological mystification; and both argued for hypertext as a way to break down academic and professional specialization in order to help people increase knowledge. The articulation of functional hypertext appropriates and submerges these forces (even while frequently citing them in principle) as it maps out functional texts on the landscape of technical efficiency, rather than one of ethics or social interaction. Katz (1992), discussing the ethical implications of technological expediency in Nazi rhetoric, argued that technological culture generates an ethic of technical efficiency:

> With expediency, the only ethical criterion necessary is the perceptible movement toward the technical goal to be achieved—including expediency itself. Indeed, expediency is the only ethic that can be "measured".... While expediency can be the basis of desire and emotion (like greed or the lust for power), the ethic of expediency is an exclusively logical, systematic, even quantifiable one, can lead to a rationality grounded in no other ethic but its own, and is symptomatic of a highly scientific, technological age. (p. 266)

I am not about extend a brief analysis of the rhetoric of expediency constructing this genre of Nazi prose to blanket contemporary functional hypertext; I only wish to tease out and complicate one of the primary tendencies articulating functional hypertext (and, to some extent, hypertext in general). The rise in technical efficiency becomes articulated as the fundamental goal, almost exclusive of other concerns.[1] Other possible articulations for efficiency become secondary if considered at all. Broader social issues, for example, can be addressed by different articulations of efficiency, such as quality of life, including measures such as emotional well-being, ecological stability and sustainability, social relationships, and so on. But as Feenberg (1991) argued, "soft" variables such as clean air are frequently overshadowed by "hard" variables that are more amenable to quantification—cash flow or net increase of output of goods, for example (p. 127). Technology obviously cannot completely enclose writers or readers in the discourse of technique—ecological activists have, at least partially, succeeded in making the environment a factor in definitions of efficiency.[2] The automation never succeeds in making the writer or reader fully disappear into the machine. But concepts such as technical efficiency, automation, and speed remain the primary criteria for judging and developing functional hypertexts, whereas other goals—social change, for example—are frequently secondary if admitted at all. The discourse of functional hypertext provides a powerful definition of our positions in relationship to technology. As Hall (1983) asserted, "how we act in certain situations depends on what our definitions of the situation are" (p. 77). And Slack (1989) reminded us that, "The more powerful the articulations by which we live, the more closed off we become to alternative practices and possibilities as well as to the very critical faculty that allows us to know that we are living out social choices, not necessities" (p. 335).

The network of forces surrounding the ideology of automation in functional hypertext naturalize (seem to necessitate) the subordination of users to a part of what is conceptually a little machine, an automatic text that admits little creativity, construction, or overt political thinking or action.

This development occurs in a complex network of social and technological forces: not only automation, but also models of communication, speed, technical efficiency, and the social and corporate structures of control inherent to late capitalism—not merely visible, coercive control but also, perhaps especially, hegemonic arrangements of subordination, con-

---

[1] Obviously other issues remain—moral issues involving a range of topics, from the loss of human life to ecological disasters—but these issues are also too easily submerged, as illustrated by the difficulty with which automobile passive-restraint devices such as airbags have become adopted by automakers, or the ease with which environmental damage can be more than "balanced out" by the number of citizens employed by the factory or corporation causing the damage.

[2] However, this new articulation between environmentalism and capitalism has resulted in confusions over the definition of "environmentally friendly" or "ecologically sound," as witnessed by the green revolution in marketing.

trol through fragmentation and internalization. The way in which efficiency is articulated by these numerous forces as "technical" or "mechanical" immediately suggests a binary division in which "functional" documents are opposed to "dysfunctional" documents, things that either do not work or work lazily or inefficiently, like broken machines. (The latter class would seem to include such texts as essays, letters, novels, poetry, and everyday conversation.) Automation in hypertext, in fact, exerts force beyond functional hypertext, influencing in a less visible way the construction and use of other forms of hypertext in technical communication in general as well as literature, scholarship, and collaboration.

All hypertext, to some extent, relies on automation—the automation of turning pages, exchanging commentary, constructing a new text from old pieces. But functional hypertext as it is most frequently articulated prioritizes this automation. In the quotes opening this chapter, when Ellul, Hirschhorn, and Deleuze and Guattari invoke the term *machine* in three different meanings—technical, social, and psychoanalytical—they illustrate not only the divisions but the connections among these discourses. What must be taken from each of their comments is the necessity of critique and self-examination, the resistance to the idea that this version of automation is ever the only possibility or always the primary one. The same quality of linguistic leakage allowing the term *machine* to critique common mechanical devices can be applied to the key terms (*node* and *link*) connoting various articulations of hypertext.

The goal of simple technical efficiency supplies this particular construction of hypertext with a force so persistent that it seems both natural and immovable. Work on functional hypertext use, especially in important development areas such as human factors and cognitive research, inevitably compares the "old" way of reading (paper or online hierarchical-linear) with the "new" way (hypertext; see, e.g., Horton, 1991, p. 23). The distinction between old and new technologies is articulated to other strong social forces—such as the processes of developing new technologies and ideologies of human progress. "The specific articulation between the development of new technology and progress is neither determined nor necessary," Slack (1989) notes:

> Rather, it was brought into existence and is held in place only in conjunction with a whole series of other social forces, including but not limited to, the privileging of the individual in Western culture, the legal fiction and cultural convention of attributing the invention of new technologies to individuals, capitalist economic practice in which ideas and inventions are considered intellectual property, the belief that progress is the evolution of humankind from a state of primitiveness to increasing sophistication and perfection, and the practice of essentializing the role of technology through the designation of principle effects versus side effects.... The nature of technologies matters less

> than their novelty, their sophistication, their ability to accomplish something
> faster and more efficiently than could previously be accomplished. (p. 331)

This articulation of technological progress requires that researchers map out (explicitly or implicitly, purposefully or accidentally) the scope and possible connections between specific technologies, creating genres, uses, and distinctions. Early uses of the telephone, for example, were mapped to such areas as the radio, with operators reading news, stock reports, and weather, and transmitting concerts (Marvin, 1988). The articulation of the telephone as a device affording verbal conversation (business or personal) took some time to gain strength (Fischer, 1991; Marvin, 1988). Neither designers nor users are free to map a technology in any way; some mappings are more likely—profitable and perceivable—than others. The relative cultural strengths of the goals of mechanical efficiency against those of interpersonal communication, at least in the workplace, help us to account for the success of mapping hypertext as little machines rather than other possible (even perceivable) articulations.

Although from time to time mapping is seen as creative and constructive, most frequently it is termed *discovery*; the terms *invention* and *discovery* have gained a near-synonymous relationship in our society in terms of technological progress. This slippage is not new: As Pratt (1992) pointed out, Sir Richard Burton (1860/1961) "creates" as much as "discovers" new lands in his travel writings. Even if the original act is conceived of as a creative invention, it must be marketed by placing it on the map and relating it to older technologies, a move that naturalizes novelty in a way that makes it marketable. As Deleuze and Guattari (1987) took pains to point out, such maps are too often conceived of by their makers and users as disinterested reflections of reality, "tracings on something that comes readymade.... [T]racings are like the leaves of a tree" (p. 12).

The idea of tracing reality in the research and development of functional hypertext encourages a naturalization of, among other things, powerful ideas about the goals and ways of using the technology. But as researchers articulate a particular technology such as functional hypertext—mapping (while calling it tracing) that technology's historical relationship with other technologies and forces—they are constructing one particular instantiation: They are articulating hypertext as the new, improved book machine. Designers encourage users to see the articulation as a natural evolution of the book. What is missing from these maps are considerations of how and why it became possible to connect books and machines, what specific articulation of communication provides the bridge between the two deceivingly simple terms, and how we might more explicitly engage in mapping and rearticulation.

In the final section of this chapter, and again in Chapter 6, I begin placing tracings back on maps. This activity serves as a way of encouraging both developers and users to see this particular articulation as only one construction among many, as well as to see their own actual and potential roles in these articulations. Identifying the contradictions inherent in the network of relations structuring hypertext in the particular discourse of a function acts as a way of opening potentialities. Such ruptures open possibilities for rearticulating functional hypertext use away from a goal of increased technical efficiency through simplistic automation (without losing sight of the very real benefits of some sort of technical efficiency and automation) and toward a more socially situated construction of functional hypertext. The recent emphasis in both business and academe on constructing and nurturing a more collaborative atmosphere (Bruffee, 1973; Ede & Lunsford, 1990; Johnson-Lenz & Johnson-Lenz, 1992; Kanter, 1989; Sproull & Kiesler, 1991; Trimbur, 1989) offers a potentially rearticulatory force against some of the negative aspects of the automation and/or disappearance of writing and reading in functional hypertext.

AN AUTOMATIC BOOK: THE HyperCard Help Stack

At first glance, functional hypertext appears to emulate print versions of functional texts—consultive documents in which hypertext helps readers find information faster and more easily. The differences between a print functional text and a functional hypertext are deceptively simple; normally, a virtual version of the print text is overlaid with conceptually simple searching and navigational mechanisms. Figure 3.2 shows an online help document distributed with early versions of Apple Computer's popular HyperCard. HyperCard was included with all Macintosh computers sold between November 1987 and September 1992 (Cohen, 1993). Although HyperCard is clearly only one particular instantiation of the general idea of hypertext, the prevalence of the program and Apple Computer's vision of hypertext are closely related to popular conceptions of the technology.

The HyperCard Help Stack contains 414 interconnected cards. Its structure and size are typical of functional or technical hypertext. Users working in HyperCard—either using or designing hypertext documents—can access help by holding down the command and question-mark keys on the keyboard simultaneously or by choosing a Help menu command in the program. As with many HyperCard documents, the appearance of the Help Stack emulates a print-text counterpart, in this case the spiral-bound manuals often distributed with the Apple Macintosh[3]. The "page" size is con-

---

[3] The HyperCard Help Stack is simulacra, however; it emulates a book that never was— this Help document exists only on screen and does not imitate any real-world paper document, as far as users can tell.

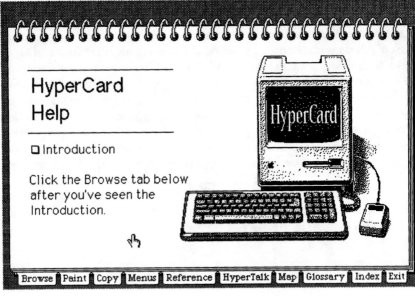

FIGURE 3.2. Opening screen from the HYPERCARD HELP STACK.

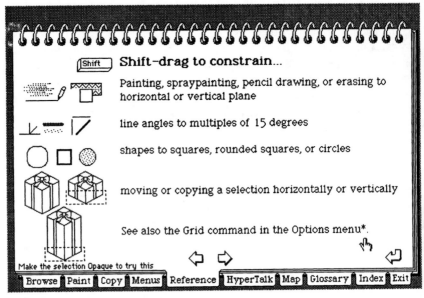

FIGURE 3.3. Information in reference section HYPERCARD HELP STACK.

densed to fit on the original 9-inch Macintosh screen and tabbed dividers allow users to move directly to the general section in which they are interested. Users clicking on the Paint tab can navigate hypertextually from a description of general painting functions to cross-indexed information in the Reference section of the manual. Users can move from the Reference screen shown in Figure 3.3 to other related items such as an entry on the screen grid (Figure 3.4; the cross-reference is indicated by the asterisk in the sentence "See also the Grid command in the Options menu*" near the bottom of the screen in Figure 3.3).

Numerous entries in the HYPERCARD HELP STACK are cross-referenced in this manner. Users clicking on the Map index tab can view a hierarchical map of the stack (Figure 3.5) and from there an additional version of the map showing the presence of cross-links in the stack (Figure 3.6). From either of these maps, users can move directly to relevant sections of the text by clicking on icons on the map.

We can gain some insight into the social forces articulating the HYPERCARD HELP STACK and similar forms of functional hypertext by examining the distinctions that can be made between the print book and the online book. Although it might be argued that a successor technology is not necessarily an

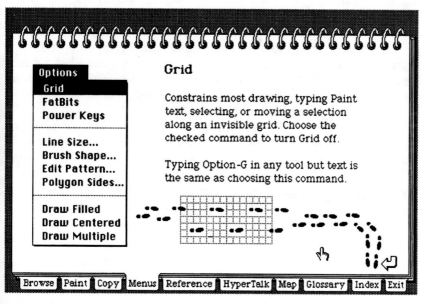

FIGURE 3.4. Cross-reference to related material.

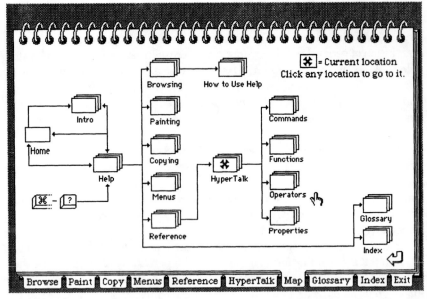

FIGURE 3.5. Tree-structured reference map in the HYPERCARD HELP STACK.

improvement over its predecessor,[4] the changes from one technology to the next are not arbitrary, but responses to the shifts in tension brought about in the cultural movement from book to screen and the placement of activities in a web of power relationships (Slack, 1989). Although the most visible aspects of this hypertext appear to be natural outgrowths of previous print mechanisms, what is important here is less what is said than what remains unsaid—from where does this technological progress spring? The virtualization of the book in the HYPERCARD stack encourages an evolutionary view of hypertext, clearly "descended" from the book.

For our project, one of the most interesting aspects of the shift from book to screen is the way in which key aspects of reading the text have been automated. The stack automates the apparently tedious (and potentially confusing) print-based task of manually retrieving a text from a shelf, turning to an index or endnotes page, memorizing a page number, turning to the relevant page, reading material (which might include subdeviations based on other references in that text portion), and, if necessary, returning to the

---

[4] The problem in determining how much "progress" or "efficiency" is exhibited by a technology is, as should be evident by this point, that the meanings of these terms are frequently constructed in a self-interested, self-validating manner (Ellul, 1964; Slack, 1989; Winner, 1986).

point at which the reader began the departure. This automation affords a host of perceived benefits, most notably the increased speed of "navigating" a virtual space over a physical one (Horn, 1990; Horton, 1990, 1991; Lai & Manber, 1991; Marchionini & Shneiderman, 1988). In addition, automating aspects of reading appears to make the act of communication less open to chance misinterpretations or misreadings (Bush, 1945/1987; Frisse, 1987; Horn, 1990; vanLehn, 1985). In this way, the HELP STACK functions as a more neutral or transparent channel for information transfer. From the viewpoints of typical hypertext developers and users, communication in hypertext is more efficient than communication in print because hypertext exerts smaller effects on the "real" message (or, perhaps, in print the medium is the message but that is a flaw of print).

As online help in general has evolved from the early example of the HYPERCARD HELP STACK, designers have been able to jettison explicit markers relating the online help to the book (shadowed pages, ring binders, etc.), retaining the crucial elements of easy navigation, relatively closed-ended solutions. As automation increases its force on this articulation, online help begins to automate the task itself rather than merely the act of locating information (Figure 3.7).

In this process of automation, the HYPERCARD HELP STACK articulates the use of functional hypertext as, at least partially, a mechanical activity—even more mechanical than print text use, because the machine operates

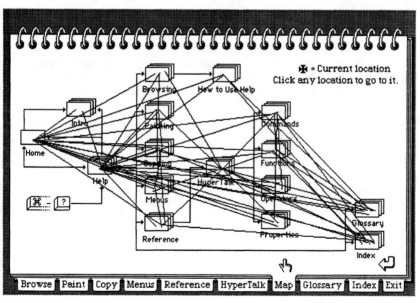

FIGURE 3.6. Network map in HYPERCARD HELP STACK.

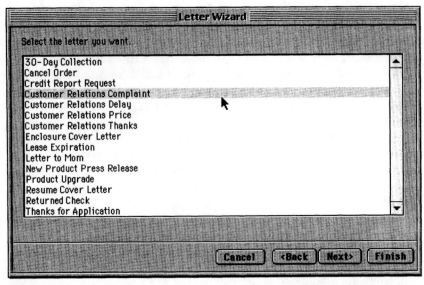

FIGURE 3.7. Boilerplate text for letters available in MICROSOFT WORD 6.0.

more efficiently than older, "manual" manuals.[5] Finding information in a text should not involve a great deal of thought; better that the process of locating information is removed as much as possible from the picture. Reading and understanding should be automatic. Turning pages in order to find a pertinent section merely distracts the reader from the "real" task. This mechanical view is given even greater and broader force through the model of communication held by many technical communication theorists and practitioners. Reading a functional document should be as simple and easy as possible; the less the reader makes choices in using or interpreting the text (which page to turn to next or how to decode a specific sentence), the better (Flower, Hayes, & Swarts, 1983; Horn, 1990; Horton, 1990; Price & Korman, 1993; Woolever & Loeb, 1994). Here, hypertext is not merely a machine, but a better machine than print because hypertext is a technically more efficient machine.

The emphasis here on transparency in technical communication is not a surprising or even recent development. Technical communication has long been framed by its practitioners as an activity and discipline in which the medium should (ideally) be transparent: Connors' (1982) history of technical communication identifies the splitting off of technical communication

---

[5] The machine view of the book exists in print as well, with information being transferred from author to reader or sender to receiver.

from English departments as due in part to the heightened sense of a need for efficiency in functional and technical prose. And, although maintaining a critical stance on both the fluidity and power of definitions,[6] Dobrin (1983) notes that "technical writing's greatest success comes when it is swallowed easily and digested quickly" (p. 247). Flower et al.'s (1983) guidelines for writers of functional documents—what they call the "scenario principle"—suggests to writers that good documents are those that readers fit into most readily. As Mathes and Stevenson (1991) put it, organizational writers must "address the needs of individual people" (p. 18).

Whether these goals for technical communication are good or bad is not really under consideration here; I would not want to use functional documentation that made communication difficult for no apparent reason. What is at issue is the apparent prohibition on questioning the validity and overwhelming strength of simple, technical efficiency in this discourse. What I want to consider is the force of the model at work in common approaches to technical communication and functional hypertext. The Cartesian assumptions behind the information transmission model construct an environment in which information moves in and out of individual minds (even as those minds are connected by corporate and other social structures). The external structures connecting individuals provide, for the writer, channels through which information can run, applying force when it strikes the mind at the other end.

A text such as the HYPERCARD HELP STACK operates in this environment at two primary levels: First, the text appears to the reader as a space offering greater than the usual number of choices; compared to print, hypertext in general is perceived as giving users more freedom. Hypertext is "an enabling rather than directive environment, offering unusually high levels of user control" (Marchionini, 1988, p. 8). This development in hypertext is frequently articulated to a specific type of freedom for the reader, in that he or she now determines which specific path may best address the current situation.

At the second level, less pronounced but more powerful, the hypertext restricts the reader's freedom by constructing an unnoticed paradox: Whereas an overly restricted and/or difficult-to-use functional text might give users a critical position in relation to the technology (see Winograd & Flores, 1987), a fluid, very fast functional text that appears to respond directly to the user's immediate needs constructs accommodating users. Dobrin's (1983) definition of technical communication as "writing that accommodates technology to the user" (p. 242) is intended to complicate this exchange, but functional hypertext helps users naturalize those accommo-

---

[6] "Technical writing doesn't just happen to occur alongside technology; it is a technological product, a residue of technological management" (Dobrin, 1983, p. 243).

dations. Functional hypertext is able to address the needs (defined in a limited way) of a heterogeneous audience more effectively than previous media. Whereas print texts in this context functioned as machines that moved meaning from writer to reader, the operation was less efficient in print than is possible in hypertext: Flipping pages, finding and consulting indices and tables of contents, and limitations in ordering and structuring material interfered with a reader's perceived ability to go where he or she wanted to go. As the text broke down, the reader was forced to consider relations to technology, the way in which the machine was never completely in his or her control. The lines of power became apparent. The user's technical needs are, after all, only one need among many types of needs; a "dysfunctional" hypertext (i.e., one that admits other concerns besides technical efficiency) brings to the surface not only a critique of technical efficiency, but also the lack of control many users have in their relations to technology and the limitations of technology. But in the functional articulation of hypertext, the text is made automatic, into a better little machine. Readers take their places "naturally" in a system of forces, appreciating the increased ease with which they entered into the technological system—they are less likely to reflect on their relations to technology.

HOW TO READ A BOOK:
THE LEGACY OF SHANNON AND WEAVER

Although communication theorists have recently begun investigating more complex models of technical communication (see, e.g., Slack, Miller, & Doak, 1993; Sullivan, 1990), most functional documents are constructed under the influence of a mechanical model of human communication. The HYPERCARD HELP STACK positions books as vehicles of movement and speed, transmission and reception. These little machines operate to carry information from writer to reader or technology to reader, something like the way that a vending machine delivers a particular item to a consumer according to the consumer's choice. As I discuss in Chapter 4, the connections between freedom and consumerism become especially strong in cases where information is more explicitly commodified (in fact, it is possible to envision functional texts that have strengthened the commodity force so that reading online help involves incremental fees—similar to, but more efficient than, the increasing use of toll phone numbers and pay-per-minute lines for software support).

Writers and readers in this model are encouraged to see reading as (ideally) automatic movement and transfer. For the writer, the words and structure of the text control the reader's movement and, consequently, how the reader will construct or receive knowledge based on that text. Information transmitted to the reader depends on his or her current location in the text: In occupying a specific place in the machine, the reader opens his or her mind to receive specific pieces of information automatically from the author or technology. From the reader's standpoint, the questions of movement and transmission are related to the task of following the path suggested by the text in order to receive information. Content-area novices in particular have difficulties rejecting this model and are less likely to critique its implications. "First-year students tend to... regard any bound volume as a *program for reading*" (Kaplan & Moulthrop, 1991, p. 8, italics in original). The reader here becomes a computer, a virtual machine whose subjectivity depends primarily on the codes of the program.

Models of Communication

From the standpoint of this transmission model, people write in order to communicate their thoughts to another person; people read in order to use the information that others have written. Developed by Bell Labs researcher Claude Shannon in the early 1940s primarily to address engineering issues in communication technologies, the transmission model involves the passage of a message from sender to receiver down a channel (Figure 3.8). Although Shannon's theories most directly addressed engineering issues, Warren Weaver argued that accuracy of transmission—"the technical problem"—provides the foundation for communication issues such as the semantic content and the effectiveness of a communication (Shannon & Weaver, 1949, p. 96). Consider the early Hayes and Flower (1980) cognitive model of the writing process as information transfer between internal

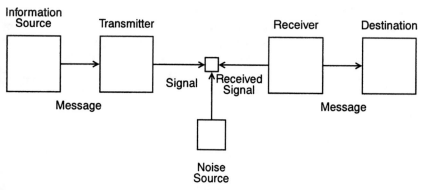

FIGURE 3.8. Shannon and Weaver Model of Communication.

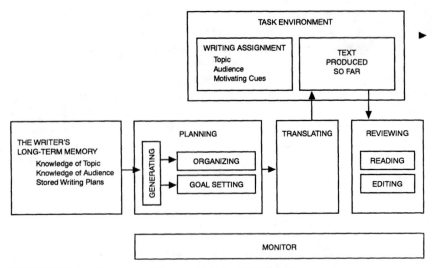

FIGURE 3.9.   Hayes and Flower Model of Writing Processes.

mental states (Figure 3.9). And both the first (1976) and the second (1991) edition of Mathes and Stevenson's widely used *Designing Technical Reports* (written for engineers rather than professional technical writers) provide a model strikingly similar to Shannon and Weaver's transmission model in order to explain the role of the engineer in a organization (Figure 3.10). Although researchers such as Flower have moved to a more social and political model (see, e.g., Flower, 1989), the transmission model continues to enjoy wide popularity in many areas, including technical communication.

In the Shannon and Weaver (1949) model, information is produced by an information source then coded or sent by a transmitter. After the coded signal passes through the channel (a passage that may introduce noise into the coded message), the receiver decodes the message (using the inverse of the coding procedure) and passes the message to the destination. The degree of information present in a message depends not on the volume of signals but on a combination of uncertainty and redundancy—highly predictable messages hold little information content. Shannon offered the example of Joyce's *Finnegan's Wake* as an unpredictable but highly informational message, and the 850-word basic English vocabulary as a system allowing the potential for messages of lesser information. Although certainly the technical problem is important to communication theory, the transmission model has come to represent the basis for broader issues such as meaning.

Even though both Shannon and Weaver (1949) sometimes wrote about the transmission model and its associated formulae as "intuitive" (p. 4) and "natural" (p. 101), the model is constructed according to the primary logic

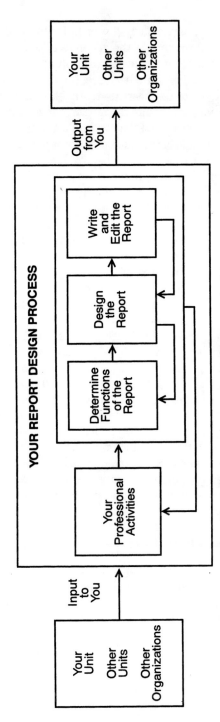

FIGURE 3.10. Mathes & Stevenson's model of organizational writing contexts.

of science and technology, particularly the need for methods amenable to quantification and measurement. As the graphics of the model testify, the earliest versions of Shannon's work saw communication as a one-way process, from sender to receiver. Furthermore, the task of the receiver is to decode a preexisting code, to discover the truth—the information—of the message; the receiver, ideally, acts as the mirror image of the sender.[7]

Shannon and Weaver articulated their idea of communication to a range of ideas about technology, one of the most important of which is the concept of noise. For Shannon and Weaver, noise is introduced only in the channel, where "the received message contains certain distortions, certain errors, certain extraneous material" (p. 109)—neither source or transmitter nor receiver or destination can introduce noise. Without noise, the sent and received messages should be identical. From the standpoint of the transmission model, the mirroring of the message in source and destination is the goal. Although noise increases the amount of information (uncertainty) in a signal, Shannon and Weaver were careful to stress that noise is undesirable, a type of information that should be avoided because "the received signal is not necessarily the same as that sent out by the transmitter" (p. 34). In order to compensate for noise, the encoding process may introduce redundancy by repeating the signal or by limiting the probability that one signal will be followed by another. The word "the," for example, has a higher probability of being followed by a noun than a verb, for example (the English language, Shannon and Weaver pointed out, is about 50% redundant). A good transmitter makes careful use of redundancy to offset noise in an efficient way. Noise is a crucial concept for their model because communicators must be able to predict ranges of error, margins for which they can account and then compensate through the introduction of just enough redundancy.

The value of a communication technology, as articulated by this model, depends on its efficiency: Channel use must be maximized. Noise becomes an important factor because the transmitter must balance the need for efficiency with the limitations of the channel. Information has to be coded, transmitted, and decoded as quickly as possible without distorting the decoder's ability to reconstruct the correct initial message. As Weaver said:

> The best transmitter... is that which codes the message in such a way that the signal has just those optimum statistical characteristics which are best suited to the channel to be used—which in fact maximize the signal (or one may say the channel) entropy and make it equal to the capacity C of the channel.
> This kind of coding leads... to the maximum rate C/H [where H is the

---

[7] Although later systems theory models began to include feedback and reversal of the sender-receiver roles, the dominant term in the model continues to be optimization of the technical aspects of communication—a search for simple, technical efficiency.

amount of information per symbol] for the transmission of symbols. But for this gain in transmission rate, one pays a price. For rather perversely it happens that as one makes coding more and more nearly ideal, one is forced to longer and longer delays *in the process of coding.* (p. 108, italics in original)

Although the transmission model of communication has been replaced with a host of (often contradictory) approaches, the idea of communication as a channel through which meaning flows from sender to receiver still remains the basis for much everyday activity as well as the majority of functional hypertext.[8] Even in technical communication, approaches that encourage a rich sense of audience may intend that awareness less as a way of thinking about the creativity and intersubjectivity surrounding the act of communication, but only as a way to determine the best packet and channel through which to send the information. Figure 3.10, taken from Mathes and Stevenson's (1991) popular *Designing Technical Reports*, provides only a slightly more complex model of communication. Characteristics of the medium that influence the "content" of a communication in any way (e.g., the effort necessary to turn pages in a book) are articulated as deficiencies in the medium. Under the influence of this model (explicit or implicit), texts are channels for transmitting information to a relatively passive receiver. In this construction, functional hypertext appears as a valuable medium because of the increased efficiency in reading that becomes possible (Charney, 1994; Horn, 1990; Horton, 1990).[9] Where in this articulation the print book was a machine in the manner of a primitive piece of technology (that, in modern times, became so common as to seem natural), functional hypertext is a machine for the future (which is to say, for today)—silent, clean, light, fast, and efficient.

Automating the Book 1:
Automation and Volume of Information Transfer

In this seemingly endless construction of technological progress, the book is articulated as old technology and hypertext as new technology—faster, easier to control, amenable to fast reproduction, distribution, and update

---

[8] Although contemporary theories of technical communication typically oppose the transmission model, most technical communicators continue to place users in this model—as the receiver of information (see critiques in Allen, 1992; Johnson-Eilola & Selber, in press; Miller, 1979; Slack et al. 1993). The primary example in this chapter, the HYPERCARD HELP STACK, provides evidence of the prevalence of this model for users of functional documents.

[9] There are other benefits as will in this relationship: increased storage capability, interactive graphics, and so forth. The rationale and utility of these other characteristics are related back into their relationships to efficiency (each picture worth a thousand words).

(Horn, 1990; Horton, 1990; Walker, 1987). Although the print book possessed some crucial mechanical aspects—a machine for transferring an author's intended meaning truthfully to a reader—those mechanics have today become so naturalized as to seem pretechnological. In general and specific instances, functional hypertext is constructed as a technological heir to the print book. But, paralleling Deleuze and Guattari's (1987) comparison between the games of chess and Go, functional hypertext, like chess, is "institutionalized, regulated, coded.... a question of arranging a closed space for oneself, thus of going from one point to another, of occupying the maximum number of squares with the minimum number of spaces" (p. 353).[10] Although functional hypertext constructs a freedom of movement for users in concert with that user's specific context, freedom is culturally defined as a system of prohibitions and approvals that regulate the user's needs. The little machine of functional hypertext operates through and is regulated by scientific management techniques and technologies constructing late capitalism, a relationship often encouraging automation as a route to increased managerial control, speed, and profit (Hirschhorn, 1984; Shaiken, 1986; Zuboff, 1988). Hypertext as a virtual medium might embody a number of forms and articulations, but the weight of this form of efficiency constructs a conservative, relatively powerless approach to writing and reading.

By conceptually and operationally connecting functional hypertext to printed books, technical communicators naturalize both the coding procedures of print communication and, at a broader level, the role of technology in our culture. As Selber (1995b) argued, "The metaphors we use to define and describe texts, nodes, and links encourage developments and uses of this technology along particular axes of disciplinary interest" (p. 65). According to Eldred and Fortune (1992), "the 'book' metaphor... implicitly encourages users to approach the hyperdocument with the same processing assumptions and strategies they would use with a conventional text" (p. 68). Eldred and Fortune's critiques are accurate, but can be extended further. The metaphor of the book is limiting for one group of theorists—Eldred and Fortune assert that hypertext-as-book constitutes a waste of technological resources—but the metaphor is very productive for those who are primarily interested in increasing their control over the technical efficiency of work. The unexamined linkage from book to hypertext (under the guise of constructing a more efficient

---

[10] The war machine, however, like Go "proceeds altogether differently, territorializing and deterritorializing" space, working to "make the outside a territory in space; consolidate that territory by the construction of a second, adjacent territory; deterritorialize the enemy by shattering his territory from within; deterritorialize oneself by renouncing, by going elsewhere" (Deleuze & Guattari, 1987, p. 353). Such movements roughly map rearticulations I work toward in Chapter 6.

machine) deepens the degree to which users are integrated into the culture of production and consumption.

But I want to discuss the more pervasive sense of automation—largely unquestioned outside of small, academic circles—inherent in much hypertext. Introducing a new metaphor for the specific technology of hypertext—more explicitly associative or collaborative rather than linear-hierarchical and product, for example—will not automatically change this aspect of hypertext use. Eldred and Fortune, for example, observed that Landow's (1992c) analysis of the INTERMEDIA hypertext system as network rather than book still commonly ends with users focusing on single works or authors (Eldred & Fortune, 1992, p. 71).[11] Even when hypertext does not look like a book, more powerful social structures encourage writers and readers to think of the medium as a channel (or at best a methodology) for automation.

The tenacity of the little machines articulation owes much to the widespread belief in the benefits of automation. In fact, we can measure some aspects of the general cultural faith in the power of little machines hypertext because the articulation remains strong despite several critiques of hypertext in general (Charney, 1987, 1994; Eldred & Fortune, 1992; Halasz, 1988; Johnson-Eilola, 1993a; Meyrowitz, 1991; Moulthrop, 1989b; Raskin, 1987), a growing body of empirical data illustrating the complexities of hypertext reading, especially when users are concerned with gains in simple technical efficiency (Hardman, 1989; McMath, Tamaru, & Rada, 1989; Monk, Walsh, & Dix, 1988; Rubens, 1991), and the abundant discussion of the difficulties of navigating in a virtual space (Begoray, 1990; Johnson-Eilola, 1991b; McAleese, 1989). As Rubens (1991) cautioned in his comparison of functional linear and hypertext documents, in order for a hypertext to be useful it must often be augmented with nonbooklike features that compensate for navigational or searching problems: Boolean operators for concatenating search criteria, trail-construction mechanisms, and so on. These concerns do not seem insurmountable, but the popularity of hypertext that prioritizes simple, technical efficiency, regardless of other possibilities, illustrates the powerful confluence of the ideas of efficiency and automation as they articulate to print culture—the power of automation to increase efficiency is seen as so strong in many cases that contemplating either the significance or purposes of the automation is never undertaken. However, Rubens' assertion about the necessity of nonbooklike aspects may open up productive and empowering possibilities, something I return to later in this chapter and again in Chapters 5 and 6.

---

[11] A more extended analysis of the structures and uses of INTERMEDIA is taken up in Chapter 5.

Automating the Book 2:
Automation and Speed of Information Transfer

Automation as a way to increase efficiency addresses not only the rate or volume of that transfer but also, perhaps especially, the accuracy of the transfer of information from sender to receiver. Empirical tests on the utility of hypertext (from an implicitly functionalist perspective) measure effects in terms of *accuracy* (comparing the information given by the text to the information the reader received) as well as *speed* (the rate at which users navigate and/or recall information or solve tasks; McKnight, Dillon, & Richardson, 1990; Monk et al., 1988; Wright & Lickorish, 1990).

Obviously there are realistic concerns here in the relationship between speed and use of a text,[12] but the significance and power of this articulation bears more than a straightforward relationship. As Slack et al. (1993) pointed out in their critique of theories of technical communication:

> The emphasis in the historical development of new technologies of communication (from walkers, runners, horses, smoke signals, semaphore, print, telegraph, telephone, television, satellites computers, fax machines, etc.) has been on the transmission of knowledge and information in such a way to *exercise control over space and people faster and farther.* (pp. 15–16)

The increase in speed becomes bound up, in a cybernetic management way, with more efficient control. In functional text, readers are expected (and expect) to follow as closely as possible the suggestions of the text; meaning appears to be less a manner of interpretation, translation, or construction than one of automatic acceptance and reception. Even though Shannon and Weaver (1949) pointed out that "information" is not synonymous with "meaning" in the transmission model, the positioning of the transmission model as the foundation of communication (rather than one particular, if useful model among many) exerts powerful influences on issues beyond the realm of accuracy of information and rates of transfer.[13] But as with the technological development mapped by Slack, Miller, and Doak, speed of information trans-

---

[12] To use the terms of cognitive psychology and functionalism in the midst of their critique, there appear to be well-observed limits to a person's capacity to memorize information. Outside of the most dogmatically expounded postmodern theories of reading, efficiency in reading text is always an issue at some level.

[13] In their bibliographic essay on communication theory and technical communication largely composed of extensions to Shannon and Weaver's work, Barnett and Hughes (1985) stated, "When the system includes people, meaning may be attributed to the information" (p. 39). Importantly, Barnett and Hughes did not make it clear exactly what or who assumes the position of the agent for attributing meaning to the information—sender, receiver, model, or some other agent or collective.

fer becomes articulated to flexibility and resolution: The medium should be able to transfer information to receivers quickly but also be able to customize the information based on the needs of specific users to the greatest degree possible. Direct-dial telephones replace switchboard operators; 500-channel cable TV and direct satellites replace 13-channel VHF; the World Wide Web replaces the Internet replaces ARPANet; single, primary structures for a specific functional text are replaced by the multiple structures and paths of functional hypertext. The transmission model tends to support one-way systems of communication over interactive discourses, a crucial consideration as our culture begins the shift from broadcast and low-bandwidth cable and telephone to integrated systems of broadband communication. Although such technologies might be articulated as expanding the ability of the population in general to engage in discussion (a vision often invoked when seeking governmental or public approval), the emphasis on delivering information to consumers tends to prioritize little more than 500-channel, limited feedback television. In a discussion of interactive media in the widely read journal *Technical Communication,* for example, O'Malley (1993) ended by admitting that "[a]lthough the term *interactive* implies a sophisticated form of communication within the CD world, especially as applied to business or education, the competitive arena of consumer television holds the most promise" (p. 622). Following this admission, O'Malley turned to an explicit discussion of the transmission model, lauding the ways in which interactive multimedia can reduce noise.

Functional hypertext attempts the automation of many of these techniques. The history of the book itself represents, in part, an attempt to construct a more portable, random-access medium (Bolter, 1991b; Eisenstein, 1979). The alphabetic organization of the encyclopedia, for example, allows readers in search of a specific entry to move directly to the pertinent volume and, by following the alphabetical organization inside that volume, quickly find the entry they need. As Bolter (1991b) pointed out:

A good contemporary encyclopedia exploits every technique of print technology to help the reader find the relevant articles, paragraphs, and even finer units of text.... Printing, which had created a new degree of textual overload, also offered the solution of alphabetical order and precise indices. (p. 91)

Other methods of organization such as the cross-referenced word (in all caps or bold text) or the index, both of which overlay a secondary organization onto the primary alphabet laid over the collection of texts, attempt to help readers move from one concept to another in the encyclopedia. The articulation of literacy to simple technical efficiency has developed over the history of print, as written works came to represent stores of external memory that should be arranged to benefit the reader's search. Similar types of conventions guide, to some extent, the writers and readers of reports, memos, technical manuals, novels, and even spoken conversation (from chapter and subsection headings, tables of contents, and even footnotes used by literary authors such as Joyce and Fowles, to anaphoric and pronominal references that create conceptual relations in written and spoken language).

Automating the Book 3: Other Genres

In addition, automation as a way of increasing technical efficiency shapes texts that appear less "functional": professional communication, popular computer-based fiction, and essay writing as well. Even when recognizing the capacity for an environment such as STORYSPACE to include radically different primary organizations to a text,[14] writers are also capable of recognizing that the strongest needs of readers are still often the linearity and hierarchy developed in print. The hypertextual version of Bolter's (1991a) WRITING SPACE, for example, is constructed largely along the linear-hierarchical model followed by most textbooks, but also includes numerous cross- and marginal-text notes. Bolter recognized that although novelty is an important measure of technological progress, that progress must be mapped as a place relatively close to home. Although associational connections are offered between a number of sections in the text, the book culture, surface structure of hierarchy encourages the reader to see these links as natural, offering themselves automatically only when needed and subordinate (or even invisible) when the reader's individual needs do not call them forth.

Similarly, Voyager's "Expanded Books" series includes translations of print texts such as Martin Gardener's augmented version of Lewis Carroll's work in *The Complete Annotated Alice*, Michael Crichton's *Jurassic Park*, Douglas Adams' *Hitch Hiker's Guide to the Galaxy*, and even Richard Lanham's *The Electronic Word*. Although Voyager claims that computers "are beginning to transform the way you read," their advertising also asserts that the software allows you to *"Read paginated, book-like text on your computer screen."* Although Voyager has admittedly included a few nonbookish facilities (mainly automatic word searching), their primary focus is emulating the book on screen. In such texts, because there is not a preexisting reason for the automation of the book to included nonlinear access, the more "disruptive" (to print readers) operations of hypertext are either ignored or downplayed.

The Electronic Books version of Lanham's popular *The Electronic Word*,

---

[14] For a discussion of the three modes of structural maps provided in STORYSPACE, see Bolter (1991b), Johnson-Eilola (1992), and Mulvihill (1992), among others.

for example, is packed with a brief print leaflet containing installation instructions and the reassurance that even though:

> [T]he Chicago Expanded Book doesn't look much like the average Chicago book. The fine binding materials, like the high-grade, acid-free paper, the smell of ink, the heft of a large scholarly tome, all the traditional physical marks of high-quality scholarly publishing are missing. But after you have installed this electronic book on your computer, you will find that all of the other things you have come to expect to be true of a book are true of the Chicago Expanded Book. It has pages, a table of contents, an index, and the usual scholarly apparatus: end notes, figures, and so on. You can write in the margins, underline passages, even dog-ear pages and insert electronic paper clips. (*A Chicago Expanded Book*, 1993)

However, the Voyager texts provide an indication of the limited ways in which the term *hypertext* is currently constructed by the computer industry at large: In 1992, the widely read *MacUser* (The 8th annual, 1993) magazine named the Expanded Books series "Editor's Choice for Best New Information Resource" (the latter two words echoing the idea of communication as goods to be transferred). In their description of the series, *MacUser* editors observed that:

> Electronic books were envisioned many years ago by hypertext pioneer Ted Nelson. But just as da Vinci's flying machines had to wait for the internal-combustion engine, Nelson's dream required the PowerBook—and the talents of The Voyager Company—before it could be realized in the form of **Expanded Books**.... Great literature no longer comes on paper alone. (The 8th annual, 1993, p. 102; emphasis in original)

Although the Expanded Books series does not offer a great deal in the way of hypertext functionality, the appearance of a print book on screen provides a strong enough indicator of hypertext to signal to consumers that this is the future of books—hypertext. The power of Nelson's name here operates as an advertising image (the renegade, forward-thinking visionary, years ahead of his time) to lend an aura of technological advancement to Expanded Books—even though Nelson's description of hypertext argued for a much more open and interconnected literature than offered here. The Expanded Books may offer a step toward "Nelson's dream" (reading fiction or literary nonfiction on screen is still relatively rare), but this may be a limiting rather than expansive movement. The Expanded Books construct a more technically efficient form of the book.

Even when the structure of the software does not push writers toward a bookish orientation—virtual stacks of paper, ring-bound notepads, and so on—the automation of concepts such as linearity, hierarchy, and marginalization still appear. Landow and Lanestedt's (1992) *THE IN MEMORIAM WEB*, a text I discuss at length in Chapter 5, constitutes student texts as marginal commentary around the central figure of Tennyson's *In Memoriam* (indeed, although students authored a large number of nodes in the web, their names are conspicuously absent on the cover). And recent initiatives such as the Association for Computing Machinery's (ACM) online publishing program explicitly recognize that what is important in signifying value is no longer print, but the publisher's imprint. So although one (very popular) view of the World Wide Web is that it obliterates the gatekeepers of traditional press publishing, such gatekeeping is certainly possible—and will likely be popular with academics and industry professionals alike. The World Wide Web, for the ACM, may offer structural advantages, but they are primarily articulated as an increase in the efficiency of delivery systems (Figure 3.11). The very flexibility and openness of the World Wide Web that

FIGURE 3.11. Home page and online magazine from the Association for Computing Machinery (ACM).

increase efficiency in the distribution of information are also considered to be dangerous characteristics, because not only can ACM send information, but anyone can. So the new emphasis on the ACM imprint (rather than the printing itself) functions to reassert hierarchy.

So the primary goals of technical communication—speed, clarity, and efficiency—appear throughout a whole range of other types of texts besides functional documents. The articulation of hypertext to the machine—of writing and reading as the acts of operating a machine—present in even fictional or expository text, attempts to construct a reader as a person taking his or her place in a relatively passive, mechanical operation.[15]

LOCATING CONTROL:
MANAGING PEOPLE AND/AS INFORMATION

To return to Hirschhorn's (1984) observations recounted at the beginning of this chapter, a conventional machine must control the distribution of power with as little unnecessary movement as possible (the articulation of "unnecessary" becomes a key issue here, being defined in this context by the constraints of simple, technical efficiency). This conception of machine power operates at two levels—(a) the mechanical sense of the actual operations of a technology in the application of mechanical force (e.g., either the connections in the drive train of an automobile or the connected actions that must be made in looking up information in a text), as well as (b) the political sense of the distribution and condensation of responsibility and control in the application and maintenance of hierarchical social forces.[16] This control follows two predominant paths—an increase in management control or the internalization of control by the worker. The early goal of increased mechanical efficiency[17] leads to the goal of increased managerial efficiency in the

---

[15] As discussed in Chapters 4 and 5, the movement in late-capitalist societies from centralized to decentralized control is closely connected to the shift in literary theories from expressive realist and modernist to postmodernist conceptions of writing and reading. This connection helps to explain the existence of little machines articulations of hypertext in literature. This mechanical construction is not as prevalent or powerful as it is in functional hypertext, a weakness partially related to the persistence of the idea of a literary author as a creative genius in popular conceptions of authorship and literature (cf. Foucault, 1977).

[16] For example, the social prohibitions discouraging a line worker—or filmmaker Michael Moore—from phoning or stopping by the office of the Chair of General Motors to chat about the problems of industrial automation.

[17] Shannon and Weaver's (1949) early model of communication, which I argued earlier is a primary force in the little machines articulation of hypertext, is and was itself a complex and shifting articulation composed at least in part of the pervasive emphasis on measurement of movement and speed inherent in capitalist cultures.

workplace, where workers lose control over tasks as their jobs become more automated: The workplace (including the workers) becomes a large-scale machine. As Braverman (1974) put it:

> The reduction of the worker to the level of an instrument in the production process is by no means exclusively associated with machinery. We must also note the attempt, either in the absence of machinery or in conjunction with individually operated machines, *to treat the workers themselves as machines.* (pp. 172–173, emphasis in original)

The interplay between pursuing technical efficiency and dehumanizing human participants surfaces in Shannon and Weaver's (1949) naturalization of the transmission model, in which he argued that even though the transmission model may be "disappointing and bizarre," Shannon's work:

> [H]as so penetratingly cleared that air that one is now, perhaps for the first time, ready for a real theory of meaning. An engineering communication theory is just like a very proper and discreet girl accepting your telegram. She pays no attention to the meaning, whether it be sad, or joyous, or embarrassing. But she must be prepared to deal with all that comes on her desk. This idea that a communication system ought to try to deal with all possible messages, and that the intelligent way to try to is to base design on the statistical character of the source, is surely not without significance for communication in general. Language must be designed (or developed) with a view of the totality of things that man may wish to say; but not being able to accomplish everything, it too should do as well as possible as often as possible. That is to say, it too should deal with its task statistically. (p. 117)

Here the ideas of technical and managerial efficiency meet (not to mention the construction of gender roles in technological capitalism), as the worker becomes a part of the machine with (ideally) no constructive part in the process of communication. Commonly, the technical communicator is not seen as an author but as the encoder or translator (Slack et al. 1993).

The paradox here between functional hypertext ceding power to the user on one hand and, on the other hand, technology being controlled by its engineers provides a sharp warning about popular notions of hypertext as largely reader-determined. On the surface, functional hypertext appears to accelerate a tendency of functional documentation in general: the acceptance of the text to multiple instantiations. The text seems to be infinitely adaptable—instead of hammering round pegs of information into the square holes of a reader's mind, functional hypertext fills differing spaces with liquid information. The indices of print text, the tabbed dividers and tables of contents of print or virtual manuals silently attest to an acceptance of indeterminacy: The author can never fully predict the mind of the reader. Authors lose their control over the specific path followed by the reader as the text becomes a networked hypertext. This liberation and freedom are expressed in the earliest articulations of hypertext by Bush, Nelson, and Englebart as well as in contemporary work by the majority of those writing about and within hypertext (Begoray, 1990; Conklin, 1986). Such articulations of hypertext closely align with the movement from hierarchical to networked workplaces: The overhead and technical efficiency of many workplaces has been replaced by an open structure in which individual workers are provided with an apparently larger degree of freedom in deciding how to accomplish a goal.

From another perspective, however, a reader working in hypertext becomes more easily subjected to their current task.[18] The control moves from the (often distant) author, engineer, or writer of a help text to the location of the workplace or management. Although an individual text may appear to offer a greater degree of control for users, the use of that text must be considered in an ecological perspective, taking into account such forces as the user's social position (academic, personal, corporate), as well as the very strong primary task in which the user is engaged (functional hypertexts are most frequently consulted as an aid to completing some other task)—the sum of these may outweigh any potential benefits the functional hypertext purports to offer. Or, rather, the text may be successful if the definition of success is carefully limited to technical efficiency issues.

Hypertext, then, integrates most successfully into the workplace not as a transformative (let alone disruptive) technology, but as a conservative process, a way of making progress in the drive toward increased technical efficiency. Engineers at Boeing, for example, argued that hypertext computer applications must fit as seamlessly as possible into the current environment (Malcolm, Poltrock, & Schuler, 1991; see also Wright, 1991). As the pace of reading increases, users are given less time for reflection. The discourse of technical efficiency attempts to code and/or repress other discourses, such as that of creativity or broad institutional power on the part of the user, indeterminacy in meaning, or the politics of technology use (Ellul, 1964; Katz, 1992; Slack, 1989; Sullivan, 1990).

Similarly, many workers in the new, posthierarchical workplaces are finding that their new positions involve enormous increases in responsibility and workload but little increase in status or pay. In fact, a growing number of these workers are temporary, to be given an even greater degree of individual freedom at the end of the project: freedom from employment, from health insurance, from paid vacation or sick leave, or from any of the other benefits normally accruing to workers. Manpower, the temporary employment agency, is currently the largest employer in the nation.

---

[18] The emphasis on choice and lack of authorial control occurs in postmodern interpretations of hypertext (Johnson-Eilola, 1993a, 1993b; Moulthrop, 1989a), although the ideas of agency and subjectivity become suspect (see Chapters 4 and 5).

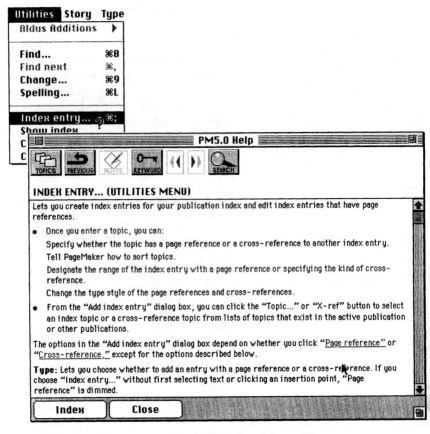

FIGURE 3.12. Context-sensitive help in PAGEMAKER 5.0A.

Hypertexts are constructed as "efficient" machines in this discourse through the contraction of time and space in functional communication (Johnson-Eilola & Selber, in press). The range of value assigned to specific texts in this discourse depends on the degree to which they can remove themselves (and conscious human action[19]) from view and history: Those documents that are not functional are dysfunctional. Because hypertext articulates, in this instance, to the dominant (but complex) idea of efficiency, critique becomes increasingly difficult—as Poster (1990) cautioned, "If communication only facilitates or impedes other activities it has no inde-

---

[19] During the writing of an early version of this chapter, I called the IRS TeleTax System's (automated) hotline to check on the status of my electronically filed 1992 Federal 1040 form. The recorded voice assured me that, "The less human interaction required in processing your return, the less chance for error.... Electronic filing: It's the way of the future."

pendent consequences" (p. 8). Although it would be a little innocent to think of communication as somehow ever completely independent of other forces, Poster's remark reminds us that communication involves parameters other than speed and volume. But functional hypertext makes these other, subordinated forces hard to think critically about, or even think of at all.

In cases where a hypertext documentation system makes work more efficient by making the help system more completely integrated with the work environment, the scope and pace of work begin to flatten with tasks beginning to lose differentiation. As with many contemporary applications, users of PAGEMAKER's (1994) online help can call up context-sensitive help screens while they are working in PAGEMAKER by clicking the Help button on the keyboard, which changes the mouse-cursor to a question mark. Users then click on the screen object for which they would like information. PAGEMAKER immediately displays the relevant section of the help document (Figure 3.12). In the case of programs that use the Apple Macintosh's Balloon Help,

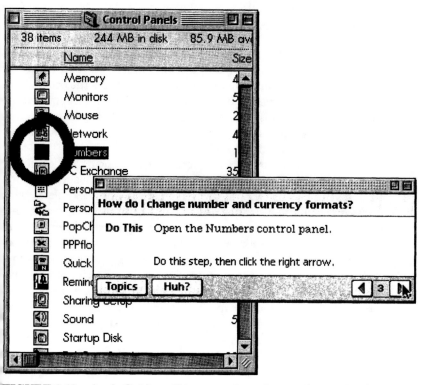

FIGURE 3.13. Apple Guide walking user through procedure to localize number and currency format. (Note circle drawn around Number icon at left to show user which Control Panel to open.)

a toggle-control can bring up help text as users pass the mouse-pointer over items on the screen (Figure 3.1). Movement from the problem space in the primary text to the functional help text appears almost unmediated and instantaneous—the spaces blur together; "help" disappears into "work."

In the PAGEMAKER example, the help text can appear as one component of the workspace rather than an external area users enter when problems arise. The introduction of semiautomating instructions (Figure 3.13) often redefines the goal of online help from helping the user gain information about a topic to completing the task for the user. In some cases, this can be helpful and empowering (I would rather have the words wrap at the end of the line than the old typewriter method: Near the end of a line, a bell sounds to warn me that I need to hit the return key and move to the next line, perhaps also figuring out where to hyphenate a word before the line break).

But the impetus to automate encroaches onto goals that are not (and may never be) amenable to automation with current technologies: Microsoft Word's wizard for designing the layout and structure for a résumé, for example (Figure 3.14), can only operate successfully by silently removing rhetorical issues such as profession, educational levels, culture, and other, concrete details crucial to finding employment. The Resume Wizard does not even mention that these things might be of concern to the user; instead, they are asked to do no more than push buttons and fill in blanks. The automation in these cases surpasses the book, which was not efficient enough even in hypertextual form because it required the user to learn something. Although it would be Luddite to oppose such forms of assistance simply because they automate a process, we must come to question what they automate and why.

Furthermore, in traditional cases workers experiencing difficulties or having questions about their task are likely to consult a colleague or supervisor for help. But because the integrated hypertext and task allows them to find quickly the information they need to complete their task, workers are less likely to consult a source outside their currently assigned work area or task (that assignment can be explicit or implicit)—physical, social, and mental patterns and processes lose distinction. Because problems in using a technology no longer provide a rupture in efficient use of the technology, critical distance contracts. The functional hypertext provides more freedom, but only by restricting how the idea of freedom is constructed by the social forces articulating technical efficiency: As Ellul (1964) argued, "The human being ends by being encased in an even broader technical framework. It will doubtless make life easier and enable him to work with a minimum of effort, but only on the condition that he follow its rules to the letter" (p. 412). Although Ellul's overall framework tends toward totalizing human activity in a way that "allows for no social, economic, or cultural conflict" (Slack, 1984a, p. 46), functional hypertext represents one contested locus in which

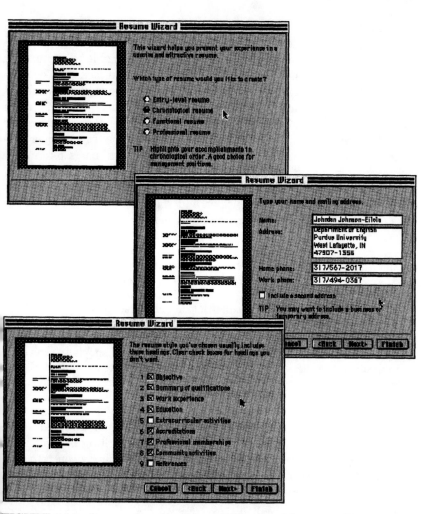

FIGURE 3.14. Screens from the Résumé Wizard in MICROSOFT WORD 6.0.

users find this paradoxical freedom to be controlled.

Where workers were once required to assume their place within the workplace, they are now limited (often without realizing it) to the keyboard and CRT of the workstation:

> The girl who pays the Consolidated Underwriters' claims sits right in front of me. There was a question on my claims form. She didn't turn around and ask me. She wrote me a letter. She didn't realize it was me. I said "Cindy, do you know that you sent me a letter?" She said, "Did I really?" (Zuboff, 1988, p. 140)

In noticing the irony of this exchange, this person suggests that the shift in the location of control is not completely unnoticed. By increasing the worker's dependency on the computer, managers are more able to account for the worker's activities. When all of a worker's assigned tasks can be completed on the computer, any worker's movements outside of the workstation represent disciplinary problems (Mosco, 1988; Shaiken, 1986). Even the act of leaving the computer presents a visible signal to a supervisor (aside from the fact that an idle keyboard can easily be tracked by a keystroke-recording program). In Internet discussion lists, users often complain that "frivolous" or "political" messages might be overseen by employers (Johnson-Eilola & Selber, 1995). Obvious critical connections exist between computer technologies and the Foucault's (1979) famous work on panoptic institutions and discursive formations:

> A whole problematic then develops: that of an architecture that is no longer built simply to be seen (as with the ostentation of palaces), or to observe the external space (cf., the geometry of fortresses), but to permit an internal, articulated and detailed control—to render visible those who are inside it; in more general terms, an architecture that would operate to transform individuals: to act on those it shelters, to provide a hold on their conduct, to carry the effects of power through them, to make it possible to know them, to alter them. Stones make people docile and knowable. The old simple schema of confinement and enclosure—thick walls, a heavy gate that prevents entering or leaving—began to be replaced by the calculation of openings, of filled and empty spaces, passages and transparencies (p. 172).

The virtuality of the computer space opens completely new lines of vision in the panopticon. Foucault here might have been writing of the virtual workspaces of computer systems. Despite their disarmingly concrete location—the isolated cubicles of an office, for example—virtual workspaces exist in a structural framework that displays the worker to observers. (The reverse is also true—workers can see, virtually, outward from their location to other places—but only to a limited and normally carefully controlled extent.) The space of the computer creates territories that workers inhabit in carefully restricted ways. More importantly, these territories specify when, where, and how workers can move about: They regulate social interaction. Distinguishing the "territory" from the "locale," Soja (1989) argued:

> Territoriality is the more general term and contains hints of such particularized notions as sovereignty, property, discipline, surveillance, and jurisdiction. It refers to the production and reproduction of spatial enclosures that not only concentrate interaction (a feature of all locales) but also intensify and enforce its boundaries.... As an expression of the territoriality of locales, regionalism is grounded in the geography of power. (pp. 150–151)

Little machines fragment socially in order to effect more efficient technical control, connecting workers up to the larger machines of late capitalism.[20] Beginning with the micro- and macrostructuring of Henry Ford's assembly line factory and Frederick Winslow Taylor's time–motion studies and moving outward (simultaneously decentralizing in post-Fordist strategies), the factory "becomes an integrated and automated complex, a megamachine that paces and disciplines the workforce. Control is, then truly structural. The time-clock and the assembly line prevail. Relations of power, subsumed into the functioning of technology, become invisible" (Robins & Webster, 1988, p. 49). The computer provides a flexible structuring system for surveillance, both external and self-imposed disciplinary operations, through the construction of a value system based in the dominant plane of the concerns of technical efficiency.

Functional hypertext and late-capitalist management construct a subject free to wander among the links of a hypertext, but also help construct the subject's tendencies to see wandering as sinful—the sin of wasting the resource of time, of not putting in "an honest day's work." As technical efficiency increases, discipline becomes less visible. Although the discourse structuring functional hypertext use is not as overpowering as Ellul (1964) might make it—functional hypertext contradicts (and intersects) the subculture that allows users to engage in "nonproductive" exchanges—the discursive suggestions and positionings are certainly very powerful. Functional hypertext encourages a dominant way of acting and being acted on—to move forward and to be taken up and spoken by the discourse of efficiency.

The coupled speed and volume articulation of efficiency in this way becomes constructed in late capitalism's drive for increased productivity, a drive emerging as a simultaneous fragmentation and specialization in factory and clerical work (Shaiken, 1986, p. 234). There are also class relations—but not bases—in the distribution of the various articulations of hypertext to different classes of employment. Managerial control also becomes exerted on middle management from upper management, which in term encourages pressure on lower-level workers by middle management: "Realizing full well the potential of the computer, middle managers are in a unique position to defend their turf, especially when the new systems are being introduced" (Shaiken, 1986, p. 230). Such defenses can impede organizational change because middle management must continue to exhibit the necessity of their positions to upper management.

Low-level workers are allowed to complete their task more quickly and efficiently, but are not allowed by their direct supervisors the opportunity to

---

[20] The transition from monopoly to late capitalism, which I turn to in chapter 4, involves the fragmentation of large social machines into smaller, more flexible, less structured, but still controlled environments.

learn or practice anything approaching a managerial decision; the display of management skills in low-level workers might illustrate to upper level supervisors that middle management is redundant. As I discuss in Chapter 6, the rapid movement by many companies to the Internet and World Wide Web and the movement to nonhierarchical workplace structures holds some potential for letting workers engage in broader, less purely functional types of communication. At the same time, however, this "freedom" may be similar to the illusory freedom of hypertext. Workers understand very well that even when many choices are available, choosing to engage in online discussion is an act fraught with dangers. As some participants on one professional e-mail list pointed out, discussions must stay within an extremely narrow definition of work-related issues: Discussions of increasing efficiency are fine, but discussions of mandatory drug testing, racial and gender-based discrimination, and the politics of the workplace are seen as an extravagant waste of the employer's resources (Johnson-Eilola & Selber, 1995). The way in which the technology has been constructed often subverts middle-management's (not to mention low-level workers') need for some degree of autonomy and privacy. The ease with which computers can track, organize, and display the wealth of data gathered in computer use for other tasks exposes both low-level workers and middle management to the view of the highest levels. In the face of this surveillance by upper management, middle management often attempts to prove its own worth by increasing the pressure for simple efficiency and by even more fully isolating workers into low-level tasks that prohibit the type of operational experience and knowledge that would threaten middle management. Although the activities of late capitalism tend toward fragmentation and apparent chaos, it is not a movement toward anarchy but also toward technical efficiency and nondistributed control. As Robins and Webster (1988) commented:

> Decentralized activities can be coordinated as if they were centralized. This is the important insight. Centralization and decentralization do not represent alternative paradigms of social organization. Rather than representing the road to freedom and democracy, decentralization refines and streamlines the effective exercises of power. (p. 56)

Even in cases where writers and readers might argue that the efficiency of the automatic book does not displace a more human-centered ethos, such as in the teaching of composition, technological rationality can possibly overtake other concerns or hide possibilities. As Harkin and Sosnoski (1992) satirically pointed out in "HyperGradeSheets," hypertext is often thought of as a potentially all-inclusive map of an external reality. The gradebook hypertexts proposed by Harkin and Sosnoski become collection spaces, ways to link in the totality of a student's life. Because of the accuracy of their insight into the potentials inherent to some types of hypertext, their description is worth quoting at length:

> Imagine... a note card screen looking exactly like a typical gradesheet. On the left hand column are the names of students. As you proceed across the spreadsheet, additional columns include grades for assignments within courses. What a hypertext makes possible is a "hotlink" from any item of information on one card screen to any other card in the file system.
>
> The link is instantaneous. "Pressing" the "button" on which the information is typed on the resident screen instantly brings up any information to which it is linked. So, if a [Hyper-GradeSheet] user wants to view the performance upon which the grade "B-" was awarded to Muffy Lippincott for Assignment #2 in English 111 (Composition I), all she would have to do is to press "B-" in that column (or hit it with the cursor) and up on the screen would come Muffy's paper, an argument that feminism equals communism. Not only this, but another button could easily be keyed to the phrase "Assignment #2." By pressing this button, the user would call up the instructor's assignment on another window of the screen and thus obtain a clearer view of the extent to which Muffy did or did not fulfill the assignment. More than this—any word on the assignment card screen could similarly call up additional information. For instance, the textbook chapter on argument which provided Muffy's model for the essay could also be surveyed.
>
> Further, were the user to press Muffy's own button, her entire academic record could come into view. And even further, Muffy's evaluation of her instructor could be called to the screen in an instant, thus giving the user information against which to check and balance the merits of Muffy's performance.
>
> But we have barely begun to scratch the surface of this technology's potential. In a hypermedic situation, we could not only call up the texts of Muffy's assignment, her textbook, and her evaluation of her teacher, but we could also see a video tape of the actual classroom and observe directly the instructions that Muffy was given. Of course, the size of the database comes into play here, but CD technology gives us almost infinite memory into which we can pour pedagogical scenarios for future reference. This, naturally, would come in quite handy in cases of student grievances. (pp. 25–26)

This description is both humorous and—like the best satire—frighteningly accurate. Harkin and Sosnoski's anecdotal definition of the possibilities of hypertext could easily be substituted for many serious proposals already presented by hypertext proponents. The text emulates a preexisting, print-based technology, making that precursor more technically efficient (the hypertext in this way gains the status of a natural object). One of the strongest defining characteristics of hypertext as defined by Bush and

Nelson (and taken up unquestioned by nearly every current proponent of hypertext) was that of inclusion: In the absence of cognitive overload, more information is always better.[21] (The fact that cognitive overload seems to be a constant problem does not negate the concept of inclusion as an ever-present goal.) Similar problems occur in discussions and popular perception of the World Wide Web, which, although it might be an extremely versatile, ambitious network of computing resources, is far from all-inclusive.

A critique similar to Harkin and Sosnoski's—although less satirical—can be found in some theories of word processing critical of the fluidity of computer-based writing. For Sudol (1991), word processing programs encourage the accumulation of information and, in the end, result in *"overproduction... a flabbiness and verbose style... and a diminution of meaning and a trivialization of content"* (pp. 923-934, italics in original). Where early proponents of word processing in composition lauded the increased fluency with which writers produced text (with the emphasis on continual making and remaking of text rather than on product), for Sudol, putting unnecessary words to paper is a waste of language. And Heim (1987), commenting directly on the automating nature of computer applications, explained the apparent disappearance of the little machine:

> The accelerated automation of word processing makes possible a new immediacy in the creation of public, typified text. Immediacy is the sense of there being no medium quod, no instrumental impediment to thinking in external symbols, only a medium quo, or pure transparent element. As I write, I can put things directly in my writing. My stream of consciousness can be paralleled by the running flow of the electronic element. Words dance on the screen. Sentences slide smoothly into place, make way for one another, while paragraphs ripple down the screen. Words become highlighted, vanish at the push of a button, then reappear instantly at will. (p. 152)

Although these critiques sometimes appear overly conservative (and nostalgic themselves, constructing literacy as innocent), they also contain valid points: When a technology such as hypertext makes an activity easier and faster, people often forget to question at what expense that ease and speed comes and who, in the end, profits. The technology, the communication

---

[21] As I discuss in greater depth in the following chapters, postmodern articulations of hypertext offer their own take on this inclusiveness: the Barthesian "open text" that can be endlessly deconstructed and attached to other texts (Barthes, 1977b; on deconstruction and hypertext, see e.g., Bolter, 1991b; Delany & Landow, 1990; Harpold, 1990; Landow, 1992c). Although technical efficiency would seem to be at odds with postmodernism, one description of what I am attempting in this chapter might be a deconstruction that brings to the surface the contradictions inherent in traditionally capitalist idea of technical efficiency—contradictions that drive the movement toward late capitalism and postmodernism.

medium, validates itself by removing itself from the picture. Instead of computer-mediated symbols, the text becomes a direct channel to some other reality (the tool for which help was requested; the thoughts of the writer's mind). In functional hypertext, the technical communicator begins to disappear from the user's view.

Most obviously, the task of management or teaching articulated onto a hypertext such as Harkin and Sosnoski's (1992) HyperGradeSheets or some of the other hypertexts previously described position their readers as objective evaluators who can, in virtual form, travel the territory inhabited by their subordinates (students or workers as information). As I have argued elsewhere (Johnson-Eilola, 1991, 1993), the perceived capability for readers to move quickly to whatever virtual location they desire can bring about the sense of total knowledge and mastery, submerging questions about the limitations of that text.

Hypertext, according to the rhetoric, composition, and literary theorists discussed in Chapter 5, is the text that deconstructs itself, denies unified subjectivity and pure authorial intention by giving control to the reader. However, functional hypertext replaces antiquated notions with a new superobjectivity, the collection and navigation of information as conquest. A flawed logic insists that because the text is always permanently open, the text must be able to contain everything. The automating nature of hypertext tends, in this articulation, to cut off thinking about the degree to which the hypertext maps a "reality" different than the signified toward which an item in the text purportedly refers. The Muffy to which HyperGradeSheets points tends to appear as a full exhaustion of that student's being. Harkin and Sosnoski realized this, but their knowledge was tinged with the dark humor that HyperGradeSheets mirrors less parodic projects. The businesses of calculating speeds and volumes of information transfer provide their own insistent goals—not merely to improve speed and volume, but to infinitely accelerate those characteristics.

ARTICULATING LITERACIES OF HYPERTEXT: MAPS AND TRACES, FUNCTIONS AND CRITIQUES

The failure of an infinitely expandable text to exhaust meaning is more than the failure of hypertext as a technology; conceptions of language are implicated here, as indicated by the earlier analyses of the Shannon and Weaver model. The information transfer model of communication relies heavily on a mechanical view of language, of the (impossible) recoverability of original contexts. Functional hypertexts purport to map an external, objective, preexisting reality rather than admit they—designer, text, user—are in the act of constructing realities. The text, they insist, should be transparent and the medium should not mediate.[22] But, as discussed earlier, in distinguishing between "maps" and "traces," Deleuze and Guattari (1987) asserted that maps construct, whereas traces represent. The hypertexts discussed earlier are seen by most users (and developers) as tracings, as objective representations of "something that comes ready-made" (p. 12). According to Poster (1990), "the structure or grammar of the database *creates* relationships among pieces of information that do not exist in those relationships outside of the database" (p. 96). But in not acknowledging, let alone reflecting on, the constitutive character of the technology, users attempt to realize an angelic promontory from which they can gain total knowledge: "The Enlightenment dream of an educated society, wherein all knowledge is available to the least individual, is now technically feasible.... A new day has certainly dawned in human history, but what that day forebodes is far from clear" (Poster, 1990, p. 72). The map is "open and connectable in all its dimensions; it is detachable, reversible, susceptible to constant modification" (Deleuze & Guattari, 1987, p. 12)—the map does not only point outward but, in the activity of its perpetual deconstruction and reconstruction, constructs the "outward," the purportedly preexisting reality. The less common (but potentially more empowering) sense of the map as generative is largely missing from the use of hypertext as an automatic book.

But if language cannot mirror reality it also cannot completely construct it; we must work to find a way "between thinking of ideology as disembodied ideas on one hand, and as nothing but a matter of certain behaviour patterns on the other" (Eagleton, 1991, p. 194). The mappings of even the most functional hypertexts occur at the intersection of physical and psychic, individual and social (and call into question those very binaries).

Although the technology of functional hypertext appears suited to the interests of late capitalism, hypertext did not spontaneously appear as such but was appropriated and constructed in that manner by this particular discourse. More importantly, "this particular discourse" is no single discourse, but a set of interconnecting and competing discourses that can never result in a single articulation of hypertext, repressive or liberating. To say that the uses of hypertext discussed in this chapter are entirely conservative—attempting only to provide a more efficient book machine—would be a grave oversimplification; my critique in this book is resistant and might therefore appear overstated. The relation between hypertext and book machine I am constructing is much more complex than a single voice can articulate. Bolter's (1991a) *Writing Space* hypertext provides both a hierarchical and network organization, even though

---

[22] As discussed earlier, in functional documentation (and functional aspects of other types of hypertexts), the "author" is frequently invisible and unconsidered to the user.

it ends by prioritizing hierarchy and line over network.

Furthermore, it is not efficiency itself that is problematic, but also (and perhaps primarily) the environment. I am not arguing here against efficiency, but against articulating efficiency as a primary and relatively exclusive goal. There is no completely deterministic reason that functional hypertext as a little machine must include the assumption that the medium is transparent. These activities are only tendential forces, characteristics constructed in specific but culturally dominant discourses. As Knoblauch (1990) argued, functional or subsistence literacies allow people to survive within relations of oppression; critical literacies look toward the transformation of such systems. The ability to navigate and use hypertext as an automated text represents a subset of functional literacy, a type of literacy that Giroux (1992a) insisted "reduces the practice of liberation to the mechanistic learning of reading and writing skills.... [conveying] the double articulation of conventional literacy as both social empowerment and ideological oppression" (p. 244). Functional hypertext literacy frees workers to engage in a more technically efficient form of communication and to integrate themselves more fully into the machine. The functional aspects of hypertext are an important starting point in reconceiving writing and reading, but they are only a starting point.

In Chapter 6, I attempt to rearticulate the little machines form of hypertext into a broader, more socialized technology. Three points discussed in the following chapters highlight forces that can be positioned in ways that add strength to this new articulation: the increasing use of the Internet and the World Wide Web by corporations and schools, the rise of posthierarchical work structures and project teams, and related emphasis on collaborative projects in education can provide to this rearticulation of online help. Whereas the little machines articulation works through the construction of the worker inside a discrete machine, the social version of online help developed in Chapter 6 allows workers the potential to communicate with one another in dialogue rather than receiving one-way transmission of information. This recontextualization helps developers and users stop thinking of online help as automation and instead prioritizing a pedagogy based on dialogue.

Chapter 4
Economies of Hyperspace: Digital Colonies and Markets

Many scholars... underestimate the extent to which the research library, in its function as a clearinghouse for information, affects the questions that they pose and the organization of the universities in which they work.

—Gregory Crane (1991, p. 339)

[C]ommunications sciences and modern biologies are constructed by a common move—*the translation of the world into a problem of coding*, a search for a common language in which all resistance to instrumental control disappears and all heterogeneity can be submitted to disassembly, reassembly, investment, and exchange.

—Donna Haraway (1985, p. 164)

Information is not a thing, an entity; it is a social relation, and in contemporary capitalist societies it expresses the characteristic and prevailing relations of power.

—Kevin Robins and Frank Webster (1988, p. 70)

In online information systems, users inhabit and navigate a virtual space; the concept of location becomes less physical and more mental, as users inhabit information space, as they move from "place" to "place" electronically, they see and manipulate information in and as a space that spans the entire earth (Figure 4.1). This chapter begins with an investigation of two articulations in which information is structured as a space instead of (or as well as) a machine for transmitting information. This form of hypertext can be glimpsed briefly in the little machines articulation of the previous chapter, although in space articulations the sense of participation and movement are normally heightened (although the two types can coexist). In these new forms of hypertext, information is not merely transported by compact virtual machines from sender to receiver, but appears as a new

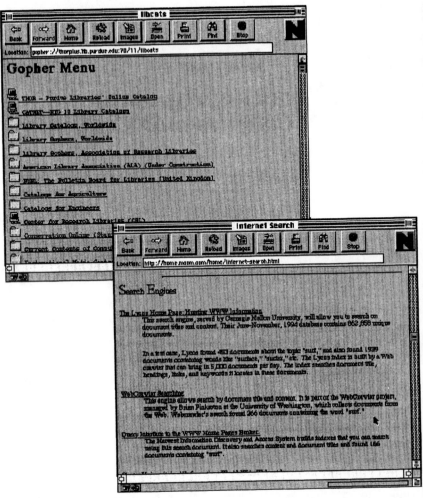

FIGURE 4.1. Points of access to World Wide Web-based on organization or location (top) or Net-wide search engines (bottom).

world for exploration, inhabitation, development, sale, and circulation. Information is not only spatialized but commodified (the spatialization, in fact, is a key component of the commodification). The global village develops a self-sustaining culture and economy.

Although composition theorists only infrequently write about online information systems, these technologies represent an increasingly important environment for our work and teaching. As with the little machines articulation of the previous chapter, our tendency to ignore these aspects of technology is particularly dangerous because, in important ways, they structure our work at all levels. Theorists have recently begun examining the social infrastructures informing (and forming) writing and reading, the intertextual relations alluded to (sometimes explicitly symbolized) in journal articles, conference presentations, and books. But we have yet to consider deeply the ways in which the very technology by which this intertext is constructed—and the current shifting in this technology from print to virtual—is implicated in the construction of the research, writing, and living of us and our students. Information is becoming a space, one in which we increasingly work, teach, and live.

Like hypertext theorists Bush and Nelson, McLuhan (1964) saw the development of a global information and communication infrastructure as fundamentally egalitarian, a way "to abolish the spatial dimension rather than enlarge it... Dialogue supersedes lecture. The greatest dignitaries hobnob with youth" (p. 225).[1] But the expansion of information networks across the world tends to abolish history rather than space—the space still exists, to be divided up, occupied, and exchanged on the market or paved for circulation. The present stages a continual postmodern nostalgia, a mourning for the now because we live always for the future; the present is already relegated to the past in the storehouse of cobwebbed memory. History becomes an archive, another space for storage of data, for navigation, occupation. History thus becomes timeless, above rather than submitted to time. Who you are matters less than where you go—where and when you go determines who you are. (Microsoft Corporation's advertisements, in fact, entice potential customers with the teaser, "Where do you want to go today?")

SPACE AS COMMODITY, SPACE AS CONSTRUCTION

These spaces are not, however, deterministically colonialist or repressive, although that formation is made more prevalent (like the little machines type of functional hypertext) in the unexamined matrix of forces involved in current technology use. Depending on the specific relations of force in each situation, the spatial articulations can take one of (at least) two forms—the *commodity* and the *construction*. In the first form, the subject

---

[1] McLuhan (1964) offered as evidence of the disintegration of class and social barrier this story: A group of Oxford students, on hearing that Rudyard Kipling was paid 10 shillings per word for his writing, sent Kipling 10 shillings and the message "Please send us one of your very best words." Kipling replied "Thanks" (p. 225). Although probably apocryphal, the tale offers a powerful suggestion about commerce as the impetus behind global communication, and perhaps about the motivations dignitaries might have for hobnobbing with youth.

of the current chapter, spatialized information is viewed primarily as a commodity for economic exchange. In the second form, discussed in Chapter 5, the electronic information space is seen as a forum for the explicitly political deconstruction and reconstruction of subject positions. These constructions, of course, do not fall easily into differing discourses, but frequently struggle for dominance in specific occurrences. From some perspectives, in fact, the two articulations are variants of the same object or activity, the late-capitalist spaces of online information services and the postmodern deconstruction of the world-as-text being different ways to think about the same movements. With their gift for enthusiastic over-statement, media philosophers Taylor and Saarinen (1994) claimed that, "In hypertext, all the border guards have been assassinated. The entire world of knowlege becomes a free-trade zone. In this common market, cur-rency is current" ("Interstanding," p. 6[2]). To complicate matters, besides frequently coexisting, these two articulations commonly occur in techno-logical situations that also include elements of technically efficient, func-tional hypertext that may add force to or contradict the dominant forms in specific uses. Still, we can examine and separate out these tendencies as part of our critical inquiry.

Numerous forces have constructed information and/or knowledge as object or space in contemporary academic, humanist research: the objecti-fication of speech in writing (and the historical movement from orality to literacy); the emphasis in the cultural literacy movement on knowledge as something to be handed down, acquired; the related infusion of multiple-choice, standardized testing as a method of intelligence measurement; dis-course communities and intertextuality; and the growing Internet and World Wide Web. These tendencies existed before the advent of large com-puter-based information spaces because we can consider print text as enmeshed in an abstract information space (space articulations of hyper-text give that space a more vivid texture). However, the proliferation and widespread use of the computer as a tool for constructing and navigating these information spaces gives new force to the ideas of discourse commu-nities and invisible colleges,[3] not to mention the global markets of the World Wide Web.

---

[2] As with many books emulating hypertext, Taylor and Saarinen's text explicitly confounds typical bibliographic references to page numbering. *Imagologies* is composed of 25 unnum-bered chapters with page numbering internal to each chapter.

[3] Also lending force to this idea are Internet college courses (in which participants hold dis-cussions and exchange papers and commentary), satellite-based classes uniting distant teach-ers and students, and the provision for registrants of conferences such as the annual Computers & Writing Conference to register as virtual attendants (participating in integrat-ed electronic discussions before, during, and after the conference).

Although knowledge has long been considered valuable (as apprentice-ships, treasure maps, bibles), the capitalist impulse to impose exchange value as the ground zero of social importance has changed considerations of what it means to "possess" knowledge, to "have" information. The social force of capital tends to appropriate information and space, to both support that construction and be supported by it as information begins to attain the status of an important new form of commodity. Knowledge has always been power, but never before have the factories, markets, and trade routes for its development and circulation been so well developed.

Concerns about the commodification of discourse in composition research and pedagogy may seem misdirected: Even if writing theorists and teachers frequently do spatialize abstract information (from specific pedagogical techniques such as outlining through the appropriation of ped-agogical strategies such as thinking about borders and social hierarchies), we also frequently attempt to overcome the emphases on product and com-modity with approaches that are explicitly humanist or political (in hyper-text work, see Johnson-Eilola, 1993a; Kaplan and Moulthrop, 1991; Smith, 1991). And when we do construct a new form of space, we often do so as a way of empowering people, such as the ways in which compositionists and sociologists construct discourse communities as virtual spaces (Bazerman, 1988; Cooper, 1989; Porter, 1986; Selfe & Eilola, 1988; Swales, 1990) in order to engender thinking about "invisible" barriers to participation (jar-gon, speech acts, etc.), or composition's struggles to define itself as territo-ry distinct from psychology, sociology, history, literature, and so forth (Bazerman, 1988; Berkenkotter, 1991; Berkenkotter, Huckin, & Ackerman, 1988; Phelps, 1991).

Despite this critical mode, we also find that it is easy (and often useful) to think of abstract things spatially. But our propensity to spatialize lends force to other activities and objects even though this was not our intention. As with the invisibility of the little machines articulation for functional hypertext, information spatialization has become so prevalent that it seems natural. How else could we think about information except as locat-ed in some physical location, as located in our heads, of course, but also printed in books, pressed into CD-ROMs, laid out across sheets of newspa-per, or organized hierarchically in tables of contents, associationally in indices, on a high shelf on the third floor of the campus library, or as a World Wide Web of citation, appropriation, commentary, and conversation? Information space encourages activities similar to those undertaken in more apparently physical spaces—encourages us to think of information to be browsed as if on a store shelf. Not coincidentally, the term *browser* applies to both shopping and reading on the World Wide Web. Composition teachers must consider the ways in which these articulations construct a range of possibilities that can either open up or (as is now frequently the case) invisibly limit what it means to write, read, and think in and with information spaces.

SCHOLARSHIP IN THE LATE AGE OF PRINT

[M]any intriguing questions about the effects of the new technology remain. For example, what changes occur when students have access to bibliographic retrieval systems instead of card catalogs and index books for their research papers?

—Jeanne W. Halpern and Sarah Liggett (1984, p. 85)

Although we may commonly consider the act of constructing a self in a computer environment as a sort of escapist fantasy fit for cyberpunk teens, many of us already spend at least part of our lives in virtual spaces of one sort or another; these spaces, though, are often taken for granted. Too often, our transition from one environment to its technological successor appears as a smooth movement. If we remark on the fact that we have moved from one technology to another, these thoughts fade quickly: I no longer understand how people wrote on typewriters even though I used to do so. We have learned to think more deeply about social spaces—Bartholomae's (1985) students "Inventing the University" or Berkenkotter et al.'s (1988) doctoral student "Nate" reconstructing himself to align with the discourses of academia, for example, help us to think about our students' attempts to enter particular discursive spaces. These spaces are constructed according to the rules of different literacy technologies, although we do not comment on this as frequently, except to note how unnatural or nonintuitive some spaces are. We want different (faster, bigger, more expensive) but the same (no transitions, no interruptions, no learning new ways of thinking). Ease of technology use is an important aspect, but also potentially a mystifying characteristic, hiding the very real differences often occurring in technology shifts.

For example, while researching material for an early version of this chapter, I went to Michigan Technological University's campus library to use one of the CD-ROM-equipped computers to run a quick check on recent publications about databases. My research focus quickly switched from an abstract question about database users to a series of questions about myself as one of those user-inhabitants. Alongside the now-familiar PCs and CD-ROM players stood an impressive display of information technology: A bibliographic information system called "ProQuest" that consisted of a PC-compatible computer topped by a dual-page, grayscale monitor. To the left stood a squat 6-drive CD-ROM jukebox; four 2-foot-high carousel racks of CD-ROMs flanked the user—640 CD ROMs that stored something in the neighborhood of 300 or 400 gigabytes of information.[4] Five of the six drives in the CD-ROM player contain the normal title and index information held by the other workstations (although the other systems at our library only access one CD of title and index information); the sixth CD-ROM held disks switched in and out from the towers.

The information on the ProQuest disks spanned an enormous range of publications and genres. According to the manual for the system, ProQuest covers the fields of "scientific and technical, business and management, social sciences and humanities, and general-interest information. Sources include conference proceedings, dissertations, newspapers, business journals and weeklies, and general periodicals." In this broad grouping are over 800 business and management journals; newspapers such as *The Christian Science Monitor*, *The Washington Post*, and *The Wall Street Journal*; social sciences indices; and the more than 80 journals covered under the umbrella of IEEE/IEE (the professional organizations of, respectively, U.S. and British electrical engineers). Most of the collections are updated monthly (the IEEE/IEE set, for example, adds 15,000 pages per month of titles, abstracts, and full text). The time span covered by the system varies by topic and title, with most going back 4 or 5 years. Updates to the CD-ROMs cost approximately $16,000 per year.

In ProQuest, users look up material by topic, subject, author searches with all of the usual augmentations of Boolean searching, date-constraining, and so on. But once the titles and abstracts are retrieved, users can frequently also read full-page reproductions of the scanned articles themselves, including figures, tables, and pictures (the business, newspaper, and IEEE/IEE sections include full text). Such an environment is becoming increasingly common for both students and teachers of composition. In the case of a system such as ProQuest, not only are the indices and titles contained in the space (as with most online library catalogs and services such as Dialog), but the works themselves are present in this new electronic information space.

The ProQuest today seems quaint—it is so physical, so obtrusive, so local ("Look children," we can almost hear a tour guide tell a group of schoolchildren. "How primitive! They needed a physical copy of the information at each site!") compared to the new spaces of USENET discussion groups and the World Wide Web, not to mention the growth of pay-per-use information

---

[4] The amount varies depending on how full each CD-ROM is—for update disks, at least, the amount of information issued will not be divisible evenly into the 650-megabyte capacity of most CDs. If each disk was full, the amount would approach 615,000,000 kilobytes, or around 650 gigabytes.

spaces like Carl/UnCover or InfoSeek (Figure 4.2). But the ProQuest system, existing at the boundary in which the physical library becomes virtual, can help us look critically at the present and future of research spaces. We work today in a landscape of information but do not think about it very often once we figure out how to move around easily. Even before learning to comfortably navigate the World Wide Web, most of us learned to write and think under the influence of an education that emphasizes ideas such as

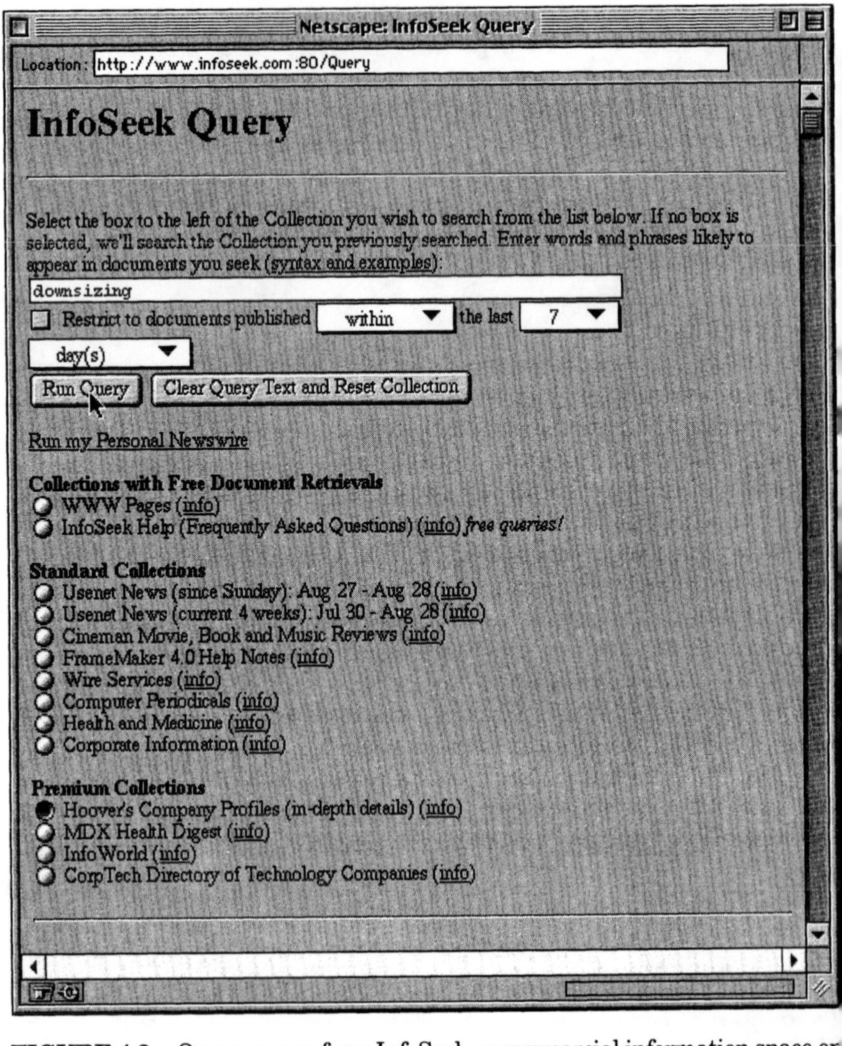

FIGURE 4.2.   Query screen from InfoSeek, a commercial information space on the World Wide Web.

communities of scholars, *discourses* (literally meaning "to move across"), and *intertextual* relations. In our research and writing, we work to develop a sense of context for both our individual and collective selves, a virtual community placing our own thoughts in a matrix of relations to the work of other scholars, both as a way to signal a setting for readers as well as to legitimate our own work. This positioning—and the naturalization such constructions quickly achieve—make our work particularly susceptible to more powerful forces that situate information not merely as spatial but as a commodity in the growing economy of hyperspace.

Although humanities scholars and teachers have begun publishing an increasing amount of critical thinking about the use of word-processing programs, writing about hypertext from the same group has focused largely on the implications of hypertext environments for process in composition (Johnson-Eilola, 1992; Joyce, 1988; Smith, Weiss, & Ferguson, 1987; Smith et al., 1986), literary scholarship (Bolter, 1991b; Landow, 1992c; Landow & Delany, 1990), or as a form of literature (Harpold, 1990; Moulthrop & Kaplan, 1994). Issues relating hypertext to the objectification of information in the service of colonialism or capitalism have gone relatively unmentioned, with few exceptions (see, for e.g., Johnson-Eilola, 1993a; Moulthrop, 1989b; Smith, 1994; Ulmer, 1992). When online information spaces are mentioned, it is frequently in a general and uncritical way, following the basic, largely positive concepts given by Bush and Nelson—the goal becomes a relatively unquestioned pursuit of more information and a more transparent interface: bigger spaces, faster and easier to pilot vehicles for moving through them.[5]

A similar silence about the information as a commodified spaced exists in work explicitly aimed at research-based writing.[6] Although writing teachers have begun to address the issue of library research—students often think of research papers as collections of information rather than constructed arguments about complex, difficult to solve problems or issues (e.g., Capossela, 1991; Gage, 1987)—most information spaces give primacy to that very accumulative goal. And, partially because of the diversity of types of information spaces, texts on research-based writing continue to offer advice for students that is vague and easily ignored. Although Hairston and Ruszkiewicz's (1988) widely used *Scott, Foresman Handbook for Writers* contains a page discussing online databases, their advice is (nec-

---

[5] This transparency is the goal of much current computer research. This is both pleasing and troubling: No one wants to make the technology baffling and difficult to use. However, we also have to remember the ways in which comfort can subvert critique.

[6] One of the exceptions to this silence, WRITING ABOUT LITERATURE, is discussed in a later section of this chapter.

essarily) vague, telling students to think about specifying years, whether or not foreign language terms or works should be included, and the like. And, as they noted, frequently the power of such systems is not only veiled behind complex operating systems but is also incredibly expensive. (Actually, Hairston & Ruszkiewicz only note "they cost money" [p. 592].) The 1992 edition of Fowler, Aaron, and Limburg's *The Little, Brown Handbook* offers slightly more information but, in the end, the text's treatment of online research boils down to the advice that students should use accurate keywords but not be too narrow or broad. Little, Brown's advice on the economics bears striking similarity to Hairston and Ruszkiewicz's: "[Y]ou may be charged a fee" (p. 562).

In some ways, these silences are understandable (and difficult to discuss in specific terms): Online information spaces are currently very heterogeneous, with each system apparently supporting different organizations, search engines and methods, disciplines, time spans, comprehensiveness, and fee structure. But still troubling is the absence of even an abstract, vague warning that some fields or disciplines may not be covered as extensively as others (based on either the economics of disciplines at large, or on the library's political and economic situations), or that online spaces frequently do not cover material more than a handful of years old. (Libraries are quicker, however, to point out to patrons that the old technologies—the print card catalogs—are obsolete, announcing with signs that no new materials have been added for years.) For the authors of these research handbooks, using an online information space may require arcane search lexicons or even money, but the basic idea of searching for references is a mechanical task, something easily (and necessarily) divorced from ideological questions.

The conception of these spaces as nonideological certainly agrees with the approaches of Hairston (1990, 1992) and Ruszkiewicz (1992). As Hairston (1992) envisioned the discipline, "Writing courses, especially required freshman courses, should not be *for* anything or *about* anything other than writing itself, and how one uses it to learn and think and communicate" (p. 179, italics in original). Although a reform-minded teacher could easily interpret "how one uses it to learn and think and communicate" to mean critical theory and radical pedagogy, Hairston's overall project attempts to negate such questioning, and this stance encourages a primarily functionalist approach to writing instruction in general. Even though it is impossible to write without content, Hairston was arguing that the content of the writing should agree with the dominant ideology, at least her version of it. From this stance, issues such as the way in which information is objectified and spatialized (except that these activities make the technology easier to use) or the economics of hypertext are not merely meaningless, but damaging.

Although ProQuest appears as a very different technology than hypertexts like Joyce's *Afternoon*, ProQuest points toward at least one branch—an extremely popular and profitable branch—of hypertext, commodified information spaces. Also constructed here is the position of the user as a consumer of information. Rather than discrete texts to be consulted, these hypertexts are constructed as immense, dynamic spaces through which users move; the goal for such systems is often to create "seamless information environments" (Yankelovich, Haan, Meyrowitz, & Drucker, 1988). In many ways, ProQuest and similar systems bear the mark of early predictions about hypertext as landscape, a space in which the implicit network of texts in and between disciplines could be transformed into a navigable information space—Netscape users surfing the World Wide Web.

Nelson's (1982) "docuverse" explicitly maps text onto world; Bush's (1945/1987) "trailblazers" would constitute "a new profession... who would find delight in the task of establishing useful trails through the enormous mass of the public record" (p. 52). Mapmakers are often the people society considers the most knowledgeable about a space.[7] Such visions are both valuable and ominous in the way that a seamless virtual space denies its gaps. Students and teachers must learn to question the technology itself and our ways of thinking about it, the limits and necessary biases of the patterns of information storage and retrieval.[8] Both teachers and students must address the forces articulating these online spaces.

LANGUAGE AND SPACE

A hypermedia presentation implies that image, script, and sound are inherently congenial; a hyperfiction novel implies that reading *is* writing; a hypertext database implies that users somewhat independently forge links, make knowledge.... What is significant is the extent to which the user is, or appears to be, empowered, and the degree to which the network itself becomes the overriding metaphor for the mind, each terminal analogous to a neural node. A truly contemporary freeway: Just log-in and watch the signs. But how free?...

—Joe Amato (1992, p. 46)

Although recent theory certainly makes more complex the causal relations between words and worlds, the perceived connection between language

---

[7] As a CNN art director recalls, during the Gulf War, parents and concerned loved ones of soldiers "would call the graphics department and ask if the map designers knew which way a troop movement had gone, or where the 103rd Airborne was" (Meggs, 1991, p. 61).

[8] As always, this problem occurs in other media as well, but the computer appears to accentuate the problem.

and landscape, information and space, is not a new one. The Greek *topoi*, its modern translation *topics*, and the modern geographical term *topography* are etymologically related. In rhetoric, a topic is the place "to which one resorted in order to find something to say on a given subject" (Corbett, 1987, p. 35). For Perelman and Olbrechts-Tyteca (1969), the *loci* are "an indispensable arsenal on which a person wishing to persuade another person will have to draw" (p. 84). Similarly, the *ars memoria* of ancient oral rhetoricians included the metaphorical set of rooms in which the speaker had "placed" portions of an oration; during delivery, the speaker mentally walked through the rooms as a mnemonic strategy (Yates, 1966). But although language here assumed some important spatial qualities, writing (and especially print) made the space of information a more accepted view.

Print as Space

> Our complacency in thinking of words as signs is due to the tendency, perhaps incipient in oral cultures but clearly marked in chirographic cultures and far more marked in typographic cultures, to reduce all sensation and indeed all human experience to visual analogues. Sound is an event in time, and "time marches on," relentlessly, with no stop or division. Time is seemingly tamed if we treat it spatially on a calendar or the face of a clock, where we can make it appear as divided into separate units next to each other.... Reduced to space, time seems more under control—but only seems to be, for real, indivisible time carries us to real death. (This is not to deny that spatial reductionism is immeasurably useful and technologically necessary, but only to say that its accomplishments are intellectually limiting, and can be deceiving.)
> —Walter Ong (1982, p. 77)

Although scholarly research and discussion via computer technologies is relatively new to humanities, thinking about information as an object and space are much older. Language presupposes a connection between the spatial and objective world and speech, even though that connection is arbitrary, dynamic, and socially constructed. As a shared system, *langue* is not fixed or completely structured by a preexisting physical world (or vice versa). As Saussure (1959) explained, "the arbitrary nature of the sign is really what protects language from any attempt to modify it" (p. 73): Language does not derive as a given system from reality, but neither does language exist separate from the physical world. Language and reality are, in terms of human thought, mutually constructing. We can attribute some of the objectification and spatialization of thought to the socially shared agreement on connections between language and world. We cannot, however, take the development of our current forms of spatialization as "natural" unless we were resigned to fatalism. We need to think carefully about spatializing as a way of controlling (or feeling control) over information as well as the social and political aspects of that control. Precisely because the physical world does not provide the motivation between sign and referent, we can begin to investigate the forces that do operate to shape our discourses.

Despite this ambiguous relationship between word and world existing in even oral cultures, print succeeded most fully in turning word into object. Printed books are easily subsumable into capitalist production, distribution, and consumption; contemporary copyright laws reinforce the idea of consumption and ownership where they might otherwise break down under the observation that reading or photocopying books do not consume a product in the same way food or fuel is consumed. As Plato's Socrates warned, print has a life of its own, and is not simply the device we send out as our presence to speak as us when we are absent. Appropriating Plato's cautionary text, Derrida (1977) argued that writing takes on a life of its own, moving and moved by an "essential drift" and "cut off from all absolute responsibility" (p. 181). Deconstruction began with print, as the idea of a physical presence behind speech (the speaker voicing language) came under increasing attack. Postmodernism textualizes all; "speech, consciousness, meaning, presence, truth, etc." are now only an effect of writing (Derrida, 1977, p. 189). The information space writes us. I am not willing to push such a position to deterministic extremes, but I think we must recognize the ways in which specific articulations of hypertext work to decenter and decontextualize users.

Although the relationship between sign and referent is in some sense arbitrary, the system of signs is also in some sense coherent and not completely arbitrary. Metaphors of space ("Good is up; bad is down") exhibit a tendency toward systemic structure. To use Lakoff and Johnson's (1980) example, "I'm feeling *up* today"; "He's at the *peak* of his health"; "I am on *top* of the situation"; versus "He came *down* with the flu"; "He *sank* into a coma"; "Things are at an all time *low*" (pp. 17–18). Although Lakoff and Johnson acceded that the physical world provides the foundation for language, they also indicated that "it is difficult for us to imagine any alternative metaphor that might structure the concept" although exceptions hint at other possibilities—we can explain "I'm feeling expansive" as an exception to the up–down orientation (p. 18). Similarly, border pedagogies and linguistic contact zones rely on the implied relations between geographical and cultural borders. We can no longer think so easily of our writing as emanating from some isolated soul outward into the world, but now consider our writing—our thoughts themselves—as constituted socially to an important degree, in conflict and agreement with the groups into which we enter. In our postmodern lives, we begin to think of our own identities as the conjunctions of discourses (the contended nexus marking our current position, a heteroglossia of voices: teacher, learner, mentor, mentee, spouse, parent, child, employee, citizen).

So text as information has long seemed spatial, although hyperspace appears to expand and transform that space, much as the automobile transformed the scope and nature of navigation. The car is not merely a horseless carriage, but a transformation of the concept of what a carriage was, how and who should use it, and for what purposes. Much as the first automobile passengers must have felt a curious blend of old and new, working in electronic information spaces does resemble the old ways of working with traditional card catalog and print indices. People attempt to follow different paths in order to answer a question or find types of information. The three distinct physical card catalogs (author, title, subject) parallel the three different points of access to our library's online card catalog.

Constructing an Electronic Textual Space

Acknowledging intellectual debts has long been an important part of writing, but modern ideas of intertextuality and social construction give new emphasis to the idea of discourse as network. Although capitalist relations have also exerted a profound influence on the objectification and spatialization of information, the social forces discussed previously have also contributed to (and been strengthened by) the spread of network electronic text. The capacity for print to make words into objects (clearly physical artifacts such as books, separated from their author), coupled with the rising literate orientation of Western society (which values print over oral in most official but nonritual situations), the idea of culture as a possession rather than an activity, and the development of social constructivist and deconstructivist movements engaged in conceiving of intellect as a social rather than internal capacity construct a situation encouraging the development of technologies such as online databases and the World Wide Web. In an electronic information space such as the ProQuest system, however, the network of text becomes spatial—navigable—in a way not feasible before. And this, recall, predates the increasingly popular World Wide Web, which seems to globalize the idea of text as space.

Although in writing we begin to see the way in which information and knowledge begin to appear as objects, the grain size remains fairly large: Books, or even essays, are difficult to break down. The mechanics of print (in terms of production and consumption) discouraged the type of breakdown common in electronic text.

The basic writings on hypertext by Nelson and Bush emphasized global networks of knowledge. By itself, the immense size of many virtual information spaces may encourage a qualitatively different type of research, with both new benefits and new difficulties—not only functional but also cultural. After the information becomes spatialized, it also becomes naturalized and can more easily be constituted as a vast space in its own right, apart from an apparent geographical "support system" of people—akin but far superior to the puny spaces of the old paper indices and catalogs. Automation always transforms, but often does so in a rush that hides the important alterations of the activity. Although 10 years ago switching from a subject–word search to an author-word search was certainly a possibility, students were probably much less likely to undertake such switching when it meant a 15-yard walk from one set of index cards to another, the hope that another person was not already using the specific drawer needed, and the "tedious" search for the relevant card. Even a hit meant walking upstairs, sometimes a number of flights, and wandering the stacks. Certainly there is nothing wrong with a little exercise, but the ease with which modern textbases allow fluid, interconnected access to sources has begun to change the nature of scholarship.

For example, even when online time is not measured in dollars per second of connect time, or bytes of information transfer, the vast amount of information in such databases requires that students learn how to focus their searches: Searching in the card catalog of a traditional card catalog for the title word *data processing* might yield 100 entries to be skimmed, whereas a large online database could easily yield thousands.[9] Anyone who has used the World Wide Web experiences two quick realizations: There is an incredible amount of information out there, and it is extremely difficult to find specific things. And in pay-per-use systems such as DIALOG, a miskeyed or overly general search query could result in hundreds or even thousands of dollars of unneeded information. In the face of increased information, teachers must also reinforce the distinction between information and knowledge; it becomes more tempting to merely "let the sources speak" than to sift through, interpret, and synthesize that information. At the same time, this value judgment raises the question, shouldn't the mere act of associating sources in a specific pattern be enough? Why can't the sources "speak"? Where systems such as online card catalogs are frequently articulated primarily by the forces of automation and technical efficiency, broader technologies such as ProQuest or DIALOG represent a qualitatively different experience: The technology does not merely automate the use of a reference work, but now exists as a space that can be entered, browsed, and purchased from like a market.

---

[9] The University of California/California State University-sponsored MELVYL system of over 6 million titles, responds to the query "FIND [subject word] COMPUTER" with the warning that the resulting query will contain over 10,000 records. Helpfully, the system allows users to show the first 200 records answering the query in order to evaluate the problems with their search strategies.

INFORMATION AS MARKET AND COMMODITY

> To the single individual, distribution naturally appears as a social law, which determines his position within the framework of production, and within which he produces; distribution thus being antecedent to production. An individual who has neither capital nor landed property of his own is dependent on wage-labour from his birth as a consequence of social distribution. But this dependence is itself the result of the existence of capital and landed property as independent factors of production.
>
> —Karl Marx (1988, p. 136)

These spaces, in corporate ownership and use, develop along the lines of spaces already controlled by corporations. The articulation of information as both object and space affords the circulation of commodities and the development and sale of the space itself. Consider, for example, the history of the development of the massive databases of Project EDGAR (Electronic Data Gathering, Analysis, and Retrieval) by Mead Data Central with funding by the U. S. government. Mead's commodity, in this instance, is information released by companies and individuals filing reports (ostensibly public) with the Securities and Exchange Commission (SEC). Such information is required by law to be published for disclosure of numerous financial reports, from corporations' stock ownership reports and prospectuses, 10-K reports, and other financially useful information for both investors and competitors. Although this information is technically public, it is unmanageable (unnavigable) in its print version by virtue of sheer volume without the devoted efforts of a staff of specialists, something few small businesses possess. The case provides an important warning about the potential dangers of the commodification of information.

As Nicol and Darnowski (1989) reported, EDGAR "computerize[s] the receiving, processing, and dissemination of the millions of pages of paper received by the [Securities Exchange Commission (SEC)] each year from companies that offer securities to the public" (p. 28).[10] The increased ease of navigation in and speed of access to an information space are important attributes for a host of businesses, "necessary for decision-making by financial executives, bankers, accountants, management consultants, marketing and advertising professionals, and attorneys" (p. 28). The way in which the information space affords virtual navigation—compared to a similar amount of print information, even when well indexed—would seem to

---

[10] In order to highlight the potentials for subversion, or at least critique, of these information spaces, I want to note that I retrieved Nicol and Darnowski's (1989) article during my initial uses of the ProQuest system discussed earlier.

empower not only large companies with numerous highly paid financial professionals, but also smaller companies with correspondingly smaller cash flows. Except for one factor: the cost at which Mead is marketing this public information. Although the SEC has paid over $13.5 million in government funds to Mead so far for the product, Mead has limited their market to high-capital organizations. As Love and Nader (1993) warned, Mead's initial plans were to limit access to EDGAR so that "the only remote access will be at an estimated cost of $340,000 per year per site" (p. 18). This, despite a 1989 study cited by Love and Nader indicating that:

> It would cost less than $5 million in computing and telecommunications hardware to provide 2.2 million hours of prime-time remote on-line access to EDGAR—or about $2.30 for each annual hour of access, plus 27 cents per hour in operating expenses for access to one of the richest veins of information in the federal government. (p. 18)

After numerous protests in this vein, Mead agreed to publish the information on the Internet, but for only a brief time. (In the latest in a series of flip-flops over the future of the system, the SEC has just announced that they will fund and provide free access to the information.) Mead Data Central's project enacts two key aspects of Nelson's philosophy of hypertext: the spatialization of information in a navigable docuverse and the support of this system through a system of royalties for access. But in Nelson's plan, access was articulated in a much different manner—even the capitalistic portions such as Xanadu franchises—were aimed at a low-cost, accessible network of information. Mead targets a small number of high-paying customers rather than, as Nelson encouraged, a large number of low-paying customers. The existing market, as Mead sees it, is constructed along different lines.

SPACE AND COMMODITY IN ONLINE INFORMATION SYSTEMS

> At issue is the claim that the machines, structures, and systems of modern material culture can be accurately judged not only for their contributions to the efficiency and productivity and their positive and negative side effects, but also for the ways in which they can embody specific forms of power and authority.
>
> —Langdon Winner (1986, p. 19)

As writing spatialized and fixed thought and speech, successive technologies of writing have created (and been created within) their own particular spaces. Bolter's (1991a, 1991b) *Writing Space* situates hypertext as part of a technological evolution of literacy (papyrus roll, codex, manuscript, book, linear data file, hypertext), with each technology encouraging (and allowing) differing physical, conceptual, and mental spaces for writing and reading. The scroll, for example, engenders a reading space auxiliary to the performance of the text. Because of the constraints of access, the scroll was designed and used primarily as an aid to memorization or an archive to be consulted only infrequently. Texts during the age of the scroll were not associated with single texts but with networks of related fragments. Only after the spread of printing did the concept of the book as an isolated, closed space develop. In oral cultures, the necessary ties between physical presence and speech tended to downplay the idea of language as a cultural artifact. Or, rather, in an oral performance (and in general in oral cultures), the group of conversants seem to constitute a group in a way much different than do author–reader relationships:

> When a speaker is addressing an audience, the members of the audience normally become a unity, with themselves and the speaker. If the speaker asks the audience to read a handout provided for them, the unity of the audience is shattered, to be re-established only when oral speech begins again. (Ong, 1982, p. 74)

In Bolter's influential scholarship on hypertext, he explored the historical spaces offered by different media, from oral and chirographic cultures through hypertext. Bolter's (1991b) categories of visual, conceptual, and intellectual spaces articulate an important set of intersections among space, media, and thought. Although the concept of association exists in print, with individual texts alluding to or explicitly citing others (as in my own associations, implicit and explicit, to other work such as Bolter's), references to outside texts remain subordinated to the closure of the book, with the network structure existing largely in readers' and writers' minds. Even internal network or hierarchical structures must be subordinated to the linear, front-to-back dimensions of the physical book. These structures can be resisted (consider the reader of a telephone book, or many postmodern novels) but the physical structures are commonly accepted in most contexts.

As Bolter (1991b) pointed out, "A library amasses books; an encyclopedia condenses them" (p. 88). But in modern times, accumulation is more common than condensation: early encyclopedias frequently attempted to offer some grand scheme of organization (the seven liberal arts, geographical/astral principles of association, the mental faculties) but the physical constraints of the book, combined with the multiple relations and categories that contradicted each other, resulted in the (apparently) objective alphabetical ordering.

Primary to Bolter's ideas of the new spaces engendered by hypertext is the network as it plays out across the computer screen, in the conceptual relations between texts, and in the minds of hypertext writers and readers. The space of hypertext is different operationally from print because the text exists as an explicit network rather than the relatively unopposed left–right/top–down/front–back line in which most books are read. (This claim, frequent in commentary on hypertext, ignores the everyday, self-directed readings enacted by users of texts such as instructions or online help.) The sense of the network in the text is related to the categories (somewhat overlapping) of concepts and minds. Hypertext suggests more forcefully—or reflects our sense of—the operations of the (seemingly contradictory) theories of deconstruction, intertextuality, and artificial intelligence. For Bolter and other literary theorists studying hypertexts, the network of the hypertext continually deconstructs itself by refusing a single form and by making the reader complicit in each concrete instantiation of the text. The deconstructing text, however, is for Bolter also a symbol of the mechanical view of intelligent behavior as constructed by cognitive psychology—thought as a spatial, discrete system. Deconstruction—the death of the author—returns under the guise of the debate over artificial intelligence:

> After 5000 years of phonetic writing and thousands more of picture writing, we can hardly conceive of the mind without the metaphor of writer and writing surface. As the latest technology for writing, the computer is now our most convincing expression of that metaphor. When artificial intelligence claims to be modeling the mind, the claim is therefore tautologous. Every computer program models the mind, as it reflects the interplay of writer and writing surface. The study of artificial intelligence is simply the search for a new mechanism to elaborate the writing metaphor. It is no surprise, then, that a cognitive science based on the computer explains human intelligence in terms of the mechanisms of symbol manipulation (which is another way of saying electronic writing); it cannot do otherwise. (p. 175)

Hypertext here lends force to both the unraveling of network text in deconstruction as well as the network of symbols in AI. The idea of information as a network is ambiguous enough to be appropriated to very different projects. Hypertexts illustrate convincingly (often without admitting to it) the strong forces articulating text as a space, as well as the way in which hypertext spaces differ (not merely at the visible level but also at the mental and broadly social levels) from other possible articulations of space (the point, the line, the plane, the hierarchy, the sphere, fractals, the equations of calculus, or the mental constructs of n-dimensional space, not to mention aural, tactile, olfactory, or taste constructs that, because they are sensory experiences, can be conceived of as spatial experiences).[11] What Bolter did not do was interrogate the network conception in order to show other possible articulations—non-Euclidean geometries, for example, which would seem to be connoted from the prefix "hyper," suggesting extra-linear relations between texts as something like the astronomical black holes, white holes, and wormholes that offer a shortcut to the traditional "shortest distance between two points." But because our conceptual structures, especially in reading, are based on Euclidean, planar geometry, other ways of visualizing or objectifying text are articulated as unnatural.

The difficulties of the networked space of hypertext are noted in separate reviews of Bolter's *Writing Space* by Amato (1991), Tuman (1992b), and Kaufer and Neuwirth (1992). Although each of the reviewers lauded the book's insight and intellectual breadth, they also noted the difficulty of relating the fragmented network of hypertext (the self-centered construction that each reader constructs as they navigate this space) to contemporary society's fragmentation and dispersion. Although Tuman dismissed Bolter's optimistic view of the open, democratic "network" as "neo-conservative" (p. 262), and Kaufer and Neuwirth observed the frequently undemocratic tendencies of existing computer networks (also see, e.g., Janangelo, 1991; Zuboff, 1988), what seems to be occurring at the base level of not only Bolter's vision of hypertext as open network but also the broader writing on hypertext is an affirmation (and furthering) of the postmodern fragmentation of culture—a process that is both empowering and repressive at differing times and sites. It is important to remember in these critiques that what Tuman sensed as Bolter's "neo-conservatism" is probably the dual result of Bolter's keen observation and his enthusiasm about hypertext.

The problems of constructing an overarching scheme of culture and knowledge become even more apparent with the success of the ideas of possession and objectification inherent in the cultural literacy movement. The first sentence of *Cultural Literacy* (Hirsch, 1987) asserts that to be culturally literate "is to possess the basic information needed to thrive in the modern world" (p. xiii). Culture is articulated to information owned, something that is passed down from elder to unquestioning youth, a birthright like land or a castle. One has to do little to receive this birthright except for have the proper parents (in one case, royalty, in the other, customers of the right bookstores or prep schools). Although even some of Hirsch's harshest critics agree that communally shared knowledge is an important aspect of education (Bizzell, 1990; Lazere, 1992), cultural literacy tends to prioritize

---

[11] Smith et al., (1987) added the metaphor of a funnel, connoting the contraction of possibility across the drafting of a text, with an inverted funnel connected to illustrate the expansion of possible meanings in reading. Joyce (1990) also brought a sense of the temporal to the network, reflected most clearly in tangles webs of space and time in AFTERNOON, A STORY.

isolated, disjointed bits of information. Although proponents of cultural literacy would explicitly argue that their goals involve increasing our senses of cultural history as a way to bring people together, they appear much more activist in abolishing history and replacing it with a timeless structure of decontextualized facts (a tension I discuss at greater length in Chapter 5). From and for these goals arise the various dictionaries of cultural literacy, accumulations of information to be consulted in the manner of little machines. A similar idea motivates the structure of many traditional teacher–student relationships into the distribution of information from one person to another. The banking concept of education, as Freire (1990) cynically called it, constructs students as receptacles for knowledge, repositories that are filled up with information during education to be drawn on later as needed by society.

The sense of knowledge or culture as the distribution of objects is not limited to conservative cultural movements. The social constructionist movement also exhibits similar spatializing tendencies; although the interpretation and intention of these activities differ significantly from those of the cultural literacy movement, both groups add weight to the force of the equation between information and space. Genre studies such as those undertaken by Bazerman (1988), Myers (1991), and Berkenkotter (1991), for example, look at the way in which discursive formations are constructed along textual rather than geographical lines. The intertextual relations between academic discourses are conceived of as linking together in a network of cocitation, not always explicit, binding together disciplines or other types of groups.

Attempting to define the concept of discourse communities, Swales (1990) argued that these virtual spaces share primary characteristics: public goals, methods of intercommunication used for both information and feedback, genres, common lexicons, and threshold proportion of experts to enculturate novices into the community. The geographical and social distribution of members and communication in these communities—strengthened by the metaphorical use of the term *community*—enforces the idea that information and knowledge shared by these communities also shares a spatial dimension. Information spans and binds space.

THE ECONOMY OF THE INTERFACE

The encouragement to ignore the shape and tendencies of this new space is strengthened by the unspoken assumption that working in an electronic information space should be similar to working in a physical information space (such as a card catalog or wandering the stacks). It is possible to work productively under the goal of increased technical efficiency, but when composition theorists or teachers uncritically transfer their expectations and strategies onto a new medium (and especially when those expectations and strategies were not sufficiently critiqued in terms of the old medium), they miss critical issues. The computer refers both to some external textual network and to new constructs, possibilities, and impediments peculiar to the computer-supported space. The terms of access—how queries can be constructed and by whom, what a specific system allows in the way of complex searching capabilities—affects the whole process of research, writing, and thinking itself on both individual and social scales (as much as these can even be separated).

Consider, for example, the way in which the cost of information might affect the research process. On one hand, expensive information systems financially penalize those who have not carefully ("economically" in all senses of the word) considered their research agendas. Whenever I use such systems, I find myself clenching my teeth and holding my breath in the pause between the submission of a search query and the results—not in happy anticipation of finding information I want, but in terror of over-drawing my account, of purchasing too much information. On the other hand, publicly funded online environments (such as most places in the current version of the World Wide Web) encourage opportunistic browsing, a sometimes valuable wandering in which the researcher allows chance and the structure of the information in the system, the architecture of the interface, and half-formed dispositions organize the construction of their research—the paradox here is the way in which an open, free electronic space discourages, at least initially, any sort of predetermined research strategy. But because students will undoubtedly continue to be trained in free rather than pay-per-use information spaces, students may be less likely to see the costly implications of their unstructured research strategies once they move into larger spaces such as DIALOG. Although the Internet seems to be expanding without limit, it would be foolish to assume that users will ever be able to access the same types and amount of information for free on the World Wide Web as they can in for-profit spaces. More likely will be an extension of the Carl/UnCover approach, which mixes free-access indices with the delivery of source material for a fee.

In addition, the immense amount of information in any large information space may actually act to hide important items from the browser (Johnson-Eilola, 1991a; Moulthrop, 1989b). As Landow (1992c) noted, online information spaces may indeed contain more information than the paper spaces available to most students; what needs to be guarded against is the notion that even the broadest space is complete.

Students in my research-based writing classes are now resistant to using the "manual" paper indices of periodical literature—even though most online indices only covered a 5-year span of a limited number of sources. Anything older than this brief history was less important for these writers, or at least unlikely to be investigated by them. Unless actively opposed or at least critically examined, the information space can exert great and invisible force on researchers. This is true not merely for students (who we would like to think of as naive but who are often actually more technologically and politically savvy than we think) but also for theorists and teachers.

Moving in Space

The idea that texts are spatial is due not only to forces such as the metaphorical use of "discourse" to describe sets of texts, but also ideas of space existing in discrete texts. STORYSPACE (1991), for example, includes a "rosette" of controls to navigate up, down, left, and right through a network and a central button to "drop down into" a text node (Figure 4.3).[12] Conceptual relations between ideas across text sections are objectified into graphical links connecting the network of text. Sections of text—rectangular boxes in the iconography of the program—can both be navigated and re-structured:[13] Nodes can be "hoisted" to bring them conceptually closer to

FIGURE 4.3. "Rosette" control for navigating in STORYSPACE texts.

---

[12] Similar directional icons can be found in other hypertext systems, but, as I discuss later, the influence of the inventors of STORYSPACE—Bolter, Joyce, and Smith—in hypertext theory forefronts how important spatiality is to hypertext theory as will as practice.

[13] Although there is not space here to develop a critique of the aspect, current information spaces such as DIALOG and ProQuest are primarily read-only technologies, encouraging users (much as print did) to see research as reception of information, an act that may subordinate student writing.

the viewer (the action removes all but a single node or space from the viewer); structures can be expanded, collapsed, deepened or flattened (activities that hide, show, or move sections of a hierarchical outline). Similarly, visual effects in HYPERCARD (1987) and multimedia development environments—special-effect transitions from one node of information to another—give readers a sense of a spatial and conceptual movement as information changes. Scrolls and wipes connote one piece of information pushing out another; irises and zooms indicate to users that the level of detail of the node is either increasing or decreasing (see, e.g., Shafer, 1988, pp. 235–236). These transmutations of text into graph and space make working with the text easier in many ways, especially when our sense of text as space increases.

The texts created with these programs display a similar sense of spatiality. Moulthrop's FORKING PATHS (1987) and VICTORY GARDEN (1991) each explicitly refer to this idea; McDaid's (1993) UNCLE BUDDY'S PHANTOM FUNHOUSE allows readers to wander through the households full of interconnected artifacts and narratives. Joyce's AFTERNOON, A STORY (1990) can be read as a spatialization of both information and time across a single afternoon.

The seemingly innocuous up–down/left–right controls in programs such as STORYSPACE are more vital to a reader's sense of textual structure than they might seem at first. FORKING PATHS, Moulthrop's hypertextual revision of Borges' (1962) "The Garden of Forking Paths," supports movement via double-clicking on terms in the text (found in many hypertext systems) as well as by clicking directional arrows to move from node to node in a network. Moulthrop intended that his readers navigate by the first mode, double-clicking terms, in order to develop a sense of the lexical and conceptual network connecting the chunks of text. But as Douglas found when her class read Moulthrop's hypertext, readers quickly translated the directional arrows of the navigational controls onto a two-dimensional textual structure:

> Among other things, [Jane Douglas and her students] wanted to know why the narrative did not follow a coherent line of development when its constituent nodes were read in left-to-right sequence. This seemed an odd question, since I had never envisioned anyone trying to read FORKING PATHS in that way.... As I understood it the map [the graphic representation with which Moulthrop had structured FORKING PATHS] would not have been accessible to Douglas' students, who were using ReadingSpace, a subset of the main system that did not allow readers to modify or manipulate text.

> Indeed, the student readers could not see the actual map, but I had forgotten that ReadingSpace as it was then configured included a set of functions (Right, Left, Up, Down) that permitted "blind navigation" of the hypertext. In

fact, Jane Douglas informed me, virtually all of her students had given up trying to find verbal cues after a few nodes, and had opted instead to browse the text with these spatial operators. They were intuitively reconstructing the map they could not actually see. The student readers did not think of FORKING PATHS as a continuous stream of language but as a labyrinthine structure existing in two-dimensional space. (Moulthrop, 1990, pp. 127–128)

Finding that Moulthrop's experimental text did not hold up well to reading as left-to-right movement, the readers instead began browsing in the text. Whereas traditional literary experience proceeds through the linear accumulation of fragment by fragment, action by action, chapter by chapter to metonymically construct a metaphorical whole (closure), but hypertext, as Moulthrop saw it, inverts this relationship:

> The initial metaphor in hypertext is not an imperfect annunciation destined for fulfillment. Instead, it is a system which is already present in totality, but which invites the reader not to ratify its wholeness, but to deconstruct it. Metonymy does not simply serve metaphor in hypertextual fiction, rather it coexists with metaphor in a complex dialectical relationship. (p. 129)

Unlike Moulthrop's FORKING PATHS, current online environments may already be beyond the conceptual scope of researchers, especially novices. The information load may even now be so high that the only metaphor with which to begin is not the vast, virtual library, but an untamed wilderness— the classification of the library overwhelmed by not only the mass of information but also the need to facilitate cross-disciplinary work and texts. The popular phrases for research and information reveal this tendency: Information is a *flood*, something that must be *sifted, pinpointed, mapped, navigated,* and *managed.*

In a strange paradox, text is made a space and compared to a library in order to make it seem less restricted than the library. The spatialization of information here constructs a landscape of information, then naturalizes that landscape, simultaneously constructing the idea that information space is less restrictive than physical space. A user can go wherever they wish as long as they have learned how to navigate. The student readers of FORKING PATHS understood, without seeing it, that the spatial structure of this hypertext was at least as important as the temporal progression of narrative.

Colonizing Space

Navigating large information spaces can enact the archetypal narrative of the conquering warrior or explorer (Johnson-Eilola, 1993a; Ulmer, 1992). Less warlike impulses, however, often encourage users to release control to specialists—the untamed wilderness of information promotes the idea that one should hire a specially trained safari guide—something Moulthrop (1989b) sensed in Nelson's (1987b) proposed Xanadu Hypercorps™, the specially trained hypertext navigators staffing the SilverStands.[14] As with the early writings of explorers, text becomes space, the medium in which conquest is both constituted and validated. In the travel writings produced during the 19th-century quest for the source of the Nile by explorers such as Sir Richard Burton, travelers relied heavily on what Pratt (1992) called "promontory writings" in order to discover and map new lands in and through language. Pratt quoted a section of Burton's *Lake Regions of Central Africa* (1860/1961) as a powerful example of this "monarch-of-all-I-survey" genre:

> Nothing, in sooth, could be more picturesque than this first view of the Tanganyika Lake, as it lay in the lap of the mountains, basking in the gorgeous tropical sunshine. Below and beyond a short foreground of rugged and precipitous hill-fold, down which the foot-path zigzags painfully, a narrow strip of emerald green, never sere and marvelously fertile, shelves towards a ribbon of glistening yellow sand, here bordered by sedgy rushes, there cleanly and clearly cut by the breaking wavelets. Further in front stretch the waters, an expanse of the lightest and softest blue, in breadth varying from thirty to thirty-five miles, and sprinkled by the crisp east-wind with tiny crescents of snowy foam. The background in front is a high and broken wall of steel-coloured mountains, here flecked and capped with pearly mist, there standing sharply penciled against the azure air; its yawning chasms, marked by a deeper plum-colour, fall towards dwarf hills of mound-like proportions, which apparently dip their feet in the wave. To the south, and opposite the long, low point, behind the Malagarazi River discharges the red loam suspended in its violent stream, lies the bluff headlands and capes of Uguhha, and, as the eye dilates, it falls upon a cluster of outlying islets, speckling a sea horizon. Villages, cultivated lands, the frequent canoes of the fishermen on the waters, and on a nearer approach the murmurs of the waves breaking upon the shore, give a something of variety, of movements, of life to the landscape, which, like all the fairest prospects of these regions, wants but a little of the neatness and finish of art—mosques and kiosks, palaces and villas, gardens and orchards—contrasting with the profuse lavishness and magnificence of nature, and diversifying the unbroken coup d'oeil of excessive vegetation to rival, if not excel,

---

[14] As always, we have to be careful to balance this—assistance in using a technology is not only helpful but normally necessary; working without assistance is in no way innocent of ideology. But, for the same reason, giving over control even partially to a more experienced user should never be an automatic, unquestioned action. In my use of ProQuest (not to mention DIALOG), library staff members were very protective of—and nearly verbally offensive in occupying—their technological turf.

the most admired scenery of the classic regions. (Burton, 1860/1961 p. 43; quoted in Pratt, 1992, pp. 201–202).

Burton's richly textured prose constructs for readers a verbal painting, a snapshot that both replicates and (at an unacknowledged level) creates a new place for readers. For his readers, Burton's talent is not only in the completion of the arduous physical voyage, but primarily in his keen vision as it is expressed in text, a narrative that constructs an apparently innocent recounting of the real world. But as Pratt noted, Burton's discovery "only gets 'made' real after the traveler (or other survivor) returns home, and brings it into being through texts" (p. 204). In texts such as Burton's, the lands of the Other are discovered for the first time, "a gesture of converting local knowledges (discourses) into European national and continental knowledges associated with European forms and relations of power" (p. 202). Notable in the passage are Burton's additions of "mosques and kiosks, palaces and villas, gardens and orchards": Burton views the present from his superior vantage point (both physically and culturally) as well as the future—the European conquest that will appropriate and civilize the land.

The conquest is twofold: (a) the physical land is now owned in some way by Burton via his textual construction and colonization (the speculative addition European structures), and (b) the power of language makes real something that did not exist in the same way before. Discourses construct subjectivities, determine who speaks, about what topics, and from what position. Text structures space. Burton's verbal painting operates as a simulation in the Baudrillardian sense, rehearsing the precession of simulacra: from reflection of reality (Burton's visions reflect something that he saw) through the penultimate phase of "mask[ing] the *absence* of a basic reality" (*Simulations* 11)—the land does not exist for most Europeans until Burton's privileged writings call it into being.[15]

The conquest and construction continue in hyperspace. Harkin and Sosnoski's parodic HyperGradeSheets, discussed in the previous chapter, resemble promontory narratives: The "truth" about individual students develops out of the gradual accretion and connection of "facts." Bush's original conceptions of hypertext aimed at least as much at the spread of a new, more powerful, scientific objectivity as they attempted

---

[15] In more powerfully textualizing situations—Wall Street, for example—the landscape approaches Baudrillard's (1983) "pure simulacrum," a simulation that "bears no relation to any reality whatever" (p. 11). In this situation we begin to see the electronic spaces of finance, where symbols become so utterly divorced from the world that they cease to have meaning except as markers of pure exchange value.

to support collaboration. "Presumably man's spirit should be elevated," asserted Bush (1945/1987):

> [I]f he can better review his shady past and analyze more completely and objectively his present problems. He has built a civilization so complex that he needs to mechanize his records more fully if he is to push his experiment to its logical conclusion and not merely become bogged down part way there by overtaxing his limited memory. (p. 1/54)

Articulations of efficient machine and commodified space can coexist and even support each other. Bush's memex is less a simple, innocent tool than a cyborg, a confusing blur between human and machine, text and physical reality. Although the cyborg is an ambiguous conjunction that may offer a site for opposition to patriarchy (Haraway, 1985), current articulations of the cyborg often merely add force to already dominant strands. What the memex inhabitant is able to "review" and "analyze"—and create—is not merely some neutral reflection of an external reality but also just as much a generation of new truths through the operations of the text machine. Unacknowledged, there is the sense of simultaneous discovery and of creation, much in the way Burton's promontory texts created for readers a completely new land.[16] Because this paradox is generally left unquestioned, both terms, *discover* and *create*, operate at full strength. (As Corbett [1987] noted, *inventio* can be taken to mean both "discovery" and "creation" [p. 33].) The spatialization of hypertext is articulated as conquest, overdetermined by the forces of colonialism, patriarchy, and capitalism.

Virtual space potentially calls into question—at both philosophical and experiential levels—our normally secure sense of location. Unfortunately, this questioning is most deeply felt by novices, where it is often easily dismissed as technophobia or computer illiteracy. For example, a few years ago I attempted to explain to a colleague the commands necessary to download information from a university mainframe to a local, personal computer at which we were sitting. In order to effect this transfer of files across the campus network, we had to type commands to both the remote machine (in this case the mainframe) and the local machine (the PC). The confusion about where the user was located gained particular visibility when we began by typing the "Send file" command followed immediately by "Receive file" command. The first command was directed to the mainframe, the second to the

---

[16] Taking into account the frequent distortions wrought by the explorer's texts (e.g., the complete dismissal of indigent cultures), these texts—Burton's promontory writing, Bush's historical searches, teacher's HuGS student databases—all begin to create a set of conceptual relations bound up with concrete articulations: "He" as an impersonal pronoun refers to either male or female; this student is "learning disabled."

PC—but the typing of the commands occurred in the same "real" location, the keyboard and the CRT before which we sat. To veteran users, the distinction between "local" and "remote" commands may seem so obvious to be trivial,[17] but the sense of dislocation is very real to novices, who must work through the experience of working simultaneously in multiple virtual locations. It is only as this feeling fades that experienced users begin to take the new spatiality of online movement for granted.

And when this multiple-location becomes naturalized and internalized—something that current World Wide Web browsers are very good at doing—users lose not only the vertigo experienced by some novices but also the opportunity to develop and analyze the ways in which the technology is structuring their world. The apparent infinity of existing connections becomes easily translated into the notion that everything is connected: Carolyn, my 7-year-old daughter, is incredulous when she discovers someone who does not have an e-mail address.

This is the revenge of the map: If the map is useful, mapping mirrors a single, knowable reality rather than constructing an interested and political interpretation. Like functional documentation, the map succeeds when it becomes invisible, when the reality it suggests cannot be questioned. We spend, literally, years learning to read maps, to understand the ways in which the map indexes the world and our operations in it—learning to read text (and differing discourses), to understand the conventions by which such maps operate, to operate the technologies of print and computer, and learning to index our own thinking against the map's multiple indices. I do not mean by any of this to portray maps as "artificial" and the world as "natural" (the distinction itself troubles me for the same reasons that it bothers me when people think of writing with pen and paper as natural and with a computer as artificial). Rather, I am trying to point out that we have all participated in learning ways to naturalize the operations of maps. Maps, as Wood (1992) said, are ways of living:

> Conventionally we have been asked to think about these as different *uses* of maps—navigation, planning—but both exploit the map's inherent indexicality to link territories in question with what comes with them, here perhaps shoal water, there perhaps an active fault. The *uses* are less different than the *livings* that incorporate into their present the endless labor all maps embody.... It is all labor, it is all work; and when we draw upon them—for even the most mundane activity—we are bringing forward into the present this wealth we have laid up through the sweat of our brows. (pp. 14–15)

The network and the information space, are metaphors in this strong

---

[17] I had, in fact, largely forgotten about the distinction until I tried to explain it to this user.

sense—not merely borrowed and useful ways of thinking, but also new ways of seeing, of living information and knowledge. Interfaces are cultural borders, built on prevailing structures of power, knowledge, and privilege (Selfe & Selfe, 1994; Turkle & Papert, 1990).

Thinking of conceptual references in disciplines is a powerful metaphor—whether it is the nutshelling exercises in Flower's (1985) *Writing With a Purpose* or the organizational charts that portray the hierarchies of corporate life as inverted pyramids.[18] The cyberpunk writings of Gibson (1984) have become standard explanations of computer-based information, where corporations exist most visibly as data constructs, the "consensual hallucinations" of cyberspace populated by "green pyramids and blue spheres" of postmodern transnational corporations. Although Gibson's work is fictional, the same cultural forces drive the projects and business plans of current cyberspace developers. The front cover of a collection from the 1990 and 1991 Conferences on Cyberspace (Benedikt, 1992)—including work by academic and corporate theorists from places such as University of California at San Diego, Bull Worldwide Information Systems, Autodesk, Inc. (the current owners of the rights to Ted Nelson's Xanadu), and IBM—is illustrated with a futuristic data construct, a neon-pink and purple grid supporting a complex cluster of metallic-gray blocks arranged in a postmodern architecture of information. The line separating Gibson's Matrix and Benedikt's near-now-future blurs. The space and commodity articulation of hypertext maps information space as an industrial park.

Living in the Colonies/Colonizing Ourselves

We do not merely make outposts and extract commodities; we also live in these new spaces. The spaces of information services are very real, even though not often as imaginatively rendered as Gibson's Matrix. As Amato (1992) warned of the immense excitement over hypermedia environments:

> This learning loop would seem to provide no potential for reflexive negative feedback; hence, once within it, it is difficult to envision a way out, however many hypermedia one has at one's disposal.... It is all too likely that students in a computer-based classroom will begin to regard their machines as fully-equipped entities; what is not somehow accessible through the terminal, is not. (p. 47)

The visions of hypertext as pure release from the constraints of lineari-

---

18 Other metaphors such as a discipline engaging in conversation via print texts, to adapt Burke's metaphor, are themselves spatializations and anthropomorphisms.

ty and isolated texts, when pushed to their extremes, exhibit as well the release from the constraints of time. On maps, "Time has collapsed into space" (Wood, 1992, p. 129):

> Somehow we've gotten the idea that maps have nothing to do with time. We'll indicate a date of publication and perhaps a time frame for data collection, but that's about as far as it goes—and those gestures have more to do with the status of the map as a document than with any issue of *map time*. We shrug that off, if a bit nervously, because we've learned to make maps in terms they can resolve: *anything that changes fast enough to render the map genuinely obsolete doesn't belong on the map in the first place.* (p. 125; cf. Lefebvre, 1991; Soja, 1989)

Virtual space—fluid, navigable, decentralized but still controlled—solves the dilemma of map time by condensing the idea of the world and map, mystifying the paradoxical way that the space can apparently offer the mythical angelic promontory and the streetwise, gritty perspective of the back-alley citizen, in and out of time at will. Ong (1982) put this (futile) sense of control at the rise of print culture: "Reduced to space, time seems more under control" (p. 77). Common geometrical incarnations of hypertext reverse the postmodern critical emphasis on dislocation (temporal, contextual) by attempting to name the unnamable (Rosenberg, 1992), a sort of postmodernism positivism. The iterability, the inherent objectifying tendencies of the texts seem to promise (but can never deliver) a dimensionless point of stop-time or reversible time in which writer and readers can see the one true name of the text.[19] In such a space, it seems difficult to keep in mind Moulthrop's (1990) argument that:

> To conceive of a text as a navigable space is not the same as seeing it in terms of a single, predetermined reading. The early intimations of wholeness provided by conventional fiction necessitate and authorized the chain of particulars out of which the telling is constituted, but in hypertext the metaphor of the map does not prefer any one metonymic system. Rather it enables the reader to construct a large number of such systems. The initial metaphor in hypertext is not an imperfect annunciation destined for fulfillment. Instead it is a system which is already present as a totality, but which invites the reader not to ratify its wholeness, but to deconstruct it. (p. 129)

However, as the readers of Moulthrop and Borges' (1987) version of FORKING PATHS illustrated, the map is still there, orchestrating readings:

---

[19] I am reminded here of Superman erasing the evidence of his inability to be in all places at all times—occupied with one evil-doer while a second committed crimes—by spinning the earth backward (a belief something like thinking that turning the hands of a clock backward reverses time).

Users have both the totalizing map and the contingent, specific reading. Either perspective can be used to explain away the flaws of the other. The map implies some sense of a grasp on the totality (that is its purpose) contradicted by the necessity of choosing one path to follow at any single instant (one can often backtrack and follow a different path, but that activity does not undo the previous, temporally located decision).

Deconstructing this tension is something we now frequently attempt to help our students do with literary texts, but only to a lesser degree with other types of information spaces. The equation between information and space seems natural. The ease with which the term information highway can be used to describe the Internet attests to the strength of the connection between information and space. Other transnational communication systems have been articulated in a different fashion. People would be less open to parallel terms such as describing telephone lines as the "talk highway" because they do not consider themselves as traveling, but as sending forth their voice; my grandmother always yelled into the phone, not because she was hard of hearing, but so that her voice would better span those 600 miles between us. Information today not only travels across space but also constitutes the space in which we move. Information is (apparently) tangible, and can seem to both occupy and constitute a space in a way that the telephone cannot—most phone conversations continue to be one bodied person talking to another, and the conversations construct a different sort of secondary orality than the hybrid text and action nature of cyberspace.

The contours and channels of hyperspace control the circulation of information and virtual users. Even to users trained to be resistant to the linear pull of narrative—those who deconstruct print texts—may by disarmed by the apparent openness, the vast spaces of online information systems (even Bolter asserted that hypertexts deconstruct themselves). Online information systems promise (explicitly and implicitly) more than they can deliver: Landow (1992c), for example, defended a similar accusation thus:

> After I had shown some of the ways that INTERMEDIA enabled students to follow far more connections than ever before possible between texts and context, [the questioner] asked if I was not worried because hypertext limited the students too much, because it restricted them only to what was available on the system. My first response then as now was to remark that as long as I used print technology and the limited resources of a very poor university library, no administrator or member of the faculty ever worried that I found myself unable to suggest more than a very limited number of connections, say, five or six, in a normal class discussion; now that I can suggest six or ten times that number, thus permitting students a far richer, less controlled experience of text, helpful educators suddenly begin to worry that I am "limiting" students by allowing them access to some potentially totalitarian system. (p. 177)

The point, however, is that we should have been complaining about the limitations of print. In hypertextual form, when users comment frequently on the apparently limitless space they navigate, the problems are only exacerbated. Certainly most online information systems greatly expand on the amount of material readily available to users, often in important ways. However, the impact of hypertext is sometimes so overpowering as to give users the sense of infinity rather than increase (Johnson-Eilola, 1994b). If you ask a user of the World Wide Web what types of information are available to them, they will often say "everything" rather than "a lot" or "an enormous range." Although this may seem to be a quibbling point, in the minor slippage from "much" to "all," users begin to overlook the inherent limits of technologies, the ways in which they structure work in numerous ways, and the ways the Web makes invisible whole "other" worldwide webs. The landscape of the computer provides the environment for a deterritorialization and a reterritorialization; most frequently, though, the redrawing occurs across preexisting, unconsidered terrain—and making anew that terrain as it goes, including, like all colonialism, the inhabitants. As urban planner and social theorist Virilio (1986) argued, in order to disperse potentially revolutionary energy, the ruling class can offer the masses the streets:

> As soon as it takes power, the Nazi government offers the German proletariat sport and transport. No more riots, no need for much repression; to empty the streets, it's enough to promise everyone the highway.... The stroke of genius will consist in doing away with the direct repression of riots, and the political discourse itself, by unveiling the essence of this discourse: the transportation capacity created by the mass production of automobiles (since 1914 with Ford) can become a social assault, a revolution sufficient and able to modify the citizen's way of life by transforming all the consumer's needs, by totally remodeling a territory that (need we be reminded of it?) at the beginning had no more than 400 kilometers of road. (pp. 24–25)

The vastness of electronic space, however, encourages users to think of it as borderless, just as in the beginning of the network of highways, 400 kilometers undoubtedly seemed inexhaustible. Travel across hyperspace is fast and fluid (the vertigo quickly subsides). Structures exert power even more effectively as they become invisible and unthinkable. As Wood (1992) said, "It is this *isolation* of everything *not* on the map that so potently *naturalizes* what's on it (what's not on the map... *isn't real)*" (p. 87, italics and ellipses in original). The network of text, like the network of highways, both answers and creates needs—the network creates need for more of itself. As the space becomes more heavily navigated, users begin to notice cracks in the fabric, places they want to go to but are missing. The space must expand in order to perpetuate the idea of free navigation. The highway map only asks the question "Which of these paths will you take?" not "What paths have I made invisible?"

RECLAIMING TERRITORY

There are notable exceptions to the dominant articulations discussed previously. Like DIALOG, systems such as NETSCAPE (1994) and MOSAIC (1994) allow users to explore not merely local information, but also resources stored in the far-flung reaches of the Internet and the World Wide Web (see Figure 4.4). These spaces hold potential as a site for constructing oppositional articulations for information space. The senses of collaboration, construction, and political action (not to mention the current but fading "underground" tone to the Internet and World Wide Web) are often stronger in members of the various communities connected here than it may be in corporate spaces. The number of specializations and discrete information spaces—not to mention the sheer volume of each space—is both delightful and overwhelming. But, as I discuss later, these spaces are currently threatened by governmental directives designed to aid business rather than educational institutions, and often to collapse educational goals into business interests, a tendency in U.S. education (Aronowitz & Giroux, 1985; Killingsworth, 1993; Ohmann, 1985; Shor, 1985). Not only is it boggling to work as a professional within the electronic space of the millions of unorganized resources available through the World Wide Web, but now I must also consider how I would teach students to work within such a system in their research—students who frequently are not so pessimistic about technology as I am and, in addition, are frequently not already enmeshed in the specialized categories and catchwords of their disciplines.

In an effort to address questions of navigating information spaces, some first steps have been taken toward constructing pedagogies for online research. Addressing issues of pedagogy in this new space are programs such as WRITING ABOUT LITERATURE (Hocks & Clark, 1992) stacks designed to help students learn how to research and write from research online. WRITING ABOUT LITERATURE (Figure 4.5) limits the scope of information in an attempt to help writers learn to construct and deconstruct spaces before exposing them to the full library or information network. And the often-used Internet and Web Scavenger Hunts help users to learn searching and filtering techniques (although these projects usually emphasize information space as limitless rather than limited). Similarly, McKenzie (1993) writing to academics in humanities, provided a graduated list of online

FIGURE 4.4. Opening screens from NETSCAPE and MOSAIC, two popular World Wide Web browsers.

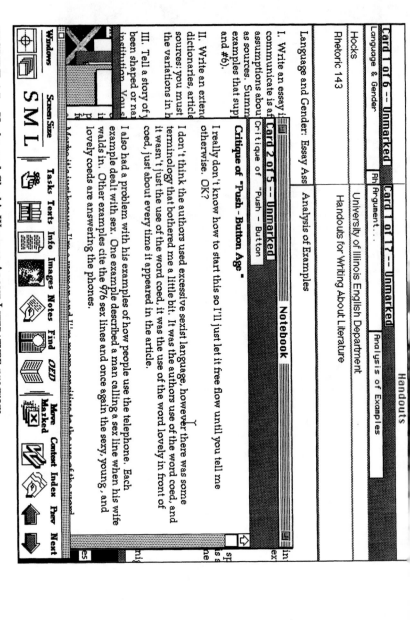

FIGURE 4.5. Hocks and Clark's WRITING ABOUT LITERATURE program.

spaces aimed at helping researchers slowly gain familiarity with increasingly large bodies of information. McKenzie cautioned them that:

> It used to be the humanist's text that sometimes got mislaid, but now humanists can, temporarily, lose themselves [in online research spaces]. This frequent disorientation can be salutary, humbling, or infuriating, depending on your personality and mood and the sense of urgency with which you sat down at the keyboard.... . Academics who have been drawn into the networks can survive and even thrive there. But I recommend that you begin with familiar territory and then venture forth gradually. (p. 205)

These resources provide an important learning environment for students and faculty, a sort of training wheels for cyberspace. Such spaces include only a relatively small number of sources rather than tens of thousands or millions of entries. Students can learn necessary skills such as how to focus or expand a keyword search query, how to move back and forth between the local-level information in the database and their own, broader research agendas. WRITING ABOUT LITERATURE includes not only indices and basic note-taking facilities but also graphics, links to the *OED*, and a set of high-end search functions for locating information in large textbases (either source material or class writing).

As valuable as these environments are, they may encourage a functional literacy of electronic space—how to get around, but not necessarily how to critique, integrate, and present information. Not present in these spaces is something often integrated on a case-by-case basis by composition teachers in each concrete instance: a class plan that encourages the student to critique both the form and the content of the technology and the information. Little has been written, however, about this crucial activity. Although information spaces such as the World Wide Web and pedagogical environments such as WRITING ABOUT LITERATURE certainly offer useful ways in which to navigate information spaces, the issue of access is still unresolved; pedagogical activities may end up necessarily adopting the stance of training students to be consumers.[20]

Information space is not necessarily repressive, but the current articulation of that space as commodity is so tenacious as to resist disarticulation. It is not clear that, even with increased government funding of public library projects, such low-end information systems will ever be allowed to compete with corporate-owned information systems. As Demac (1988) noted, the U. S. Office of Management and Budget (OMB) has explicitly stated that OMB information services would not compete with the private sector—or even with spaces the private sector was likely to develop in the future. The OMB

---

[20] This already happens, of course.

controls a large amount of public information—consumer and health information, Housing and Urban Development reports, cost of living figures of geographic areas, government statistical programs, privacy regulations, and plans for the introduction of computer technologies in government. And although the OMB's suggestions are not law for other government agencies, their publications provide guidelines in matters such as fiscal reviews of other divisions. The political and charged nature of OMB's decision was clear to even the decision makers, as Demac pointed out:

> In the circular, OMB acknowledges the importance and value of government information to society, the economy, and the management of government. The free flow of information from the government to its citizens and vice versa is said to be essential to a democratic society. But the circular also emphasizes that government information is itself a commodity with economic value in the marketplace and makes explicit a policy not to compete with the private sector. (p. 141)

In addition, the OMB makes a distinction between having to provide access to information to the public and the role of disseminating information. In order to avoid the perception that OMB is competing with corporate (or "private") interests by constructing its own information spaces, the OMB denies access to the metaphorical space itself, providing specific pieces of information on request only. Once this distinction is made and enforced, Demac argued, much information becomes invisible; people cannot request information from the OMB unless they know the OMB has the information. The OMB, however, is no longer responsible for disseminating information about what information they have—that is, they take pains to avoid the perception that they are providing an information space.

The effects of the decision to submit democratic concerns to corporate ones can be seen not only in EDGAR or OMB reports, but also in the activities undertaken by public libraries. Social theorists Schiller and Schiller (1988) provided a litany of impediments to public-access systems of information, including many cases in which public information access has been converted to private spaces for corporate use or income. In a presidential task force report by The National Commission on Libraries and Information Science (NCLIS; a group, Schiller & Schiller cynically noted, containing "an over-representation of private sector members"), the NCLIS (1982) provided justification for the privatization of information. As Schiller and Schiller quoted from the report, "It is not so much a matter of 'capitalism vs. Socialism'.... [but] a matter of whether or not the government should provide *any* service that could be provided by the non-governmental sector" (p. 160, emphasis added). The position of the OMB—nonparticipation in constructing information spaces—is also taken up here by the NCLIS.

Access in the space and commodity articulation is subordinated to profit. Where the ideology of public libraries conflicts with that of capitalism, the libraries exert a much weaker force on the construction and inhabitation of information spaces—it seems nearly impossible, in these instances, that information space could be articulated away from commodification. Even in cases where the library is allowed to act as a point of access to a commercial service—DIALOG or the increasingly popular CARL/UnCover, for example—the commercial sector still dictates the ground rules. As Schiller and Schiller (1988) warned, commercialization of information is an unequal affair. The president of Lockheed, the parent company of DIA-LOG, asserts that the company cannot afford to carry databases that "are not going to earn their keep and pay back their development costs." Responding to questions about which databases were not pulling their weight, the president replied "Humanities" (p. 161).[21]

Although much press has been given over to the increasing use of the Internet and the World Wide Web by the U.S. government, the emphasis on downsizing and privatizing government coupled with the legal battles corporations are willing to wage in order to maintain markets for information will undoubtedly keep the Internet and World Wide Web from ever becoming a diverse and open research space comparable to those developed by private interests.

For although information space is something that can be occupied by people interacting in important ways with one another (as discussed in Chapters 5 and 6), it too frequently becomes a place of ownership and purchase: Consider the terminology of the World Wide Web, where people own their own "home" pages (file ownership is a crucial feature of both the web and the UNIX file system on which much of the web is supported), where they "navigate" and "explore" other sites by following the addresses of "Universal Resource Locaters," where they "browse" (like shoppers).

The World Wide Web is a no longer an anarchic, cobbled-together community of researchers, teachers, and students, but now a marketplace. At this point, the places coexist, like advertisements for textbooks in an academic print journal, or the juxtaposition of essays criticizing the establishment alongside ads for upper income products in both the print and World Wide Web versions of *Wired* (Figure 4.6). The initial public offering of Netscape stock ended its first week with Netscape being supported with $2.7 billion in capital. This figure is probably not an indicator of financial possibilities—investment experts consider the stock overvalued—but it is an accurate sign of the sorts of massive push on to realize a profit via the World Wide Web.

---

[21] Schiller and Schiller here were quoting from page 1 of a report by Summit (1986).

FIGURE 4.6. Screens from online version of *Wired* (http://www.hotwired.com).

We can see vividly here the ways in which technologies develop and are used along lines of existing cultural force; although many hypertext theorists from the composition and literature disciplines assert a hypertext that displays openness, multiplicity, blurring roles, and other postmodern tendencies, that very fragmentation and sliding control are shaped by the forces of (disorganized) capitalist production and marketing. The historical commodification of information in other media provides a clear precedent. The earliest notions of "patent" were based on the concept of inherent rights to design, such as those initially given to silk weavers (Slack, 1984a). Inherent rights were nontransferable and nonexpiring—they were not a commodity. Only with the rise of a different articulation of patent rights (initially given to capitalists rather than inventors, in order to protect investments in technology) did information become a commodity in the modern sense. The transferable patent objectified intellectual work and allowed it to assume a place in the circulation of capital. In applying her analysis of intellectual property and patent law to the ownership of computer software, Slack (1984a) constructed a critique that can extend to the new information spaces:

> Under capitalist law, persons are constituted as isolated individuals who are free and equal. They share equal rights to own property and sell their labor power. More specifically, they have the right to "own" certain ideas, which can qualify as inventions, and the right to own and organize the labor power of inventors. Nobody has any more legal right to the protection of ideas or inventions than anyone else, but individuals are equally free under the law to sell or give away their ideas and inventions as well as their inventive practice. As people act in accordance with the legal strictures to buy, sell, or protect property rights in their inventions or inventive practices, they live the humanist ideology of isolated individuals who are free and equal, as well as the ideology of the individual's right to own inventions. The ideology is so pervasive that it is difficult to see that property rights in invention are only created by the law, and, until a patent is obtained, there are really no rights at all. Yet the ideology is so powerful that we typically live the belief in inherent rights in our ideas. The effect of this is that we come to think of and treat technologies and the process of inventing them in that ideology; we live in part as subjects constituted by the juridical level. (p. 106)

Patent law, however, has proven inadequate to seal a company's interest in electronic information as a commodity. Copyright laws, sole licenses to distribute a product, have replaced the use of patent law so the information itself becomes the commodity.

By appropriating—and encouraging—the construction of information as a landscape, monetary concerns are able to foster a rethinking of information as a commodity, like land, that can be bought, sold, and rented. Although Bush (1945/1987) and Nelson (1974/1987a, 1987b) situated the technology at conjunctions between a variety of forces (including not only capitalism but science, ethics, democracy, and authorship), hypertext's development has been more strongly shaped by the forces of technical efficiency (as discussed in the previous chapter) and capitalism. Love and Nader (1993) noted a dangerous precedent to this articulation: "Federal data, which represents billions of dollars worth of research paid for by the taxpayer, is the Information Age equivalent of the public lands snatched up by the railroads and land speculators during the settling of the Old West" (p. 18). Centralized concerns begin to find decentralized opportunities.

There exist within the commodity space important contradictory potentials, which I discuss at length in Chapter 6. In brief, although the movement to spatializing information frequently operates as a way to transport those goods from seller to buyer, these spaces can also be occupied, held, and lived as communities. We see both forms coexisting on the Internet and

World Wide Web, with companies using the network as a place to advertise goods and services or to transmit paid-for information to buyers at the same time communities on the internet are engaging in dialogue and collaborative construction. The decontextualization and fragmentation necessary to move commodities is difficult to maintain in situations where a user occupies a space, where communities come to call a space their own. But in order to prevent the current public support for Internet access from disappearing in waves of government privitization and budget cutting, we must increase the sense that the World Wide Web is more of a community than a conduit or marketplace, two views that are gaining strength rapidly as companies come to recognize the potential for profit.

Chapter 5
X-Ray Vision and Perpetual Motion: Hypertext as Postmodern Space

The great obsession of the nineteenth century was, as we know, history: with its themes of development and of suspension, of crisis and cycle, themes of the ever-accumulating past, with its great preponderance of dead men and the menacing glaciation of the world. The nineteenth century found its essential mythological resources in the second principle of thermodynamics. The present epoch will perhaps be above all the epoch of space. We are in the epoch of simultaneity: we are in the epoch of juxtaposition, the epoch of the near and the far, of the side-by-side, of the dispersed. We are at the moment, I believe, when our experience of the world is less that of a long life developing through time than that of a network that connects points and intersects with its own skein. One could perhaps say that certain ideological conflicts animating present-day polemics oppose the pious descendants of time and the determined inhabitants of space.

—Michel Foucault (1984/1986, p. 23)

The windowpane is what allows us to *see*, and the rail, what allows us to *move through*. These are two complementary modes of separation. The first creates the spectator's distance: You shall not touch; the more you see the less you hold—a dispossession of the hand in favor of a greater trajectory for the eye. The second inscribes, indefinitely, the injunction to pass on; it is its order, written in a single but endless line: go, leave, this is not your country, and neither is that—an imperative of separation which obliges one to pay for an abstract ocular domination of space by leaving behind any proper place, by losing one's footing.

—Michel de Certeau (1984, p. 112)

Hypertext, its postmodern adherents argue, makes tangible many of deconstruction's provocative claims. But unlike print, the technology on which Derrida focused most of his attention, hypertext "takes us beyond the paradox of deconstruction" (Bolter, 1991b, p. 166), "creates an almost embarrassingly literal embodiment of [Derridean de-centering and Barthesian writerly texts]" (Landow & Delany, 1990, p. 6), and provides "true freedom from the tyranny of the line" (Coover, 1992, p. 23). The normal hierarchical arrangement of reading time regulating spatial movement becomes inverted in this articulation of postmodern space, with space portioning out time, regulating time. Thinking about hypertext in this way, readers are no longer reliant on the writer to lead them temporally from border to border in the span of a tale; readers walk around, deconstruct and build, move over and under, exterior and interior.

As Baudrillard might say, the death of the book is a simulated assassination, a method by which the text comes to subvert anxieties about the limitations of the culture of the book—an ideology that traditionally works by "suppressing the processes and conditions of the production of literary texts... helping to create a world of autonomous subjects who 'work by themselves' in subjection to the existing social formation" (Belsey, 1980, p. 128). In this apparent subversion of print, the fluid, open nature of hypertext (the attributes that seem the most in opposition to print text) may actually be even more conservative than other media, which can not as easily subsume critique and resistance. By partly naming its inadequacies, an ideology may be able to "tighten rather than loosen its grip" with a self-deprecating honesty that appears to acknowledge its own flaws by showing a "limited degree of ironic self-awareness" that can mask and/or subvert important struggles (Eagleton, 1991, p. 61; see also Baudrillard, 1983; Moulthrop, 1989b). It is not merely isolated, concrete technological objects that enforce conventional ways of reading books, but society—books are machines for transmitting authority and disseminations of cultural capital. Dismantling the technology of the print book does not necessarily remove the social forces that articulated the classic book text. Hypertext might be capable of orchestrating the reader and writer movement more effectively than a print text in some cases, as in the little machines articulation discussed in Chapter 3, or, as discussed in this chapter, when the new medium is taken to be an automatic, hands-off deconstruction of itself that does not require the reader to engage in the mental struggles normally required to deconstruct a print text. The space of hypertext constructed here may offer a vista, a way of accumulating both time and space not very different than the commodity spaces discussed in the previous chapter.

But by constructing a less totalizing text (building a place encouraging deconstruction and dispersal, a free play of meaning) hypertext may end by affording only a postmodernist forum in which everything (writer, reader, society) becomes simultaneously totalized and fragmented, simulated on the computer screen and in magnetic memory. We should not be surprised at this condensation of agents, objects, and subjects: The collapse of subject method, object, and interpretation is immanent from a poststructuralist standpoint (Tompkins, 1988); in the eyes of some postmodern theorists, hypertext accelerates this tendency. The theoretical flattening of textual identity is not an innocent construction on the part of theorists. Postmodernists, Giroux (1992a) cautioned, sometimes forget that "it is ideologically convenient and politically suspect for Western intellectuals to talk about the disappearance of the speaking subject from within institutions of power" (p. 27). Consider, for example, the disempowering tendencies of what Ebert (1991) termed "ludic" postmodern feminism, "a theatre for the free-floating play... of images, disembodied signifiers and difference, as in the works of Lyotard, Baudrillard, and Derrida" (p. 887). Ebert argued convincingly that this fragmented strand of feminism—which resembles some articulations of postmodern hypertext space—ignores the value of considering patriarchy as a systematic oppression, a social totality that "congeal[s] at specific historical movements" (p. 900), in addition to oppression as a local, specific, personal, textual construction. There exists the potential for hypertext environments to become places in which contradictory positions do not so much intersect at a few points as collapse into each other, dissent being absorbed in the action of linking in counterexamples: By providing a forum for dissent and criticism, Moulthrop (1989b) argued, the existing power structure can "pre-empt any real questioning of authority" (p. 21). A text short-circuits critique by taking over the activity, inoculating readers against the force of a negative appraisal when it appears from the margins or as a shout from the back of the room.

Traditional narration depends on the contradictory ideas of movement and immobility: The narrator constitutes passageways across landscape; the classical reader rides these rails from station to station, story to story, inscribed by their itinerary. Postmodern articulations of this hypertext space, theorists commonly argue, encourage us to think of reading beyond the train tracks. There are no longer, it seems, fixed train tracks at all—only the process of readers continually retracking the landscape, becoming writers. Writing and reading become less clearly distinct, polarized activities.

The time–space oppositions—*langue–parole*, synchrony–diachrony, and product–process—provide Phelps (1988) with a hinge for deconstructing the contemporary debate in print-based composition between product and process. Composition teaching, as Phelps articulated it, becomes the activity of not merely choosing to emphasize space or time, but a way to blur the two into the space–time of dance, existing only when in process. For Phelps (1987), "discourse is essentially dance, event, or pattern of symbolic energies in which the discourser participates" (p. 156), and text (in part) is the historical progression of drafting (p. 157). The unresolved difficulty confronting Phelps, however—the problem of many contemporary theorists and pedagogues—is the general meanings given to print technology in our culture: Print cannot sustain a dance.

As composition and literary theory discuss invisible and/or dynamic aspects of texts—slippage in the sign system, intertextuality, reader response, and so on—what the term *book* signifies comes to seem dead and static, unable to support the theory constructed about (and within) it. The book is redefined, its meaning shifted. The dislocation in the chain of signifiers is even greater in the growing discussion of hypertext.

The increasing and often contested overlap between postmodernism and composition theory provides a starting point from which we can begin to critically investigate and rearticulate a hypertext for composition theory and practice. As Schilb (1988) noted, postmodernism provides vital theoretical mappings that can explicitly address questions of social power, whereas composition theory and pedagogy provide an insistence on real-world activity. And Faigley (1989) observed that "the expressive and rationalist traditions of teaching writing... deny the role of language in constructing selves" (p. 410), and can be implicated in pedagogies unknowingly supportive of capitalism such as ownership of text and authentic voices that seem to spring from some romanticized self.

The terminology of contemporary approaches to text provides a useful site for critical inquiry about hypertext—the death of the author, the writerly text, indeterminacy, collaboration. Literary theory maps hypertext use in one way, but this mapping is neither natural nor necessary. At the same time, the mapping is also a potentially useful denaturalizing act, provided that the motivations and effects of these connections are made apparent and open for critique. A text existing as an open, associational web may afford a postmodernist approach, but it no way guarantees it, especially when hypertext reading is constructed as the (automatic and necessary) opposite of classical reading.

The shift in composition theory from product to process offers a useful precedent for discussions of hypertext. Phelps (1988) noted, for example, the often damaging ways in which process movement opposes itself to product: Constructing the process of writing as the most important activity does not remove the product, but acts to make the product text even more static and immovable in order to heighten the values of process. In a broad sense, of course, some type of conservatism might be called for (e.g. retaining at least some sense of continuity between the present and the near future seems necessary) but calling hypertext "revolutionary" can also subvert real social change. When Postman (1992) argued that technological developments—the telegraph, penny press, television, and now computer—brought about profound and sweeping changes in our culture, he articulated technology in powerful, deterministic ways: "Such changes occur quickly, surely, and, in a sense, silently" (p. 8). Certainly I would agree that technologies have been involved in important cultural shifts, but demonizing specific, isolated technologies does little to help us recognize that they can also act conservatively (even when they appear to be making radical changes). Even in the context of literary theories such as postmodernism, hypertext can easily remain a primarily conservative rather than radical forum. The deterministic position, from an optimistic or pessimistic perspective, can discourage people from thinking about acting constructively or resistantly within technological systems.

But we cannot complete a deconstruction or completely capture history as product (the "final" draft of writing) by merely mapping time, taking historical progressions of snapshots during the journey. In this chapter I discuss two key ways of thinking about postmodern space: geometrical and geographical.[1] In practice, these abstract terms conflict with and constitute each other (and other spaces, such as commodity)—but making this simple cut allows the critique to begin.

GEOMETRY AND GEOGRAPHY

What's important to recognize is not the impossible duality of the poles, but what happens *between* them. You might say it's What We Learn, what we actually experience in space-time as we conceive ourselves, as we conceive space-time.

—Carolyn Guyer (1992)

Geometry and geography write related but different versions of the relationship between time and space in text; looking at the two critically may allow us to rearticulate hypertext space (both postmodern and commodity) in a potentially empowering manner. The division between two terms, like most pairs, represents a somewhat artificial distinction, as each can be perceived in its other. However, the division helps to rupture the generic idea of hypertext as space completely and innocently open to any use. Articulations of hypertext space differ in their form and in the activities and ways of thinking they encourage users to engage in.

We think of the physical world—the "real" world—as a *geographical* place, something that we can change only slowly and incompletely (barring nuclear catastrophe). Cyberspace and the other information spaces discussed in Chapter 4, however, are more closely tied to *geometrical* relations.

---

[1] The reductive "two" limiting the field is necessary in order to begin the discussion. Later, I introduce other ways of thinking about postmodern space in hypertext that question this easy division (in particular, mapping the functional and commodity spaces of the previous chapters to the spaces of this chapter).

The mathematical formulae totalize virtual space; substitution of terms in a simple equation can drastically, completely, and instantaneously change the structure of the space. And although it may be comforting to humanists to dismiss such spaces as unreal fantasies, like language they are ways of understanding the world that exert tangible effects. The work of contemporary geographers such as Wood (1992) and Soja (1989) along with post-Lacanian theorists Deleuze and Guattari (1987) serve to remind us that the virtual, apparently psychic space of the map arranges our inhabitation of physical space.

Landscapes cannot be known in the same sense as a geometrical figure, due to their occupation by both physical and psychic selves, the complex forces of nature, and the enormity of factors influencing the structure and behavior of the space. The seemingly complex structures of fractal space, for example, even when they are used to present strikingly realistic portrayals of the "real" world, can be completely described by relatively simple equations: The seemingly chaotic Mandelbrot set is described by the short equation $z = z^2 + c$ where z begins with zero and c is a complex number. Figures generated by the Mandelbrot equation appear real although the spaces they create are artificial; fractals map reality in a generative sense but do not exhaust the physical world. *Chaos* has become a misnomer in that chaos theory is actually the science of systems that seem unruly but possess a mathematically specifiable, underlying pattern (at the very least, at the statistical level).

The difficulty with articulating the differences is in the common overlap between geometry and geography. Geographies are frequently represented as geometries. The grid of the map, for example, divides up and names geographies. But we can use the idea that a geography is a traversed landscape. Navigating a landscape, especially in a culture that relies on maps as heavily as Western culture, conjoins conceptual geometry and lived geography. Different maps and different landscapes vary in how they position subjects (colonist, invader, smuggler, emissary, immigrant, emigrant). This is not a binary opposition, but a social struggle over the composition of space.

Although de Certeau (1984) used space in a much more restrictive manner than I am doing here, his distinction between *place* and *space* parallels in some ways the division between geometry and geography:

> A place (*lieu*) is the order (of whatever kind) in accord with which elements are distributed in relationships of coexistence. It thus excludes the possibility of two things being in the same location (*place*). The law of the "proper" rules in this place: the elements taken into consideration are *beside* one another, each situated in its own "proper" and distinct location, a location it

defines. A place is thus an instantaneous configuration of positions. It implies an indication of stability.

A *space* exists when one takes into consideration vectors of direction, velocities, and time variables. Thus space is composed of intersections of mobile elements....

In short, *space is a practiced place.* (p. 117, emphasis in original)

We can equate the place with geometry and space with geography. Geography or space is lived or practiced more than geometry or place, which, if it is not timeless, always attempts to place time in a subordinate position.

From the perspective of composition theory, we can roughly associate geometry with the current–traditional, product-oriented approach to writing instruction, something Berlin (1984) termed "the triumph of the scientific and technical worldview" (p. 62). The final product maps out the student's knowledge from a timeless perspective (not ignorant of time, but encompassing all time); each component executed efficiently and in its proper place. In the process paradigm, the text is never there as a product but only as a shifting, infinite movement of rewriting, a geography to be walked through by teachers in their evaluation. Print, however, is the contradiction that prevents process from removing product. Although current composition theory and pedagogy sometimes seem to exclude the product, these extremes are often also debilitating: Geometries are necessary ways of mapping relations among histories and constructing tactics of resistance that tie local to global concerns. In practice, the geographies and geometries of composition co-exist as teachers gather, for example, slices across the geography of text in portfolios to construct a geometry of the writing process.

HYPERTEXT, POSTMODERNISM, AND SUBJECTIVITY

Given the effective empowerment of a neo-conservative opposition bent on burying again the exploitative instrumentality of spatial restructuring, it becomes even more urgent that all progressive social forces—feminism, the "Greens," the peace movement, organized and disorganized labour, movements for national liberation and for radical urban and regional change— become consciously and explicitly spatial movements as well.
—Edward Soja (1989, p. 173)

The histories of composition and literary theory are themselves complex articulations, constructed in an endless struggle over language—author, reader, society, and text. Although traditionally the two discourses have maintained (a respectful) distance, connecting the two more fully can help us articulate a theory and pedagogy of composition concerned with both politics and practice (see arguments, e.g., in Berlin, 1988, 1992; Dasenbrock, 1988; Harkin & Schilb, 1991; Schilb, 1988). Literary theory offers a way of grasping the relations between text and late capitalism or postmodernism, addressing issues important to composition theorists and teachers, including questions of social construction, gender, and the structures of power. Hypertext enters into relationship with these discourses and terms not as an isolated new entity (although some social groups in this introduction claim such novelties), but emerges in a preexisting (but shifting) web of forces—contradictory projects such as cultural literacy and critical literacy; traditional interpretation and deconstruction; and geometry, geography, and narrative.

Postmodern hypertext spaces of the type I discuss in this chapter are constructed in a complicated matrix of approaches to and issues within composition and literary theory: intertextuality, the social construction of knowledge, the roles of readers and writers, the indeterminacy of context and meaning, the formation of language in subjectivity, the multiplicity of discourses in which subjects are immersed, and so on. My conflation of this range of theoretical and pedagogical positions is not meant to remove their very real differences. Many of these gaps—for example, the difficulties of the loss of productive identity or agency in postmodernism and deconstruction compared to other movements such as critical pedagogy—resurface later in this chapter. For the moment, however, the (overly) general umbrella of "postmodern space" serves to contrast these political (and post-political) approaches and stances to the little machines of Chapter 3 and commodity space articulations of Chapter 4, also highlighting the shared spatial aspects of both capitalism and postmodernism alluded to earlier and in the previous chapters.

Postmodern theorists of hypertext concentrate much of their attention on a particular class of concepts and terms that connect literary theory and hypertext. This connection is frequently displayed as a textual or literary evolution, with current uses of hypertext descending naturally out of the work of theorists such as Barthes and Derrida (see e.g., Bolter, 1991b; Johnson-Eilola, 1994b; Landow, 1992c; Landow & Delany, 1990; Moulthrop, 1989a,1989b). We should recall that although early discussions of hypertext by Bush, Nelson, and Englebart discussed concepts such as intertextuality, the hypertext systems they envisioned and created were not intended to support the postmodern activities many now claim for them.[2] Certainly

---

[2] Jameson identified a similar cannibalization as one of the defining features of postmodern architecture.

Bush would have had serious difficulties accepting a text such as AFTERNOON as literature (Johnson-Eilola, 1994) or finding merit in the potential for hypertext to encourage a "[d]iscursive promiscuousness... a flattening of hierarchies and a revision or dissemination of authority" (Moulthrop, 1993). The originators of hypertext were, to return to Foucault's (1984/1986) distinction between modernists and postmodernists, "the pious descendants of time" who today are opposed by "the determined inhabitants of space" (p. 23). Bush's project was explicitly scientific, aiming for a structure, language, and whole calculus of objective human history. Prior to a more sustained critique of the current situation of hypertext in composition and literary theory, I provide brief overviews of two of the most frequently discussed attributes of space and subject hypertext use, the blurring between the roles of writer and reader and the decentering of the subject.

Blurring Lines: Writer and Reader

One of the most striking features of space and subject hypertext is the way in which the technology apparently breaks down the distinctions between writer and reader, especially the commonsense notions of these roles as polar opposites. Theorists see the blurring of the line between writer and reader as extending recent theoretical positions in literary theory—hypertext, in this articulation, makes visible something that has long been theorized (see, e.g., Johnson-Eilola, 1992; Landow & Delany, 1990; McDaid, 1991a, 1991b; Moulthrop, 1989a). In hypertexts, Bolter (1991b) contended, "readers cannot avoid writing the text itself, since every choice they make is an act of writing" (p. 144).

The same fundamental node–link structure that motivates hypertext as machine and hypertext as commodity space becomes, under the influence of contemporary literary theory, an explicitly postmodern blurring of the lines of responsibility between reader and writer.[3] Compared to hypertext, print does not seem as capable of collapsing the reader and writer in the visible, surface-level manner enacted by hypertext writers and readers. Hypertext, according to Landow and Delany (1990), "creates an almost embarrassingly literal embodiment" of the theoretical work of poststructuralists such as Barthes and Derrida (p. 6). In "The Death of the Author,"

---

[3] Such postmodern blurrings may be commonplace in all uses of hypertext, although with decidedly different characters from one articulation to another. As the previous chapter illustrates, the fragmentation and disconnection inherent in hypertext do not automatically become articulated to empowering projects—late capitalism is very capable of orchestrating a disorganized field. The current chapter is more concerned with exploring those postmodern articulations that are explicitly reformist political.

for example, Barthes (1977a) claimed that "In the multiplicity of writing, everything is to be *disentangled,* nothing *deciphered;* the structure can be followed, 'run' (like a thread of a stocking) at every point and every level...." (p. 147). In "From Work to Text," Barthes (1977b) extended this idea, making each reader also partially a writer: "The Text.... asks of the reader a practical collaboration..." (p. 163; see also Scholes, 1989, p. 5). But where Barthes' transformation of reader to collaborative writer is primarily mental and unseen, hypertext appears to make the intertextual, networked text visible and active for the writer and reader (Moulthrop, 1989b), with the reader an explicit rather than merely psychic collaborator with the writer (Joyce, 1988). In addition, some teachers assert that the importance given to linking texts or segments in hypertext may also encourage students to make associative connections in their own thought processes and to think in a pluralistic, nonlinear fashion (Beck & Spicer, 1988; Beeman et al., 1987). As Landow and Delany (1990) described some of the key benefits of hypertext:

> Critical thinking relies upon relating many things to one another. Since the essence of hypertext lies in its making connections, it accustoms students to make connections among materials they encounter. A major component of critical thinking consists in the habits of seeking the way various causes impinge upon a single phenomenon or event and then evaluating their relative importance; and hypertext encourages such habits.
>
> Hypertext also helps a novice reader to learn the habit of nonsequential reading characteristic of more advanced study. Scholarly and scientific writing require readers to leave the main text and venture out to consider footnotes, evidence of statistics and other authorities, and the like; they must then integrate their scattered evidence into a complex intellectual structure. The Brown [University] experience suggests that using INTERMEDIA teaches students to read in this sophisticated way. (p. 22)

The multiple nature of this space is made manifest to readers in the graphical displays of node–link relations contained in the most popular platforms for postmodern hypertext—INTERMEDIA and STORYSPACE, as illustrated in graphics in previous chapters. Those who construct, teach, and use postmodern hypertext spaces provide and immerse users in a space of text and encourage the appropriation of terms such as *blurring lines, social networks, intertextuality, navigation, mapping,* and so on. As I discuss in later sections, when hypertext is articulated as postmodern space it most frequently authorizes one of two primary ways of thinking about space—the geometrical or the geographical—that in turn support very different ways of thinking about text and society.

More than in other articulations, people using postmodern hypertext are seen as neither solely readers nor solely writers of hypertext—users are told that they take both roles simultaneously and visibly. But even nonliterary texts such as corporate memos appear subject to such drastic shifts. In hypertexts, Moulthrop (1989a) asserted:

> [A]ny writing can be linked or woven into a de-centered matrix of information, its affiliation with specific, identifiable speech acts comes into question…. The changes that have come to the technology of writing take us out of the realm of self-validating truths and decrees and places us instead in a context that requires negotiation, cross-reference, and a constant awareness of diversity. (p. 259)

According to postmodern hypertext theorists, a hypertext not only invites readers to participate in making the text, but forces them to do so, requiring both readers and writers to become "co-learners" (Joyce, 1988, p. 12).

Of course, a reader's experience with any text is always a negotiation with text, writer, society, and self. But the stability of traditional texts is both physical and psychological; the physical, stable presence of the text works to deny the intangible, psychological text the reader attempts to construct (Kaplan, 1991). Hypertext, especially as constructed in explicitly postmodern sites, appears to overcome the relative fixity of print texts. Print literacy relies heavily on the idea that a printed text should be "stable"; conventional readers count on the fact that a printed text represents the author's (relatively) final and authoritative words that the ordering of elements strongly implies the sequence in which the author intended the text to be read (Slatin, 1990; see also Landow & Delany, 1990, pp. 12–13; Ong, 1982, p. 132–133). These assumptions, in print culture, are fairly safe guidelines.

With postmodern hypertext spaces, theorists attempt to challenge the idea of stable structure, of careful ordering in a single implied sequence. In hypertexts both in online help and on the World Wide Web, among other places, the focus is typically on the links provided by the author, so some sense of stability is preserved. However, in an open, constructive postmodern space, the original author or text's authority seems to evaporate under the force of the reader's movements: Readers not only choose among the options offered by the original text, but may also add their own paths or even texts.[4] It is these types of hypertext that begin to challenge most seriously assumptions about the respective positions and functions of student

---

[4] Both Bolter (1991b) and Poster (1990) noted the openness inherent in electronic text in general, but the conceptual metaphor of the book (as e.g., is found in Bolter's [1991a] hypertext version of WRITING SPACE) tends to overcome the construction of a postmodern space with that of the little machine; the cultural weight of print can overcome other potentials.

writing and literature in the classroom. Landow and Delany (1990) observed that:

> From a literary perspective based on book technology, the effects of electronic linking may appear harmful and dangerous. The notion of an individual, discrete work becomes increasingly undermined and untenable within this form of information technology, as it already has within much contemporary critical theory.... The reader is now faced by a kind of textual randomness. The writer, conversely, loses certain basic controls over his text: the text appears to break down, to fragment and atomize into constituent elements (the *lexia* or block of text), and these reading units take on a life of their own as they become more self-contained because less dependent on what comes before or after in a linear succession. (pp. 9–10)

Moulthrop and Kaplan (1994) explored these challenges at length, asking "If we English teachers embrace this form of text production, do we abandon what we have taken to be central literary values?" (p. 222).

With very few exceptions, however, the postmodern theorists from whom these positions were drawn—Derrida, Barthes, Kristeva, Cixous, Lyotard—were writing in the (late) age of print rather than computer-based text.[5] Despite the frequent assertion that hypertext in some way affords or even requires an explicitly deconstructive stance or textual activity, traditional deconstruction is directed as an attack on a number of particularly print characteristics, as Bolter himself pointed out. In a sense, a reader's resistance to a classic work or attempts at dethroning the author may only become bureaucratized and automated in order to disperse their force—the reader's commentary adding to the author's project. As I discuss later, the way in which an open hypertext can absorb and disperse commentary (sometimes more effectively than print) may act to neutralize deconstruction as a method of resistance.

Decentering the Subject of Discourse

The shifts in writer and reader roles authorized (and necessitated) by this postmodern space are closely related to a more fundamental shift, the decentering of the subject. According to Faigley (1989), the dispersal of autonomous identity is:

> [o]ne of the most troubling ideas for the humanities and the social scientists in the last two decades.... The unified, individual consciousness coterminous

---

[5] See Poster (1990) for a discussion of Derrida's interesting comments on electronic text.

with the physical body turns out not to be the "natural" self but a Western
version with specific historical and economic origins. (p. 396)

Hypertext theorists attempt to connect postmodern theory to the medium's apparent lack of central control and multiple, concrete work to make
the decentering of the subject a visible process (Harpold, 1990; Johnson-
Eilola, 1993a). The text is no longer a linear or hierarchical string of words[6]
(an object connoting isolation and self-unity) but now an explicitly open
space of text that can apparently be entered, navigated, deconstructed,
reconstructed, and exited in nearly infinite ways. But if the idea that the
reader is also the writer is difficult to translate into pedagogy, the decentering of the subject demanded in deconstruction can be even more difficult
for students and teachers to accept, especially those writers attempting to
construct subjectivities, either postmodern agencies (Ebert, 1991;
Ellsworth, 1989; Faigley, 1992), or somewhat reductive "honest voices" in
the modernist sense (see critiques in Berlin, 1992; Dasenbrock, 1988).
Many teachers are still struggling—or refusing to struggle—with the
implications of deconstruction for readers of traditional, printed texts (and
finding that deconstruction is a difficult theory to enact in pedagogical
practice). Swearingen (1990) offered the commonsense reminder that
deconstruction can be seen by students (and instructors) as terrifying
because:

> [t]he dogmatic pronouncements of the entrapment of the reader by the text
> are themselves coercive and entrapping, mutilating and silencing. To
> announce to students that there is no such thing as accurate reference
> because there is no reality unmediated by language is an arrogant pedagog-
> ical act. (p. 220)

This situation may become even more difficult when the subject is written or read in computer-based texts, because there the subject "no longer
functions as a center in the way it did in pre-electronic writing" (Poster,
1990, p. 100). In even a relatively conventionally structured hypertext as
Bolter's (1991a) WRITING SPACE, Bolter cautioned the readers that the
author of the text, and even of the copyright notice, might not in fact be
Bolter but a subsequent reader of Bolter's text who decides to surrepti-
tiously revise the text. Electronic texts are revised much more easily than

---

[6] The conceptual map of such readings emulates a hierarchy through the production of a
macrostructural presentation (encouraged by outlines, section heads, etc. in the text) but is normally read as a rough line from start to end; even when expert readers skip around nonlinearly,
their concept of the text reconstructs this hierarchy. This is probably true to a certain extent
even for contemporary readers of hypertext who were educated in a largely print culture.

print texts. The inherent reproducibility of computer texts (which are not only reproduced in a factory like a print book, but copied from magnetic media to RAM and VRAM, shot to the screen on cathode rays) tends to complicate notions of "original" versus "copy." The visible deconstruction of writing in hypertext spaces might be even more terrifying than the psychic deconstruction of print texts, or even the deconstruction of a electric linear text: In hypertext, the characteristics of virtual text (lack of physical orienting features such as position on page; relative position of a single page to the beginning and end of the text; ease with which layout, contents, typography, graphics, etc. may be restructured; etc.) can heighten the sense of decentering.

The dispersion of subject and text in hypertext, however, can be used to situate deconstructive acts in ways that allow students to find voices (multiple) and participate in discussions that value "qualitative tolerance and selective pluralism" (Swearingen, 1990, p. 223) by not allowing the texts to be completely displaced by deconstructive force. So on first glance at least, spatializing text may offer a useful way of teaching deconstructive processes. As I discuss later and in Chapter 6, however, this articulation of hypertext must not be mistaken as an automation of deconstruction, an all-too-common tendency. Hypertext might, in some cases, provide an allegory or encouragement toward deconstruction, but it does not replace it.

One of the difficulties in deconstructing print text is that the print text is there, it can be held and pointed to. To students, learning how to do deconstruction may be too often constructed as a choice between binary opposites: the physical text is there but the deconstructed text is nowhere, "infinitely open to production, but by definition unable to exist" (Belsey, 1980, p. 145). Derrida (1977) noted writing's "essential drift" and consequent state of writing as "cut off from all absolute responsibility, from *consciousness* as the ultimate authority, orphaned and separated at birth" from the writer (p. 181). In one (simplistic but unfortunately common) way of seeing deconstruction, people have two choices: They see themselves as intellectual dupes, believing in the sanctity of the author's true vision, or see themselves as depersonalized sliding effects of discourse without any way of distinguishing between good and bad, truth or falsehood. The contradiction here for readers and writers may be that such a position seems to invalidate, as Swearingen argued, any ground on which writer or readers can stand because the text is infinitely disintegrating.

A hypertext, because it is electronic text, is never completely physically "there," never able to be completely located in physical space because it is simultaneously located in phosphor images on the computer screen; magnetic configurations of volatile, silicon computer memory; more permanent floppy, hard, and/or optical disk storage; and sometimes electrical impulses in phone lines. But even in deconstructed form, the hypertext can still be seen on the computer screen, mediating between product and process. The deconstruction of a hypertext can occur visibly, at the surface. Hypertext "accepts as strengths those very qualities—the play of signs, intertextuality, the lack of closure—that deconstruction poses as the ultimate limitations of literature and language" (Bolter, 1991b, p. 166). Even when the hypertext lacks important physical characteristics (the text is, after all, *virtually* there, not tangible in the same sense as print), hypertext's graphical networks strongly connote multidimensional space. In AFTERNOON, A STORY (1990), for example, readers are always conscious that the specific text they are reading is constructed, through their interactions with it, as one instantiation of a seemingly infinite number of possible readings. By making deconstruction visible, hypertext may help students see deconstruction not as a hopelessly relativistic, paralyzing act (Paine, 1989, pp. 565–566) but as "a matter of general textual practice" (Moulthrop, 1989a, p. 259). Hypertext, in this manner, overcomes the necessity of a deconstructive reading of a linear text existing only as "secondary interpretive layer" that remains "formally distinct from the original discourse" (Moulthrop, 1990, p. 123; see also Kaplan, 1991, pp. 17–18). The text is both contingent and material (or at least visible) in a way that might encourage students to see deconstruction as potentially an act of resistance rather than submission.

The forces articulating hypertext as a postmodern space are difficult to gauge because of their rupturing force—the decentering of the subject and the blurring of the writer–reader distinction can both subvert repression and subvert resistance, as is the case with the spaces of postmodern capitalism discussed in Chapter 3. In order to construct a stronger resistance, we need to more fully understand the ways in which geographical and geometric postmodern spaces are formed and used.

X-RAY VISION: INSTITUTIONALLY SANCTIONED GEOMETRIES

To be lifted to the summit of the World Trade Center is to be lifted out of the city's grasp. One's body is no longer clasped by the streets that turn and return it according to an anonymous law.... When one goes up here, he leaves behind the mass that carries off and mixes up in itself any identity of authors or spectators. An Icarus flying above these waters, he can ignore the devices of Daedalus in mobile and endless labyrinths far below. His elevation transfigures him into a voyeur. It puts him at a distance. It transforms the bewitching world by which one was "possessed" into a text that lies before one's eyes. It allows one to read it, to be a solar Eye, looking down like a god. The exaltation of a scopic and gnostic drive: the fiction of knowledge is related to this lust to be a viewpoint and nothing more.

—Michel de Certeau (1984, p. 92)

Noting (and extending) the borrowing of terminology from literary criticism to hypertext, theorists and teachers such as Landow (1992c) develop connections to Derrida by looking backward from the popular terminology currently used in hypertext theory (even outside of postmodern circles): "Like Barthes, Foucault, and Mikhail Bakhtin, Jacques Derrida continually uses the terms *link* (*liaison*), *web* (*toile*), *network* (*réseau*) and *interwoven* (*s'y tissent*), which cry out for hypertextuality" (p. 8). Landow situated postmodern hypertext after the discourse(s) of literary criticism to show how hypertext addresses ("naturally") the faults of print pried open in deconstruction. In answering the critiques of print, theorists such as Landow (1992c) situate hypertext as a way of making deconstruction easier, less prone to the "moody nostalgia" of print-oriented deconstructionists (p. 87).

In recasting hypertext as a constructive activity, Landow positioned the techology in positive terms normally denied to deconstructionists. Hypertext-based deconstructionists, are "excited by the future of textuality, knowledge, and writing.... from within the dawn" (Landow, 1992c, p. 87). But if Landow's theoretical position appears to offer a broad-based, accessible future for deconstruction and living in the postmodern spaces of hypertext, hypertext as it is articulated here also exhibits tendencies toward another nostalgia, one encouraging a traditional scholarly activity. This type of scholarship may be valuable for teaching students professional methods and collaborative work, but may also neutralize the important negative or resistant functions of deconstructive activities. The INTERMEDIA/STORYSPACE[7] webs created by Landow, his colleagues, and students at Brown University—CONTEXT34, (English 34 Class, 1991) DICKENS WEB (Landow, 1990), and THE IN MEMORIAM WEB (Landow & Lanestedt, 1992)—help students learn and construct a complex network of the richly connected allusions, citations, references, and critical commentary surrounding specific works or related bodies of works:

> [THE IN MEMORIAM WEB] made use of documents created as an exercise for the undergraduate seminar in Victorian Poetry that directed students to take a single section of the work and "show by an essay of no more than two pages (typed) or by a one-page diagram its connections or relations to other sections of the poem"....

> The six members of the graduate seminar added links and documents to the body of materials already on line. In addition to the 133 sections of the poem, these included several dozen files on the poet and his other poems as well as

---

[7] Initial versions of THE IN MEMORIAM WEB were developed in INTERMEDIA but were converted to the somewhat similar environment of STORYSPACE after Brown University discontinued INTERMEDIA development.

relevant materials on Victorian religion, science, history, and art. Students from the undergraduate seminar created approximately a dozen graphic or text documents and linked them to individual sections of *In Memoriam....* (Landow, 1992c, p. 142)

The resulting INTERMEDIA document (now converted to STORYSPACE) formed the basis for further work by both students and teachers, who added supporting material, connections, and commentary to the network (Figures 5.1 and 5.2). The resulting hypertext creates a space encouraging students to become more aware (and more active within) the matrix of rela-

FIGURE 5.1. Opening screen in THE IN MEMORIAM WEB (Landow & Lanestedt, 1992)

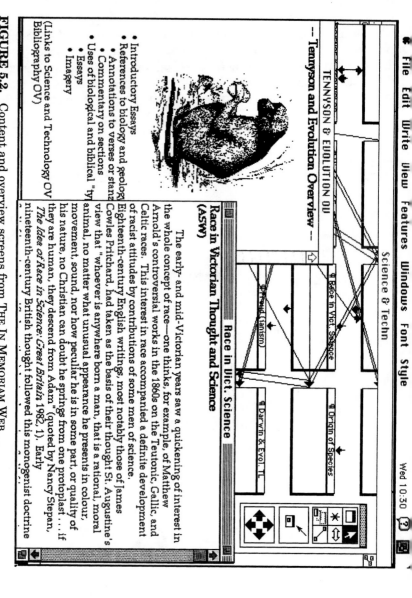

FIGURE 5.2. Content and overview screens from THE IN MEMORIAM WEB.

tions involved in literary study.[8] As Landow (1992c) summarized, "Working independently and yet together, the members of the seminar created a presentation of a major nineteenth-century literary work that makes obvious many of its internal and external relations" (p. 143). Unlike the written texts normally produced in such scholarship, "Networked hypertext systems... record and reproduce the relations among texts, one effect of which is that they permit the novice to experience the reading and thinking patterns of the expert" (p. 143).

The rift between theory and practice occurs, however, in aligning hypertext to the spaces of intertextuality and postmodernism; the two projects encompass a wide range of practices that are often but not always complementary, although Landow (1992c) appeared to see them as such: "[S]omething that Derrida and other critical theorists describe as part of a seemingly extravagant claim about language turns out precisely to describe the new economy of reading and writing with electronic, virtual, rather than physical, forms" (p. 8). The problem is that the deconstructions encouraged by these hypertexts appear bounded by a horizon of expressive realist literary scholarship as defined by Belsey (1980), in which:

> The text is seen as a way of arriving at something anterior to it: the convictions of the author, or his or her experience as part of that society at a particular time. To understand the text is to explain it in terms of the author's ideas, psychological state or social background. Books about authors often begin with a brief biography discussing the influence of the family, the environment or the society. (p. 13)

In THE IN MEMORIAM WEB, the network of text suspending Tennyson's work takes the place of the "brief biography" in order to make the critic's project more feasible. Landow seems to acknowledge the possibility of this difficulty when, with Delany (1990), he observed that "[t]he capacity to initiate the novice into a disciplinary culture suggests that this new information medium has an almost totalitarian capacity to model encounters with texts. However, the intrinsically antihierarchical nature of hypertext counteracts such a danger" (p. 23).

But this type of literary criticism is not able to sustain its antihierarchical nature because of the way that the cultural force of literary masterpieces is capable of absorbing resistance. Texts refer to each other continually, intertextually, but we would not want to call those connections revolutionary. "Technology does powerfully affect literacy," Tuman (1992c) remarked on such work in INTERMEDIA, "but Landow seems only interested in those

---

[8] This pedagogical goal extends to other discourses as well, where the intertext may be used to help students learn the conventions and backgrounds of other discourse communities (Bush's initial concepts were directed broadly at this goal).

technologies that enhance (deepen) our experience with print (p. 61). In many ways, as Brantlinger (1990) reminded us, the literary tradition is resilient enough to expand and absorb resistant forces:

> For literary humanists, the move toward cultural studies perhaps begins with the realization that reading the isolated "classic" or "great book" is not possible without also reading the larger "cultural text" into which it fits. But just what is this cultural text? Who writes it? How can it be read? Where is it located? Is it something like a gigantic library (conveniently located on a college campus), containing all the other text ever written? This would suggest not much more than an expanded versions of the literary canon or tradition.... (p. 22)

It is not enough to observe that, in hypertexts such as THE IN MEMORIAM WEB, one text opens to another, or that commentaries and historical documents can be linked into the author's text: This frequently only acts as a net rather than a disruptive force. Print literacy is founded on order and fixity; literacy, in our culture, is such a strong articulatory force that it can be felt even when the technology affords other structures.

Even when it is not necessary, for example, that Landow and Lanestedt (1992) structure the text hierarchically (hypertext, as Landow & Delany [1990] put it earlier, is "intrinsically anti-hierarchical), that hierarchy often occurs as if by default. The text itself enacts the hierarchy of professional authority—the names of Tennyson, Landow, and Lanestedt figure prominently although it is less easy to find the names of the students who worked on the text.

On one level, that forefronted by the idea of hypertext, the structure of THE IN MEMORIAM WEB is difficult to picture, being composed simultaneously of a network and a hierarchy. But a primary introduction to the text shown in Figure 5.3 illustrates the strength of print characteristics such as the Table of Contents, which organizes material in a general hierarchy.

We must separate the process of deconstruction, for example, as it is practiced on print texts from the allegory of deconstruction alluded to by hypertext. There is a very real connection here, one that has become very strongly articulated to hypertext in this instance, but the relation must not be confused with identity. Bolter similarly asserted that a hypertext—even a closed, single work such as AFTERNOON—deconstructs itself because the "margins yield," and because hypertext embodies the very contradictions of print on which deconstructionists work their havoc. However, it is not clear from the work of Landow and Bolter whether the similarity between hypertext and postmodernism allows hypertext to automate deconstruction—making it an affair of machines rather than humans—or if it encourages further subjective interventions. The writing and reading of a hypertext is like deconstruction, or might remind the writer and reader of deconstruction, but the simple act of following multiple, sometimes contradictory paths through nodes is not by

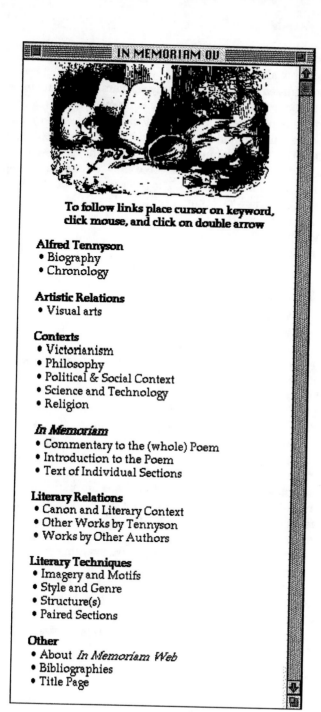

IN MEMORIAM OU

To follow links place cursor on keyword,
click mouse, and click on double arrow

Alfred Tennyson
* Biography
* Chronology

Artistic Relations
* Visual arts

Contexts
* Victorianism
* Philosophy
* Political & Social Context
* Science and Technology
* Religion

In Memoriam
* Commentary to the (whole) Poem
* Introduction to the Poem
* Text of Individual Sections

Literary Relations
* Canon and Literary Context
* Other Works by Tennyson
* Works by Other Authors

Literary Techniques
* Imagery and Motifs
* Style and Genre
* Structure(s)
* Paired Sections

Other
* About *In Memoriam Web*
* Bibliographies
* Title Page

FIGURE 5.3. Main table of contents for THE IN MEMORIAM WEB.

itself deconstructive reading. The text is not so much split as caught in a relatively static net of allusion and connotation. Although this net certainly provides an important environment for young scholars attempting to learn new genres and thinking patterns, the activity is not necessarily deconstruction, but perhaps the appropriation by conventional literary scholarship of some deconstructive techniques and concepts (and in appropriating, disarming).

Where Derrida (1977) claimed that "context is never absolutely determinable" (p. 174), Landow (1992b) asserted that "electronic linking recontextualizes individual works" (p. 79). The term context is a vague term that Landow seems to situate as original context. THE IN MEMORIAM WEB, for example, might encourage traditional scholarly techniques more than postmodern blurrings or resistant readings.

Context is an important aspect of a critical literacy of hypertext, but it must be articulated in a contingent and resistant way, not as a methodology for enshrining cultural icons. In a similar vein, Robinson (1993) said that a hypertextual corpus of work can help challenge the notion of "critical edition" as "critical reconstruction of the ideal text" (p. 272). Notably, however, Robinson did not see this new methodology as postmodernist. He closed his argument with the vision of "a clearer understanding of how some of the most important texts in our culture were shaped by their authors and received by their readers" (p. 286).

I am not debating whether or not hypertext might potentially provide an important environment for literary scholars researching the Great Works; I find such work fresh and exciting compared to earlier methods. I do, however, want to bring to the surface the difficulties of assuming that hypertext automatically and powerfully makes writing and reading deconstructive, resistant activities.

Although context remains an important issue for many postmodernists as a background for deconstructing contradictions in texts and situating cultural inequalities, THE IN MEMORIAM WEB's contextualizations frequently seem more intended to sanctify the text with an ever-expanding totalizing context (rather than the multiple, fragmenting contexts involved in deconstructing a text).

In terms of deconstruction or articulation theory, contexts are not the unified, objective grounds out of which a work grows, but ways of approaching a social relation (Slack, 1989)[9]. Although, as Landow (1992c) argued, contextualizations can both highlight unequal representations of certain classes in the canon and help include new material in the canon, we must be careful here in speaking of any sort of postmodern revolution: Hypertext

---

[9] Slack here was writing of technology rather than literature, but the observation certainly applies to the critique of Landow's sense of context (and, in addition, literature is itself a form of technology).

can provide a conservative medium for teaching institutionally sanctioned discourses. Calling such reading "automatic" deconstruction may only act to short circuit the user's perception for the need to go further than what the text offers on its surface.

Attempting to answer charges that hypertext may disarm attempts at critical reading, Landow (1992c) argued that "in linking and following links lie responsibility—political responsibility—since the reader establishes his or her own line of reading" (p. 184). This politicized reading, however, is difficult to achieve and does not necessarily follow from the technology. As Landow admitted:

> In practice most readers employ the materials developed at Brown University as a text-centered system, since they tend to focus on individual works, with the result that even if they begin sessions by entering the system to look for information about an individual author, they tend to spend most time with lexias devoted to specific texts, moving between poem and poem (Swinburne's "Laus Veneris" and Keats "La Belle Dame Sans Merci" or works centering on Ulysses by Joyce, Tennyson, and Soyinka) and between poem and informational texts ("Laus Veneris" and files on chivalry, medieval revival, courtly love, Wagner, and so on). (p. 13)

Here it seems that the social forces articulating hypertext to literary study are more concerned with the ways a web can catch objects rather than ways webs shift and reknot under various changing contexts and infinite iterations, a sort of secondary metaphysics of presence[10] in which the network of text acts as a better stand-in for the author's presence than a print text ever could (validating and surpassing the frequent criticism of postmodernism as totalizing the world in terms of text). Tennyson, Landow asserted, "created his poetry of fragments in an attempt to write with greater honesty and with greater truth about his own experience" (p. 107). Hypertext is apparently better capable of showing readers the "true" Tennyson than was the faulty technology of print.

Although a hypertext such as THE IN MEMORIAM WEB provides in one sense a way of denaturalizing writing so that it does not appear to be a mere neutral stand-in for speech[11] (and so can be used to construct new

---

[10] Derrida's metaphysics of presence or logocentrism being the view that writing is a stand-in for the presence of the speaking author.

[11] Critiquing the continued assumption by some students (and teachers) of the close identity between writing and speaking, Dasenbrock (1988) observed "[B]y refusing to employ devices that don't *sound natural*, students cut themselves off from fully learning the mechanisms of writing, some of which admittedly do not sound natural. Does anyone speak in footnotes?" (p. 5). Landow (1992c), however, may be reversing this aspect when he claimed that both Derrida and hypertext might provide a text "truer to our potential experience" (p. 8).

connections and deconstruct other texts), the text's primary use appears to be the task of recovering a lost, true context: "By making each document in the docuverse exist as part of a larger structure, INTERMEDIA places each document in what one can term the 'virtual presence' of all previously created documents and their creators" (Landow, 1992c, p. 144). Where traditional deconstruction attempted a resistance to finding the singular truth of a text, these uses of hypertext appear to work toward specifying such truths. Although such uses can never exhaust signification, they certainly hold this as their teleology.

INTERMEDIA/STORYSPACE allows the generation of contexts, but not the original context or true meaning. Although Landow refuted the idea of the network as a totalizing or centering concept (asserting that, along the lines of connectionist theories of mind, hypertext networks distribute meaning throughout the system), THE IN MEMORIAM WEB clearly constructs a textual center of gravity in the network: Tennyson's poem. Writing with Delany, Landow (1990) explicitly positioned such hypertexts as centered, with "the classical linear text, with its order and fixity, at the center of the structure... an unchanging axis from which radiate linked texts that surround it, modifying the reader's experience of this original text-in-a-new-context" (p. 9).[12] So although there is a degree of dispersal inherent in THE IN MEMORIAM WEB, the deconstruction is problematic. In Derridean deconstruction, context is both necessary and always questioned (rather than affirmed):

> Every sign, linguistic or non-linguistic, spoken or written (in the current sense of this opposition, in a small or large unit), can be *cited*, put between quotation marks; in so doing it can break with every given context, engendering an infinity of new concepts in a manner which is absolutely illimitable. (Derrida, 1977, p. 185)

Derrida was not arguing here that contexts are ever absent but that "there are only contexts without any center or absolute anchoring" (p. 186). As Spivak (1976) argued in the preface to her translation of Derrida's *O*

---

[12] Landow and Delany (1990) referred to THE IN MEMORIAM WEB in their essay, but classed it with another type of hypertext, "the adaption for hypertextual presentation of material conceived in book technology" (p. 9). Although Landow (1992c) argued that even the print structure of Tennyson's poem represents a radical "antilinear poetry of fragments," there is arguably a large difference between the nonlinearity of Tennyson's word and the nonlinearity of a fiction such as Joyce's AFTERNOON. *In Memoriam* as Tennyson constructed it (and a Landow and Lanestedt lay it out structurally in STORYSPACE) runs top to bottom in a clear order.

Grammatology, deconstruction always contains the potential of positioning the critic as master-author:

> Derrida acknowledges that the desire of deconstruction may itself be a desire to reappropriate the text actively through mastery, to show the text "what it does not know." And as she deconstructs, all protestations to the contrary, the critic necessarily assumes that she at least, and for the time being, means what she says. Even the declaration of her vulnerability must come, after all, in the controlling language of demonstration and reference. In other words, the critic provisionally forgets that her own text is necessarily self-deconstructed, always already a palimpsest. (p. lxxxvii)

But the impulse toward dominating the text cannot be switched for a complete release:

> The desire of deconstruction has also the opposite allure. Deconstruction seems to offer a way out of the closure of knowledge. By inaugurating the open-ended indefiniteness of textuality—by thus "placing in the abyss" (*mettre en abime*), as the French expression would literally have it—it shows us the lure of the abyss as freedom. The fall into the abyss of deconstruction inspires us with as much pleasure as fear.

> Thus a further deconstruction deconstructs deconstruction, both as the search for a foundation (the critic behaving as if she means what she says in her text), and as the pleasure of the bottomless. The tool for this, as indeed for any deconstruction, is our desire, itself a deconstructive and grammatological structure that forever differs from (we only desire what is not ourselves) and defers (desire is never fulfilled) the text of our selves. Deconstruction can therefore never be a positive science. (pp. lxxvii–lxxviii)

But according to many theorists, hypertext makes deconstruction positive. If we were to insist that a technology such as INTERMEDIA or STORYSPACE or a hypertext such as THE IN MEMORIAM WEB enacts rather than affords deconstruction, it might be better to point out that these things illustrate vividly the ways in which no text can ever regain an original context, the way that the text is always already promiscuous, joining with innumerable other texts and contexts—not merely one author's *oeuvre*, one genre or period, but infinitely many.[13] The number of lexia in THE IN MEMORIAM WEB must signify infinity but not contain it. In other words, the explicit signatures of those participating in the construction of the text

---

[13] Articulation theory, for example, like the poststructuralist theories from which it was deconstructed and reconstructed, depends on tension inherent in trying to think of a contradictory totality.

should not act as limits (or recaptured contexts), but as visible contradictions of the futility of single authors or meanings. The initials and names attached to commentary should act to shadow themselves with all those past and future writers and readers. "The purportedly 'ideal' structure must necessarily be such that this corruption will be 'always possible'. This *possibility* constitutes part of the *necessary* traits of the purportedly ideal structure" (Derrida, 1978, p. 218). The docuverse as a totality is itself doomed to failure—but that is one of its most valuable aspects.

The web of intertextual signification, instead of undertaking a deconstruction, works to center a work or author, to fix association in a geometry of meaning. By geometry, I mean a systemization and determination of fields of meaning, an attempt to gain exhaustive knowledge by strictly delimiting the relevant attributes of an object, what de Certeau (1984) associated with the *propre* and Deleuze and Guattari (1987) termed the gridded, arboreal, or striated space: the assignment of things to discrete locations, trapped in a web of their proper contexts.

Although certainly projects such as THE IN MEMORIAM WEB begin with the observation of material landscapes (the geography of literary production), they tend to evolve into a self-constituting, self-contained geometry. Although Landow (1992c) asserted that "[t]he hypertext document becomes a traveling Aleph" (p. 12; returning to Borges' fantastic sphere in which a viewer could see all time and all space), we must ask ourselves whether concepts such as the Aleph should be a goal for a literacy technology or the (productive) observance of an impossibility.

Landow's intertexts work (partially) toward a deconstruction of an original text (or set of texts), but in continually speaking of the way in which the intertext contextualizes the text without simultaneously and strongly highlighting the multiplicity, infinity, and frequent contradiction between these contexts, the deconstructive project is undercut: This is not Derrida's *differance*, the contextualization involved in teasing out the contradictory differences in the play of signification or the deferment of meaning, but often an attempt to recapture the authorial context. In de Certeau's terms, the INTERMEDIA web organizes a place rather than a space.[14] As Landow (1987)

---

[14] I should raise here an important distinction to be made between THE IN MEMORIAM WEB as it was constructed by students at Brown University and the one published by Eastgate Press (on which I've relied for my own work). The in-process version may have involved a great deal more deconstructive activity than seems present on reading the published version although even this caveat seems doubtful: That the text was published seems to highlight the text as product (albeit in a lesser sense than in print, because the published version of THE IN MEMORIAM WEB can be added to by writers and readers who own STORYSPACE) as well as other relatively conservative aspects mentioned earlier all seem to situate either in-class or published versions of THE IN MEMORIAM WEB at an indistinct border between postmodernism and expressive realism.

said in an earlier context, "hypertext's system of linked files conveys the strong impression that its links signify coherent, purposeful, and, above all, *useful* relationships" (p. 332). The drive for contextualization attempts to place time under the network—which should be able to bear the traces of every historical intervention or association to the father text and thereby account for history as another dimension of space—attempting to create a geometry from what might have been geography. Not incidentally, a primary difficulty of enacting critical literacies of hypertext is the danger of letting important critical (re)(de)contextualizations devolve into searches for truth. Contextualizations must always acknowledge their own politics and contingency, something THE IN MEMORIAM WEB does not frequently do.

Although all maps are generative, makers and users frequently see them in terms of a tracing or reflection rather than a construction of reality. When map users see the relations described by the map as natural reflections of reality, that reflection (which is really a construction) tends to gain primacy over other possible mappings. This geometry represents the conquest of time—when it is introduced into the map, it is articulated as a visual feature, converted into space. Time and history remain important factors, but the end goal of the project is one of conquest—in specifying historical forces, the writer or reader attempts to nail them down.

Capitalism remains an important force as well. As noted earlier, authorial presence is tightly bound up with conceptions of capital. Although in one place Landow (1992c) argued that hypertext reverses the historical development that "print technology contributed to the sense of a separate, unique text that is the product—and hence the property—of one person, the author" (pp. 92–93), Landow also argued later that "one of the primary requisites for developing a fully empowering hypertextuality is to improve, not technology, but laws concerning copyright and authorial property" (p. 198).

The current structure of the World Wide Web similarly enforces very rigid terms of ownership: In most cases, only the single owner of a site can change the text within that site. Although this would seem to protect sites from random or malicious rewriting, these restrictions also prevent readers from ever being able to contribute to the construction of the text—even to add a link of commentary—except by contacting the owner of the site and requesting that they add a link. In the current articulation of the Web, however, most readers would not even consider the idea of asking an "owner" to add in a comment or link. This possibility must be forefronted. One current initiative to encouraging such reader-sponsored writings is Moulthrop and Kaplan's Center for Responsive Electronic Writing (CREW; Figure 5.4) which allows owners to link in a graphic and pointer to an explanation of the process (and purpose) of making such a request.

In a sense, the forces acting in the space and construction articulation are akin to the forces constructing the little machines of Chapter 3:

FIGURE 5.4. CREW (Center for Responsive Electronic Writing) home page and compact.

Hypertext solves mechanical limitations of the print book (there, in ease of use and speed; here, in the isolation connoted by individual print works, an isolation that provided deconstruction the fracture that postmodern hypertexts sometimes deny in embodying this fracture). The master text absorbs its own dissent, the Oedipal myth played out as cannibalism. Although this criticism may seem to hint at a romantic notion that the text should stand on its own—that well-trained readers should be able to find the truth in the text by virtue of their abilities as readers—it is actually a criticism of the flattening of resistance and agency that may be inherent in literary uses of hypertext.

PERPETUAL MOTION: "FORKING PATHS" AND THE LOSS OF CENTER(S) IN HYPERTEXT GEOGRAPHY

[P]ersonal identity is itself the effect of a certain temporal unification of past and future with one's present... such active temporal unification is itself a function of language, or better still of the sentence, as it moves along its hermeneutic circle through time. If we are unable to unify the past, present, and future of the sentence, then we are similarly unable to unify the past, present, and future of our own biographical experience or psychic life. With the breakdown of the signifying chain, therefore, the schizophrenic is reduced to an experience of pure material signifiers, or, in other words, a series of pure and unrelated presents in time.

—Frederic Jameson (1991, p. 27)

If we sense that hypertexts such as THE IN MEMORIAM WEB may be too conservative to deliver on their promises of a postmodern writing and reading, we must also admit that a more radically postmodern approach to hypertext space is not without its own (often substantial) problems. In KARL'S FORKING RESPONSE, an important example of resistance to hypertext writing discussed by Moulthrop and Kaplan (1994), Crary attempts to resist subordinating his own text to the hypertext that is the object of his critical reading. Karl's resistance involves FORKING PATHS, a hypertext constructed by Moulthrop out of a fragmented version of Borges (1962) "Garden of Forking Paths." Aside from dividing up Borges' linear, printed text, Moulthrop introduced his own complicating text nodes, asserted multiple orderings and outcomes, and encouraged later readers to assert their own positions by writing into the text (Figure 5.5)—things that Borges could allude to but not do in print.

Crary refuses—or tries to refuse—to play the game the open hypertext encourages; instead, Crary attempts a strong, resistant reading of FORKING PATHS, critiquing and categorizing the various nodes of the text as well as Moulthrop's conception of hypertext—the "resistant" reading here being the imposition of traditional literary techniques on a relatively postmodern text (similar to the operations of THE IN MEMORIAM WEB, but at a more local level). In the end, however, Crary's attempts at resistance are futile, as his own links into the object of his critique become complicitous with his activities:

Karl Crary attempts to resist FORKING PATHS by objectifying it, establishing an aloofness from its gregarious metafictional game. Like a good strong reader (and he is a very good one), Crary senses what the text "wants" him to do and swerves from that interpretive track. He refuses to invent further variations on the Borges/Moulthrop themes. He will be sober and reflective, not fictively playful. His deviation heads him away from the narrative ground of story-space, off to the apparently separate realm of commentary, an alterna-

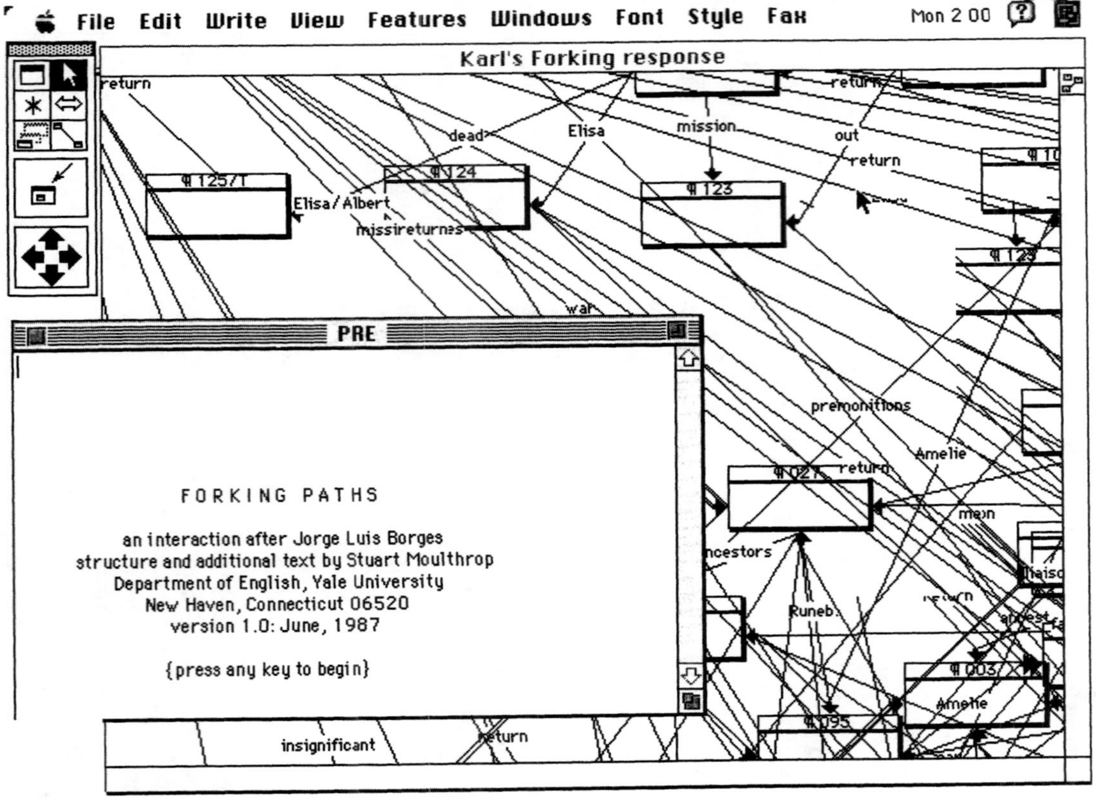
File Edit Write View Features Windows Font Style Fax
Mon 2 00
Karl's Forking response
PRE
FORKING PATHS
an interaction after Jorge Luis Borges
structure and additional text by Stuart Moulthrop
Department of English, Yale University
New Haven, Connecticut 06520
version 1.0: June, 1987
{press any key to begin}
return
dead
Elisa
mission
out
Elisa/Albert
premonitions
Amelie
insignificant

FIGURE 5.5. Opening screen from FORKING PATHS, Moulthrop's hypertextual rewrite of Borge's "In the Garden of Forking Paths."

tive theory-space. "Come inside," the prior text says, "Look... learn... build for yourself." Though Crary is happy enough to look, learn, and build, he declines the first overture, preferring to hold himself and his writing apart from the earlier texts. (Moulthrop & Kaplan, 1994, pp. 232–233)

Because Crary's writing exists in the same hypertext file as FORKING PATHS, he is already playing the game (Figure 5.6); that is, by agreeing to work within the interconnected systems of the STORYSPACE network, Crary agrees (perhaps unknowingly) to allow his text to be absorbed by FORKING PATHS. As indicated by the title to Moulthrop and Kaplan's essay, readers who have entered into this system have "became what they beheld." Although Crary's interpretive methods appear conventional—even moreso than those used by Landow and others—the postmodern text of FORKING PATHS, like all postmodern texts, eliminates most concepts of critical distance (this is one of the defining characteristics of postmodernism). As Moulthrop and Kaplan pointed out, Crary's strategy of coming to terms with the text constructs a set of categories that (apparently unwittingly) claims Crary's own text as part of FORKING PATHS. Crary (1993) recounted his process of mapping the text:

One of the most intriguing aspects of FORKING PATHS was its relation to Borges' Garden of the FORKING PATHS. Having already read Garden of the FORKING PATHS, it was interesting to watch for Borges' original text and its relation to the other text that makes up FORKING PATHS.

The text in FORKING PATHS can be divided into four types:

1) original Borges text
2) text that sounds like Borges text, but is not
3) text that does not sound like Borges text, but is still related Borges' story
4) complete digressions

Unfortunately, it is this same relationship to Borges' text that poses some great problems. The text is excellent, but its status, legally and ethically, is uncertain.

Crary here attempted to write within the geometrical grid of traditional scholarship but the space will not support it, absorbing the grid itself in the tangled network of lines structuring the text. As he is situated at the conjunction of multiple discourses, Crary is denied the possibility of existing outside or above the text. Moulthrop and Kaplan offered an interpretation of KARL'S FORKING RESPONSE that illustrates how, in the intertextual, playful realm of Moulthrop/Borges' creation, Crary's own entries appear as the text's own self-criticism. In print, Crary could at

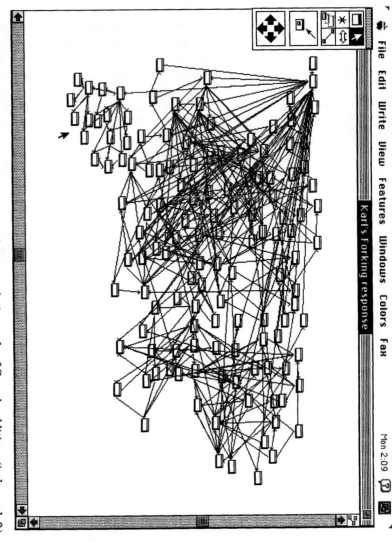

FIGURE 5.6. KARL'S FORKING RESPONSE, showing relative scale of Crary's additions (in lower left) compared to Moulthrop and Borge's text (rest of screen).

least write a critical essay that, although it oriented itself toward FORKING PATHS via citation and quotation, would be physically (if not conceptually) distinct from the text he was discussing. Once placed in a forum of explicit fragmentation and indeterminacy, each additional text is taken up and broken apart, reconnected, and held open as a process rather than a discrete, isolated, fixed object.[15] We can certainly recognize the potential benefits of this situation, as students may come to understand writing as an intertextual, social process rather than the still-common notion of writing as isolated genius. But such benefits are not an automatic consequence of hypertext. As Moulthrop and Kaplan (1994) admitted, "If Crary's attempt at creative resistance does not succeed, then our attempt at a technologically radicalized pedagogy must also be counted as a failure" (p. 236); the medium in which Crary worked automatically subsumed his attempts at resistance.

The problem here, the postmodern loss of individuality and personal control in writing and reading hypertext, corresponds to many complaints about postmodernism in general: loss of identity, the perceived politicization of the "neutral" activity of writing and reading, the imposition of a false "free market" onto interpretive activities, and so on (see, e.g., Tompkins' [1990] "Pedagogy of the Distressed" and the ensuing debate in the letter exchanges in subsequent issues of *College English*, or Hairston's [1992] "Diversity, Ideology, and the Teaching of Writing" and responses in *College Composition and Communication*). Hypertext, after all, is commonly seen as a physical embodiment of postmodern theory.

In such a context, the simple node-link structure of hypertext becomes so strongly tied to the deconstructive project that writing and reading appear to be essentially nihilistic activities. Leveling the text—acts of fragmentation and dispersal, the primary activities of deconstruction—threatens to become the prevailing function of hypertext. In such a geography, there is no future and no history, only a timeless succession of instants, what Hebdige (1988) called "the blank, empty spaces of the now" (p. 164). The text is fragmented and torn out of time and history; where communication once seemed to serve a social function, now it is merely wandering. This danger applies not only to postmodern fictions but also, as the previous chapters have demonstrated, to the breakdown of context in functional hypertext and the commodification of information in online information spaces.

If postmodernism is a space, it is one we walk through in Andy Warhol's

---

[15] We could also argue that even a print text interpretation is subsumed by the postmodern text and that hypertext only highlights this process. But obviously some methods and texts offer a better example than others.

post-political diamond dust shoes—"footgear," Jameson (1991) pointed out, "that... does not really speak to us at all" (p. 8). Where a painting such as Van Gogh's *A Pair of Boots* could, in an earlier time, engender a hermeneutic reading "in which the work in its inert, objectal form is taken as a clue or symptom for some vaster reality which replaces it as its ultimate truth" (p. 8), the expressive realist reading becomes impossible for postmodern object such as Warhol's *Diamond Dust Shoes*, Jameson argued, because:

> We have a random collection of dead objects hanging together on the canvas like so many turnips, as shorn of their earlier life world as the pile of shoes left over from Auschwitz or the remainders and tokens of some incomprehensible and tragic fire in a packed dance hall. There is therefore in Warhol no way to complete the hermeneutic gesture and restore to these oddments that whole larger lived context of the dance hall.... (p. 8)

Hypertext in postmodern space appears, at least initially, to refute interpretation as a way to articulate mastery or even resistance. As the fragmentation and dispersal of authority accelerate (in the sense of both authorship and control), every node of text exists at the same level of importance. But instead of providing a "level playing field" on which a formerly disempowered reader can construct his or her own identity, the immense gravity absorbs and levels all movement. Many readers are not yet ready to, as Joyce (1992) urged, "surrender control and in that constant declination continually render control meaningless." Surrendering control must also correspond, as Joyce (1995) noted elsewhere, with the capabilities to map (and recover) successive interdependencies and to slow down in our movements. In a completely flattened space, however, there is land to travel but no place to stop. The subject—that which joins the past and the future under the experience of the present—dissolves. Bolter (1993) made precisely the same connection when he drew railroad parallels from Paul Theroux's *The Great Railway Bazaar*:

> Even Theroux got tired of railway travel in the end. We leave him on the final page happy to be rereading the story of his trip, the linear narrative that puts everything in its place. That kind of intellectual rest and recuperation is perhaps one thing that hypertext will not give us. (p. 17)

From this perspective, Landow's intertexts invert the process implied in Crary's leveled commentary. Landow began with a monolithic geography and constructed a geometry; Karl's circumstances in FORKING PATHS reverse the problem in starting out with the purely geometrical and attempting to build a geography.

In Crary's experience, the text is a flattened, relatively undifferentiated plane.[16] Instead of time being stopped or converted to space, time is simply removed and made meaningless. The gathered nodes become a series of eternal presents, a timeless spectacle. By attempting a stance outside the text, Crary works to create a geography from the geometry of the text (Figure 5.6)—Crary's personal history of the text pulled down and left of the "main text" (Borges/Moulthrop's). By the time of Crary's arrival, however, the text is so utterly fragmented that he is unable to sustain a unified subjectivity—a distinctive voice—for long, as Moulthrop and Kaplan noted. Because Landow and colleagues as well as Crary use a somewhat conservative conception of hypertext as an interpretive vantage point that offers (or at least works toward) some angelic vision, they turn, in Jameson's terms, toward nostalgia for an earlier, innocent life. The "subject" of the space and subject articulation of hypertext appears, like hypertext, to deconstruct itself, to collapse under its own weight.

           🙠   🙠   🙠

We find ourselves standing at a problematic point in these cultural texts: The concretizing activities of THE IN MEMORIAM WEB appear as an attempt to reveal the truth about the text as a social artifact, placing all commentary in subordination to the master texts of Tennyson (or Dickens, or whomever)—a still useful method of reading, but also commonly conservative if not outright repressive. Such texts and activities are useful in training textual scholars to the workings and expectations of the profession—the geometry of a discipline—but do not seem to go very far in Landow's asserted postmodern project.

But the fragmented, flattened geography of FORKING PATHS absorbs identity in a disconcertingly disempowering manner. Time disappears in both cases, although in different manners. In extremely geometric spaces, time is totalized, frozen, mapped out. There is a sense of history, but it is closer to a reverent archaeology of the lives of past masters. In the predominantly geographic spaces, time ceases to represent anything at all—if there is movement, it is a nomadic motion made perpetual by the flattening of culture: There are no outcroppings of relatively stable identity with which we normally identify individuals; there are no plateaus on which to re-territorialize, the subject seeming to continually forget where it has

---

[16] Interestingly, Moulthrop and Kaplan did not appear to discuss Crary's earlier reading of the print version of Borges' (1962) "The Garden of Forking Paths." Although my and Moulthrop and Kaplan's use of Crary's text shows well the way in which his written response becomes absorbed by the hypertext, the discussion might have been very different had Karl been able to situate his reading more fully into the social environment of the class—including, as discussed later, collaborations with his peers.

come from in the instant it arrives at its destination (which is an identical nowhere to the previous one).

Hypertext is certainly not the simple and solitary cause of the dispersal, only a particularly vivid example, one force and symptom implicated in that displacement among many articulated by postmodern theorists. The totality of postmodern space is ungraspable, Jameson argued, requiring a new way of mapping ourselves—not the geographical, narrative itineraries of the traveler and not the geometric, cartographic measures of the traditional mapmaker, but an interplay between the two. For Jameson (1991), contemporary social life requires a "cognitive mapping" of political and physical space, a process of interplay between Althusserian Real, Imaginary, and Lacanian Symbolic. Landow's intertexts fail in this project due to their geometrical goal, an attempt to make transparent both time and space in the guise of a network of texts—a form of nostalgia that seems unable to recover a critical perspective on current social and historical spaces. Crary, on the other hand, finds nothing to resist because the fragmented text becomes removed from the Real and Imaginary—Crary attempts to resist the postmodern text that absorbs him in a pure place of the Symbolic. For Crary, geometry is absent due to any distinguishing features in the text—there is no map or grid to organize and structure the text. THE IN MEMORIAM WEB and FORKING PATHS move toward two opposing dangers of cognitive mapping as a resistance activity. Jameson (1991) warned that:

> The strength of the visual map from city to globe is so compelling that it ends up re-spatializing an operation we were supposed to think of in a different manner altogether. A new sense of global social structure was supposed to take on figuration and to displace the purely perceptual substitute of the geographical figure; cognitive mapping, which was supposed to have a kind of oxymoronic value and to transcend the limits of mapping altogether, is, as a concept, drawn back by the force of gravity of the black hole of the map itself (one of the most powerful of all human instruments) and therein cancels outs its own impossible originality. A secondary premise must, however, also be argued—namely, that the incapacity to map spatially is as crippling to political experience as the analogous incapacity to map spatially is for urban experience. It follows that an aesthetic of cognitive mapping in this sense is an integral part of any socialist political project. (p. 416)

In order to begin working on the project Jameson (1991) described as building "a pedagogical political culture which seeks to endow the individual subject with some new heightened sense of its place in the global system" (p. 54), we need to restructure postmodern articulations of hypertext so that in addition to dispersing the subject they also offer a method for learning how to situate that relatively dispersed self into an active, social matrix at the conjunction between geography and geometry.

HYPERTEXT AND THE POSTPOLITICAL WRITER AND READER

Trans-politics is the beginning of the disappearance of politics in the dwindling of the last commodity: duration. Democracy, consultation, the basis of politics, requires time. Duration is the proper of man; he is inscribed within it. For me, trans-politics is the beginning of the end.... [T]here's work to be done... in order to re-establish politics, at a time when technology no longer portions out matter and geographical space (as was the case in ancient democratic society), but when technology portions out time—and I would say: the depletion of time.

—Paul Virilio and Sylvére Lotringer (1983, p. 28)

As the plane of the text flattens—as distinctions between "my text" and "your text," "published text" and "teacher's text" and "student text," begin to disappear, as each node comes to exist at the same level of importance—hypertext potentially engenders post-political activity. The links between author and text, sign and signified that were reinforced by the physical and social structure of book discourse seem to come radically unglued. Furthermore, because hypertext is commonly conceived as merely a natural, evolutionary step from the deconstructive work of Barthes and Derrida, the link marker signifies, among other things, that this is the way it has always been—or should have been; that we were only fooling ourselves before when we said we knew who the author was.

Such a claim may be true, but it is far from reassuring. The physical boundaries of text, before the computer, seemed easy to distinguish: A book is bound and bounded. But as activity, identity, and agency are translated to the computer, reality comes to seem much more tenuous, even in day-to-day activities. One is reminded here of workers in a newly computerized wood-pulp plant interviewed by Zuboff (1988). As one anonymous plant operator expressed the anxiety,

When I go out and touch something, I know what will happen. There is a fear of not being on the floor watching things. It is like turning your back in a dark alley. You don't know what is behind you; you don't know what might be happening. It all becomes remote from you, and it makes you feel vulnerable. It was like being a new operator all over again. Today I push buttons instead of opening valves on the digester. If I push the wrong button, will I screw up? Will anything happen? (pp. 63–64)

Like the operator's uneasiness about the invisible relationship between the electronic control system and the machinery of the plant, the activity of wandering among the links, of navigating the hypertext, becomes the search for the "real" self under the signifier (the transcendental signified; Harpold, 1990, p. 174). From a textual perspective, our loss of direction in reading and writing seems to represent a loss of direction or center in our lives.

But although for critics of hypertext fiction such as Dobrin (1994) this activity appears wholly negative and oppressive (and admittedly, at times it has probably appeared to be my point as well), we can perhaps express something more constructive. If we consider the flattened plane as a transitional state or a heuristic rather than a totalizing worldview, hypertext can become an empowering forum. Dobrin fell into the argument that the technology is simultaneously effective and ineffectual, dangerous and innocuous without any middle ground that might afford a sense of purpose for the users of the technology (Landow, 1992c). Dobrin claimed not only that Crary's teachers have failed him, but that hypertext is an irrelevant medium; the medium is only a tool with which we control students.

What is missing in postmodern hypertext space (both commodity and construction forms) is an overt sense of the place of postmodernism as a method of constructive and social resistance, something Moulthrop and Kaplan began to allude to near the end of their analysis of Crary's work. By the old standards of classical interpretation, Crary's resistance is futile because he cannot dominate the text; Crary cannot construct an isolated, individual position from which to write. In this articulation, a hypertext deconstructs itself—so not only can the text not be resisted, but each subsequent writer's text is itself deconstructed.

Resistance could be directed toward a different goal, however, such as the distinction between ludic and resistance postmodernism (Ebert, 1991) discussed earlier. From the standpoint of the ludic–resistance distinction, the "negative" flattening of the text in hypertext is only a partial affair, a resistance that is never complete because it is consistently connected to the imaginary and real relations of society. Discourses are always multiple. Hypertext is important in the ways that it both realizes and problematizes things that we have been thinking about for a long time—not merely as effects of deterministic, autonomous technology, but as also influenced by late, disorganized, postmodern capitalism, social structures, and, not least, the values and powers that are tangled into the culture of the book. The book in our society tends toward authorizing and conserving power and the commodification and consumption of ideas in capitalist culture. Moulthrop and Kaplan's (1994) own final analysis of the "failure" takes this tact:

> In reading and writing hypertexts, our resistance may come to focus not on prior texts or creative precursors, but rather on the literary institutions we

have inherited from the history of print—institutions that make reading into a test of strength, authorship into a hierarchic mystery, and texts into closed books. (pp. 236–237)

So what Moulthrop, Kaplan, and Crary have accomplished is an important but only initial step away from print culture—a step that is, because of its isolation, more of a symptom than a program for action. Moulthrop and Kaplan's analysis begins with the traditional view of literary scholarship (a rhetorical move that serves to highlight the contradictions inherent in this type of reading). For such a discourse, the primary forces involve isolated reader and text; the forces of other discourse are here, but are not mapped. Dobrin's skepticism is healthy, however: Moulthrop and Kaplan's more important ideas about book culture apparently come after Crary's experiences, only being hinted at in the last few paragraphs of their essay. Hypertext is not necessarily (or perhaps even commonly) an empowering area for student work. In order to construct hypertext as a socially empowering technology, we have to expand our vision to the social, mapping the world and living the map, not merely for the types of hypertext articulated by the forces discussed in this chapter, but for all hypertext.

In Chapter 6, I illustrate a few key ways in which composition instructors and students might begin mediating between geometry and geography in hypertext by socializing the discourse. The collective activity of a community of writers can work to outweigh the weight of conventional, conservative notions of meaning. At the same time, the lived process of this activity helps to prevent the postmodernist leanings from degenerating into nihilism.

Chapter 6 in addition uses the rearticulation of space and construction as a rupture in our notions of genre that can be use in rearticulating not only "traditional" work in the composition and literature classrooms, but online research and using online help by socializing them in similar ways. Perhaps more importantly, by opening up these discourses to discussion by composition and literature theorists and teachers, I hope to begin politicizing these genres in ways that are currently absent in discussions of database design and technical communication.

Chapter 6
Angels in Rehab: Rearticulating Hypertext Writing

A structure is defined by what escapes it. Without exception, it emerges from chance, lives with and by a margin of deviation, and ends in disorder. A structure is defined by its *thresholds*—the relative limits within which it selects, perceives, and captures, more or less consistently (its margin of deviation); and the absolute limits beyond which it breaks down (chance, chaos). A structure is a regularized infolding of an aleatory outside. The closest thing there is to order is the approximate, and always temporary, prevention of disorder. The closest thing there is to determinacy is the relative containment of chance. The opposite of chance is not determinacy. It is habit.
—Brian Massumi (1992, pp. 57–58)

Since the world system of late capitalism (or postmodernity) is… inconceivable without the computerized media technology which eclipses its former spaces and faxes an unheard-of simultaneity across its branches, information technology will become virtually the representational solution as well as the representation problem of this world system's cognitive mapping, whose allegories can now always be expected to include a communicational third term.
—Frederic Jameson (1992, p. 10)

We necessarily think about technologies through nostalgia, each system structuring and being structured in matrices of existing and historical interests. Hypertext, as I have argued throughout this book, is no exception. Despite claims of radical novelty for the technology in a wide range of disciplines, the various articulations illustrate the ways we (necessarily) map the technology back against our conventional ways of acting and knowing. But even if we admit that hypertext does not automatically provide a radical rupture in our old ways of thinking and working, we can still learn a great deal from these analysis. It is vital that we think critically about these matters, both about what it was we thought we were getting into and about how we might rearticulate these technologies in better ways. If this new technology does not necessarily radically restructure our practices, how might we take advantage of contingencies? How can we identify chances? What did hypertext mean to us in the first place? The answers involve nostalgia because, although we were thinking about the future of writing, we were calling on a mythical past, one bound up in the related forces of technological development and production, literacy, late capitalism, and more: Critically examining these forces can help us rethink not only our uses of hypertext but these broader forces as well, rewriting their histories in powerful ways.

Nostalgia is a valuable feeling. Nostalgias are ideological—not in the sense of a false consciousness, but of necessarily partial and conflictual representations of social reality. In tracing that longing, we find we want not so much the past itself as what our image of the past projected our future to be. In other words, we recall a constructed history, and then place ourselves in that history imagining our future. Hypertext here is, among other things, a code word for the innocence we sometimes assume marked human existence prior to print, an impossible Eden of pure knowledge and perfect communication unmarked by the "complications" of technology. Tuman (1992c) suggested as much in noting the ways in which radical visions of hypertext articulate the technology as a nostalgic commentary about print (p. 78). We've attempted simultaneously to ascend into our afterlife and think our way backward to Eden prior to the fall. Vannevar Bush thought that hypertext-as-memex would show us Truths by laying out facts in universal, rational patterns; instead, hypertext frequently illustrates the contingency of socially constructed knowledge and habits.

This very disappointment should encourage us to analyze the situation more critically. Nostalgia reminds us that the past is never the way we imagined it was (or would be), that the world was constructed for people walking, or riding in cars, or flying in planes rather than on their own wings. We do not just get wings and take off. We have to articulate those wings to old and new possibilities, taking into account the changes we might need to make in the world itself, considering that the compelling image of being an angel might be useful, but it is also more than likely we are just people with mechanical wings strapped to our backs. It is a metaphor, nothing more (or less).

At the same time, we must also remember that we are changed, that new potentials do exist, and that our use of hypertext in writing classes and elsewhere can be used to help students think about their writing and reading as social and political activities. Where the transition from mortal to angel occurs in some mythic, instantaneous transmigration, the rearticulations of hypertext writing are always partial and incomplete ideological struggles. Mouffe (1979) counseled that:

The objective of ideological struggle is not to reject the system and all its elements but to break it down to its basic elements and then to sift through past conceptions to see which ones, with some changes of content, can serve to express the new situation. Once this is done the chosen elements are finally rearticulated into another system. (p. 192)

This is especially true when we can use the nostalgia to rethink not only isolated technologies but also the contexts in which they are constructed and maintained: the workplace, the library, the market, the classroom (and the insistent but denied intersections among these). The social order itself might be what nostalgia calls into question. We can map these nostalgias back to practices both in and out of the classroom, rearticulating what it means to write and read in hypertext.

We have no choice but to teach in a social and political environment; the question is whether or not we help our students situate their own writings explicitly in the social and the political. "Teachers who ask students to rehearse particular composing rituals in the classroom," wrote Clifford (1991), "impose an ideological agenda, admitted or not" (p. 45). And as Berlin (1988) reminded us, "A rhetoric can never be innocent, can never be a disinterested arbiter of the ideological claims of others because it is always already serving certain ideological claims" (p. 477).

As hypertext writing is articulated along the lines of print structures (as the previous chapters have argued, sociologies of the book, the library, various forms of literary critique and textual production), both writers and readers may be discouraged from questioning their positionings, from admitting the politics of writing and reading, learning and working, discussed in previous chapters. These difficulties are not caused by print per se, but are related in a complex way to the ideological structures of print in late-capitalist cultures.

Teachers who admit that all technologies are nonnecessary, temporary, social and political constructions[1] are not proclaiming anarchy. As Brantlinger (1990) argued, "the apparent assault by deconstruction on all forms of representation can be construed not as an assault at all, but as a dramatic—perhaps melodramatic—assertion of the inescapability of representation" (p. 25). Postmodernism should not be equated with the impossibility of meaning, but with the idea that meaning is a necessary, contingent, and never-universal process. Precisely because people and communities can and do construct meanings, no single person or community can determine a universal meaning.

Cultural approaches such as articulation theory can help teachers begin

---

[1] This includes, in an age of print literacy, thought itself as complicitous with technological structures.

to map the social in ways that avoid simply equating a subject's ideology with social class, a form of structural marxist antihumanism (Grossberg, 1989). As Hall (1985) explained the complexity of social structures:

> Of course a social formation is not complexly structured simply because everything interacts with everything else—that is the traditional, sociological, multifactoral approach which has no determining priorities in it. A social formation is a "structure in dominance." It has certain distinct tendencies; it has a certain configuration; it has a definite structuration. This is why the term "structure" remains important. But, nevertheless, it is a complex structure in which it is impossible to reduce one level of practice to another in some easy way. (p. 91)

Admitting the ideological nature of our teachings should make us become interested in ways in which hypertext can be rearticulated to a more explicitly social activity, a way of providing multiple mappings that do not purport to be mere (innocent) reflections of society, but explicitly political ways to live society and change it. We should still work for change even though we cannot undertake these activities with any guarantees of success; we are never completely in control.

OPPOSITION AND MOVEMENT: FROM OR *TO* AND

> The middle is by no means an average; on the contrary, it is where things pick up speed. *Between* things does not designate a localizable relation going from one thing to another and back again, but a perpendicular direction, a transversal movement that sweeps one *and* the other away, a stream without beginning or end that undermines its banks and picks up speed in the middle.
> —Gilles Deleuze and Félix Guattari (1987, p. 25)

As composition instructors, a large part of our task is helping students learn ways to cope with—to work from within and beyond—binary oppositions. Not only said–unsaid but also author–reader, literacy–orality, technology–nature, self–other, the binaries I argued at the beginning of this book defined the banks between which composition navigates. In Flower's work, for example, early models of writing that privileged the individual writer's thought processes (opposing writer and reader; e.g., Hayes & Flower, 1980) have been replaced with richer, more complex theories where "cognition and context in a sense *construct* one another" (1989, p. 287). The gap between pairs such as these constitutes the greatest power and the most dreadful dilemma for us and our students: In that gap lies intention (Dasenbrock 1988; Derrida, 1977; Searle, 1977), culture (Brantlinger, 1990; Hirsch 1987), and self-representations (Ellsworth, 1989; Swearingen, 1990).

When teachers or students automatically take one term of a pair as naturally and necessarily dominant, they risk significant problems (although, as with many unequal situations, the problems are sometimes submerged and not immediately obvious to participants). Theories of text that cede too much privilege to the writer, for example, deny the active roles taken by readers. At the opposite extreme, approaches that make the reader the determining factor in the meanings constructed from a text may end in denying writers (the problem becomes especially acute when newly valued readers begin writing their own texts). These gaps are the "spaces between" where we create the discourses of ourselves and each other (Guyer, 1992). We have to teach our students (and ourselves) tactics for movements in the range between those oppositions.

For the writer and reader of any hypertext, the gap between a link anchor (*here*) and the corresponding destination (*there*) signifies (but does not guarantee) deterritorialization, chance.[2] Abstractly, the potentials are articulated by the habits of numerous social forces: technical efficiency, late capitalism, models of literate culture, and more. These habits—the construction of dominant articulations—are not completely automatic and absolutely necessary, but they are articulated by such a divergent range of strong social forces that we do not often reflect about the energy we expend reproducing "habit."

We can use hypertext to help our students open structure to change. Naming these forces in the context of the classroom does not remove them, but can aid in the articulation of counterforces. As Giroux (1992a) argued, a border pedagogy relies on a parallel set of operations: "a recognition of those epistemological, political, cultural, and social margins that structure the language of history, power, and difference. The category of the border also prefigures cultural criticism and pedagogical processes as a set of border crossings" (p. 28).

TEACHING AS APPROPRIATING

We are finally in a position to understand how the computerization of society affects this problematic. It could become the "dream" instrument for controlling and regulating the market system, extended to include knowledge itself and governed exclusively by the performativity principle. In that case, it would inevitably involve the use of terror. But it would also aid groups discussing metaprescriptives by supplying them with the information they usually lack for making knowledgeable decisions. The line to follow for computerization to

---

[2] The gap itself is a rehearsal of Derridean *difference*.

take the second of these paths is, in principle, quite simple: give the public free access to the memory and data banks.

—Jean-François Lyotard (1984, p. 67)

Pedagogy is not as a master term able to direct the global nature of hypertextual discourses, but a local activity of specific teachers and students in concrete situations. In this final chapter, I discuss ways of using and teaching hypertext, of working transformatively within current dominant articulations. Changes in these structures are not automatically constructed by any of the tactics I discuss in the following; when people do attempt to resist or rearticulate social structures, their struggles are only sometimes successful (and, at that, always only partial). But pedagogy, especially composition pedagogy, has by now become used to the necessary difficulties of mapping local, lived experience to global theories.

Pedagogy does not work well (if at all) at the level of the universal abstract prescriptions, even though some global theories may attempt to position themselves as simply "commonsense" classroom practices, innocent of political aspects, in order to more completely structure practice.[3] This does not, however, mean that I wish to talk at length about detailed, prescriptive lesson plans and classroom techniques for using hypertext. Rather, I am interested here in providing examples of tactical approaches for writing teachers using hypertext; these tactics must be then rewritten by teachers and students in their own particular situations.

When we teach and use hypertext, we must add strength to the sense of hypertext use as social and political activity: Critique, transgress, and remake the borders normally separating discourses (e.g., functional and literary) from political perspectives. Although all articulatory forces are social and political in the broad sense of the term, I want to work here with forces that encourage people to think explicitly about the social and political aspects of their work.

This thinking begins with the work of the previous chapters, which provide a cultural critique of many common uses of hypertext. Running across all of the articulations discussed previously is the disappearance of the social as a contingent and multiple factor (of literacy technologies as fundamentally and self-reflectively social activities). Functional hypertext, for example, is articulated to print as mechanics, with technical efficiency as the primary goal. Social forces structure these readers as components in

---

[3] Grades, for example, are articulated as a commonsense, pragmatic approach to teaching writing, although (like many practices) they are constructed out of an unspoken worldview that encourages categorization and hierarchy. The conception of writing and reading as primarily skills or information transfer (Hairston, 1992; Hirsch, 1987) is another worldview that denies its theoretical goal of conserving the status quo (Brantlinger, 1990; Freire, 1990).

the machine. What is commonly unspeakable (incapable of being articulated) in the language of functional hypertext (and functional text in general) are the social forces themselves. In other words, this discourse does not ask about what escapes the structure or what is concealed by our nostalgia (which is always the foundation for constructing our futures). Online databases frequently articulate information as a commodity, extending ideas of individualism fostered by print and corresponding ideas of authorship as ownership. And whereas literary hypertexts do sometimes work to construct writing and reading as social acts, they sometimes also do so in a way that either fossilizes social activity or makes it ineffectual. Hypertext is articulated strongly to our assumptions about print, even when these assumptions are critical of print.

Our task at this point is to rearticulate some aspects of current hypertext use to explicitly social and political writing and reading. The following section lays out some of the pedagogical issues and concerns that inform the final, more concrete sections of this chapter, in which I sketch the rough outlines of a pedagogy—by example rather than master plan—for teaching ways of articulating hypertext as a more explicitly social and political technology.

But before I turn to classroom practices, I need to map out more clearly the conceptions of writing pedagogy informing my approach. As should be obvious by this point, I consider teaching of any type to be a social and political activity, whether or not teachers admit their own ideological stances. Pedagogy should engage students in activities that help them work within existing systems for positive social political change. However this vision should not be equated too quickly with a millenialist call for the end of Western culture in a revolt by the proletariat against some ominous state. We no longer live in an age of simple class politics. As Laclau and Mouffe (1985) argued, in modern times there is no longer the simple opposition of people to *ancien régime* that automatically gives people a necessary class belongingness; today, "there is no politics without hegemony" (p. 151), no single discourse (e.g., property ownership) around which each opposed group can unify its opposition to the other. Although certainly there is still a strong sense of class—management, owner, worker—the boundaries between the classes are often blurred or in movement, with single persons being hailed by multiple, competing discourses. If our culture shares any common tendency, it is one of the fragmentation of postmodernity blended with a strong belief in free, individual will. As Marcuse pointed out, the bulk of repressed citizens no longer want to challenge the system in reformist ways, but to increase their access to the upper levels of the system.

Much of the rhetoric of hypertext recounted in previous chapters is validated by the same aspects of individualism on which capitalism[4] relies—free will, increasingly complex technical systems, computerization, fragmentation, and the circulation of meaning as a commodity. Claims about individual freedom in hypertext have been a consistent theme in the history of the technology, from the early work of Bush and Nelson through the current work of Bolter and Landow. In many ways, these claims are valid as long as we define terms such as *freedom* or *individual needs* in the context of late capitalist culture, where one of the strongest tendential forces is the free-market economy.

If we simply construct and use hypertext in the classroom as an environment that appears to allow writer and readers complete freedom to wander the texts according to individual wishes, we are merely mystifying the nature of writing and reading text in general. For that matter, Lyotard's (1984) cry for complete access is itself necessarily utopian, because people will always rely on technological manners for filtering information (from card catalogs to intelligent agents), a situation that in itself complicates notions of "free access." It does no good at this point to argue about whether we created this system or this system created us; the relationship is complex and multiply determined. But in helping our students critically investigate the mutual constructions of subjectivity and social systems, we can help them identify the gaps and positionings, to reconstruct their identities and the system in empowering ways. We must provide projects that enable students to work toward some tangible goal cognitively mapped to large social arenas, to both expose the ways in which they are articulated by the ideologies of books, technological society, late capitalism, and so forth, as well as provide them with ways in which they may speak for changes in that ideology.

Subversion of dominant terms is possible because articulations are always already multiple and conflicting; they are negotiations of power relationships in language. Articulations exist more as practice than thing, as a dynamic movement occurring in the construction and deconstruction of tangled weaves of influence and power, with dominant social forces having greater strength and more ability to orchestrate social movements than subordinate ones (Grossberg & Slack, 1985; Hall, 1985; Slack, 1989). Dominant strands in the weave do not all pull uniformly in a single direc-

---

[4] Paradoxically, this situation holds for postmodern capitalism as well, which relies on the willingness of workers to construct semistable subject positions within fluctuating contexts and job positions. Even when a worker's organizational position shifts rapidly and unpredictably, successful workers are those that are able to maintain the illusion of free will by ignoring aspects out of their control (hiring and firing, transnational economics, marketing strategies, etc.) and concentrating on aspects that appear to be within their control (navigating to a discrete, correct answer in an online help system).

tion (although these forces often work to make their operation appear so unified as to seem natural and uncontestable). The weave holds together by tension—web rather than chain—some of which is between threads normally considered as operating in parallel but that actually oppose and contradict each other in many ways.[5] Weaker forces or threads of some sort are always present even if frequently ignored, pulling ineffectually against the stronger strands. By strengthening the weaker strands—strengths that potentially may come from one of the strands that also contributes to the dominant force—a resistant force may be woven through what Fiske (1989) termed "the guerrilla tactics of the subordinate" in the midst of "[t]he text's struggle to control its readings... met by the oppositional struggle of its readers to make their socially pertinent readings out of its resources" (pp. 171, 170). Everyday life in this view is understood as a continual process of inhabitation and appropriation, "a culture of concrete practices which embody and perform differences" (Fiske, 1992, p. 162). This performance—living in and as resistance—is how articulation theory attempts to explain and inform pedagogy and political action in general:

> The aim of a theoretically-informed political practice must surely be to bring about or construct the articulation between social and economic forces and those forms of politics and ideology which might lead them in practice to intervene in history in a progressive way—an articulation which has to be *constructed* through practice precisely because it is not guaranteed by how those forces are constituted in the first place. (Hall, 1985, p. 95)

Specific articulations are never guaranteed; these structures are contingent on numerous dynamic and unequal, contradictory forces, a situation that leaves openings for reform-minded teachers, theorists, and students. Our efforts to reform ideas about hypertext as we teach is potentially authorized by the complex and mutable nature of the medium itself. Even as they are constructed by dominant forces, new technologies frequently contain breaks in containment, overflows of control mechanisms that allow weaker forces the potential for rearticulating the technology to their own goals. As Marvin (1988) argued in her history of early electronic media:

> New media, broadly understood to include the new use of new communications technology for old or new purposes, new ways of using old technologies,

---

[5] Articulating forces are themselves being articulated by other forces: The force of efficiency articulating hypertext is only one possible formation of efficiency. There are also other ways to articulate efficiency. For example, Marcuse's project of restructuring technological use so that human needs in general are met would require rearticulating efficiency to include concepts of equitable treatment for all humans (something that is currently external to the definition, which would place that issue in ethics or politics).

and, in principle, all other possibilities for the exchange of social meaning, are always introduced into a pattern of tension created by the coexistence of old and new, which is far richer than any single medium that becomes the focus of interest because it is novel. *New media embody the possibility that accustomed orders are in jeopardy*, since communication is a peculiar kind of interaction that actively seeks variety. No matter how firmly a custom or instrumentality may appear to organize and contain it, it carries the seeds of its own subversion. (p. 8, italics added)

Marvin noted, for example, the tendencies (and resulting struggles and conflicts) for the telephone to erase social dividing lines and etiquette: A ringing telephone does not announce whether the caller is an equal, a superior, or a subordinate. The telephone became both the site where "Lower classes could crash barriers" (p. 86) and the focus of struggle to prohibit subordinates access to the technology. Eventually, however, the flux of possibilities begins to settle (although never becoming completely fixed). Social technologies become articulated along (relatively) conservative lines. Despite such border-crossing facilities, new technologies are most easily integrated into existing technological relations, conservation rather than disruption. Disruptions are drawbacks, side effects to be dealt with and downplayed. Today, answering machines screen our lines for wanted calls; voice-mail systems route and then store messages; caller ID announces, like a butler, each guest and offers the host the opportunity to decline admission. The early marketing of the telephone was articulated as a replacement for the telegraph—an early patent dispute between Bell and Western Union resulted in payments to Western Union by Bell for loss of business (Fischer, 1991).[6] Furthermore, although Marvin noted the many struggles that were staged over access to telephones, social forces have allowed the telephone to remain accessible to most classes of society while effectively prohibiting its widespread use as a subversive technology: The telephone continues to be used in a basically hierarchical and patriarchal manner in many areas, particularly in the corporate setting (just as in Pratt's accounts of autoethnographic writing, resistance is frequently unsuccessful at broad or even local social change). Corporate conceptions of appropriate uses for communication technology continue to provide a dominant force. Such hegemonic forces are also present in the situated uses of hypertext. Over the last 2 years, the World Wide Web has become increasingly disarticulated from discussion and rearticulated toward commerce. We would do well to ask ourselves why the phone—which shares many of the same potentials we call democratizing and egalitarian in global com-

---

[6] "Inefficient" uses of the telephone—"gossip"—only began to be advertised in the 1920s and 1930s. Fischer (1991) noted that social users were predominantly advertised as female.

puter networks—entered most areas of society in a conservative rather than revolutionary way. Consider the freedom offered by a functional hypertext, which may offer thousands of paths through a text space. Typically, however, the user's social situation prelimits the number of "correct" paths to one.

We need to also keep in mind the movement of hypertext writers and readers across and among different contexts. Because business is currently the largest sector of the software market and the area to which developers pay the most attention, composition teachers and theorists must learn how to deal tactically with corporate-oriented systems. That is, we need to avoid either merely accommodating or merely ignoring such concerns. In addition, corporations increasingly determine the goals to which compositionists teach, with the idea of "well-rounded education" being replaced with the phrase "marketable skills" (see, e.g., critiques in Berlin, 1988; Killingsworth, 1993; Ohmann, 1990).[7] Drucker (1988) reflected current corporate philosophies when, writing in the *Harvard Business Review*, he asserted that the decline of family and community places the corporate world in the position of determining moral structures. We might be comforted by this call for action if Drucker were asking management to think critically and broadly about business ethics. But Drucker meant something much more conservative and limited, as indicated by his discussion, later in the same article, about how useful it is to hire out work to freelance and contract workers, who frequently have little job security, savings, benefits, or retirement plans (Johnson-Eilola, 1993b).

As composition instructors, we can help students and designers articulate uses that foreground the constructive and intersubjective nature of reading and writing, even in terms of functional documents. Our work in writing classes, because it informs at least partially and potentially the writing and reading practices of so many students, may also act as a catalyst for change as these students become users, managers, and designers of hardware and software. In order to do this, we must learn (and teach) ways of questioning technology and transforming it as we use it. As Haraway (1985) argued, the cyborg is a "bastard offspring" of the oppressive systems of the military–industrial complex—Haraway's naming of the cyborg's heritage provides a powerful encouragement to act in our own interests (as bastards are notorious for doing) rather than automatically serving patriarchical needs in the way of most machines. When we think of hypertext as an angelic technology, perhaps we might instead think about occupying the position

---

[7] This is not to call for a return to the relatively conservative idea of an upperclass, liberal education (which, historically, was restricted to the upper classes). One force articulating the calls by industry for "marketable skills" in college is the shift occurring in the populations of higher education, which are no longer largely the realm of the elite.

of cyborg—able to inhabit and appropriate, even if only partially and rarely, the technologies of literacy. The machinery can be taken up critically and worked subversively from within, critically rather than automatically. This does not require us to deny our humanity, but it does call on us to appropriate the technologies, which in many ways construct possible ranges of response. Resistance and appropriation are not necessarily acts of doing away with the technological system. We must teach students to appropriate the technology, to construct more active and critical roles as users.

In his discussion of the ways in which readers can act from subordinate positions and occupy a text, de Certeau (1984) reminded us that even print reading can be disarticulated from passive activity and rearticulated as transformation:

> [T]he activity of reading has... all the characteristics of a silent production: the drift across the page, the metamorphosis of the text effected by the wandering eyes of the reader, the improvisation and expectation of meanings inferred from a few words, leaps over written spaces in an ephemeral dance.... He insinuates into another person's text the ruses of pleasure and appropriation: he poaches on it, is transported into it, pluralizes himself in it.... (p. xxi)

De Certeau emphasized the transformative and constructive nature of language use for both writer and reader; de Certeau's "spatial stories" parallel the maps that construct reality in process: "sayings and stories... organize places through the displacements they 'describe' (as a mobile point describes a curve)" (p. 116); "What the map cuts up, the story cuts across" (p. 129). Operating not from above (the angelic promontory), but inside of and across spaces (the place and movements of the cyborg), de Certeau's readers are Deleuze and Guattari's (1987) war machines: The book is not necessarily the little machine that automates reading, but possibly the machinic assemblage(s) in a process of contagion and connection instead of reproduction of a finite meaning. In this articulation, navigation does not lead to a timeless, geometric, totalizing hypertext, but a walked-through environment, more of a "tour" than a "map" (de Certeau, 1984, pp. 118–122).

So even if hypertext does not offer the angelic powers we sometimes think it might, it does hold at least the potential for some rearticulations, for increasing access to information for both our students and ourselves, for rethinking boundaries between discourses. The difficulty of thinking of reading as productive is that we often forget that in our culture, the writer is still by and large much more esteemed. We are only marking points of possible revolutionary action when we identify similarities between writing and reading; to collapse the two actions too readily is naive, akin to thinking that removing gender-specific language from a corporate memo removes sexism from the corporation. Both are useful starting points, but they are only starting points. As teachers we need to rethink not only our day-to-day practices, but the goals of these practices. As discussed in Chapter 1, in many ways these large information spaces approach (if not achieve) the perfect information games discussed by Lyotard (1984) in *The Postmodern Condition*. In this situation, Lyotard argued, university education must begin moving away from the acquisition and transmission of knowledge (which theoretically enabled students to become professionals capable of producing new knowledge) and toward helping students develop skills, primarily related to using computer-based systems. Critiquing traditional education for its goal of transmitting a body of knowledge to the student, Lyotard argued that "a professor is no more competent than memory bank networks in transmitting established knowledge, no more competent than interdisciplinary teams in imagining new moves or new games" (p. 53). In the age of perfect information, it is not the production of "new" information or knowledge that is valued, but the ability to make connections, to restructure information in new ways.[8] Certainly, we would like to imagine that a person can teach more effectively than a "memory bank network," but Lyotard's analysis also holds useful aspects. In fact, his critiques of education align with the critical pedagogy work of Freire and followers, who attempted to help students do more than accept the transmitted wisdom of the teacher.

One difficulty with Lyotard's conception of thinking and writing in the postmodern age, however, lies in the cybernetic system he envisioned orchestrating social activity. This conception relegates resistance to isolated and ineffectual pockets, something the system allows to let off steam or, according to Lyotard, combat entropy. Teachers are encouraged by the system to provide "performance-oriented skill" that will benefit the efficiency of the social system as a whole; "What no longer makes the grade is competence as defined by other criteria true/false, just/unjust, etc." ([sic], p. 51).

Although composition teachers may agree with Lyotard's analysis of traditional university education—many of us have daily reminders of the increased prestige and compensation given to disciplines that are able to clearly (quantitatively) show the ways in which they contribute to the performativity of the system—we are also searching for ways of subverting this order. Transgressive approaches (Hall's articulation, Giroux's border crossings, Pratt's linguistic contact zones) become especially appropriate when we begin examining the ways in which specific hypertext systems can be defined, as Massumi would have it, by what escapes them. In nearly every case discussed in the previous chapters, hypertext is commonly articulated

---

[8] The importance of this technological know-how is supported by research conducted by Forman (1990) and colleagues on computer-supported writing teams, which found that the technology experts often assumed leadership roles in the group.

lacking explicit mechanisms for mapping local, individual actions in the text against larger scale social movements. The little machines articulation, for example, isolates users from key aspects of social context(s) so that they can assume a position in the controlled contexts of machinery. Even articulations that, for the most part, are concerned with overthrowing conventional literary structures may instead act to isolate students from their peers: KARL'S FORKING RESPONSE positions a single, individual student against the cultural inertia of teacher, author, and literary system.

Helping students learn to position themselves in fragmented, confusing social spheres while also assisting them in efforts to work both within and (when needed) against that system requires us to teach in new ways. There are always contested, social and political dimensions to any technology, even if those forces are subordinated. Disarticulation and rearticulation are always possible.

The political aspects of hypertext design and use must be strengthened, because politics connect the local and global levels of technology use. Enacting only local tactics runs the risk of positioning hypertext users only as consumers. And even if the first generation of writers and readers may take some power from their appropriation of authorship, that role may soon become empty habit if not articulated to positive hegemonic projects. As Hebdige (1979) noted of the punk movement's appropriation of master codes:

> This is not to say, of course, that all punks were equally aware of the disjunction between experience and signification upon which the whole style was ultimately based. The style no doubt made sense for the first wave of self-conscious innovators at a level which remained inaccessible to those who became punks after the subculture had surfaced and been publicized. (p. 122)

Proclaiming in class or in the pages of an academic journal that hypertext gives "readers" the cultural power of "authors" sounds all well and good, as I mentioned earlier, but does it really erase the distinction between two roles that have been so long separated?

Still, hypertext can offer teachers a tactical approach to teaching political, social issues. We need to create a sense of broader, social and political forces to keep acts of resistance from degenerating into empty gestures. Nostalgia, operating in one form or another across all of the articulations discussed in the previous chapters, can be used to open up discourses to political interrogation, provided that we critically examine the nostalgia rather than letting it simply structure our uses and expectations. Otherwise, existing social forces articulate technologies and uses, making them appear natural and neutral, unavoidable.

REARTICULATING POSTMODERN SPACE:
SOCIAL AND POLITICAL FORCES

[U]nless we adopt the computer network as a part of a larger focus and effort to create safe discourse space, we are not doing anything new for our marginalized students. The adoption of the network must be part of a larger effort to assist these students.... The computer will not magically alter the relationships of gender, power, class, and race that so strongly and pervasively underlie classroom practice.

—Pamela Takayoshi (1994, p. 33)

The two primary examples from Chapter 5—THE IN MEMORIAM WEB and FORKING PATHS—offer useful starting points for a discussion about politicizing and socializing hypertext because much that has been written about these texts already invokes such projects. But the apparent obviousness of these texts is itself a structure that must be critically examined. Both the material construction of the hypertexts and the social context in which these texts are found tend to undercut the postmodern intentions of the teachers. THE IN MEMORIAM WEB, for example, by its choice of primary text may tend to construct students as commentators on the work of one of the great masters (replacing Great Books with Great Programs—something Lanham explicitly suggested as a positive outcome for hypertext). Because this type of writing is so common (especially in students' perceptions of literature and literary criticism), students are not encouraged by culture to resist this articulation of the genre. The agenda for classroom activity is undoubtedly clear to students (even despite their teachers' assertions of different goals).

The literary response genre inherent in FORKING PATHS, radical as it is, is similarly incapable of helping students rearticulate their relationships to literature, although for different reasons. Moulthrop so fragmented Borges' text that it cannot be approached as traditional literature, even though Crary attempted to do so. Because the text is ever-shifting and indeterminate, the application of traditional literary critique (the geometrical grid) is devoured by the text; there is no "author" or even concrete "work" to attack. But even as the text seems to attempt its own undoing, the cultural structure in which the text and reader are positioned encourages Crary to attempt a traditional literary critique—he attempted, as the previous chapter puts it, to construct a geometrical grid on an undifferentiated geography that will not support such as construction. Just like the classic text, this postmodern one succeeds when it absorbs its reader.

In both cases, students are positioned as respondents or commentators to the father-text. At one extreme, students are overcome by the weight of history partially constructing literary work in our culture; at the other extreme, students are overcome by the lack of history in the text. We still need a middle ground, where we and our students can appropriate various forces to construct a postmodern social and political articulation.

We need to help students learn to construct and appropriate their own ways of mapping local against global, and ways to cope with—and even draw tactical possibilities from—the necessary incompleteness of these maps. We can begin by articulating hypertext as a technology that should be seen as both local and global (personal and political) by adding force to (and revising) theories and pedagogies of collaboration, something that is already a popular topic in both composition and hypertext theory and practice. As McCabe (1992) pointed out in his preface to Jameson's *The Geopolitical Aesthetic*:

> [C]ognitive mapping is a way of understanding how the individual's representation of his or her social world can escape the traditional critique of representation because the mapping is intimately related to practice—to the individual's successful negotiation of urban space. Cognitive mapping in this sense is the metaphor for the processes of the political unconscious. It is also, however, the model for how we might begin to articulate the local and the global. It provides a way of linking the most intimately local—our particular path through the world—and the most global—the crucial features of our political planet. (p. xiv)

Such maps require a careful negotiation and articulation of social spheres, one area in which numerous hypertext researches have shown great interest. Hypertext is often considered an eminently collaborative medium in both its earliest articulations (Bush, 1945/1987; Nelson 1974/1987a) and its contemporary uses (Conklin & Begeman, 1987 Landow, 1992c; Slatin, 1988), a characterization that we might attempt to articulate into *post*-postmodernism in hypertext, constructing a social space for the appropriation, deconstruction, and reconstruction of other (overlapping) social spaces. At the same time, we have to recognize that hypertext is about much more than simply allowing anyone to add to the text; such articulations may end in doing little more than absorbing attempts a reform (local or global). Collaboration should not be seen as a way of gaining pleasant and tranquil agreement among group members. Collaborative theory has recently questioned its earlier characterization of collaboration as a search for consensus. As George (1989) pointed out, for example, even in cases where students are writing to other students (and not to authoritative texts or to only the instructor), there exist unequal distributions of power: Some students are more fully in possession of the discourses that are traditionally valued in academia; some have larger repertoires for asserting control over others (p. 6; Williams, 1983, pp. 75–76).

Collaboration, in fact, can become more valuable from these differences

First, the benefits of collaboration exist precisely because group members make different contributions to topics. A revised notion of consensus, Trimbur (1989) argued, "would provide students with a critical measure to identify the relations of power in the formation of expert judgment" (p. 613), a process that would "open gaps in the conversation through which differences may emerge" (p. 614). Second, groups can temporarily and partially coalesce around single important issues when needed, articulating a contingent but collective force from many smaller groups. Such groups are composed of members who disagree, sometimes vehemently, on other important issues but are able to combine forces on key issues when necessary. We must take care that students are able to construct—and understand the process of the construction of—their own identities, even if they are multiple and conflicting and the constructions are never completely within their control. As Laclau and Mouffe (1985) wrote:

> Between the logic of complete identity and that of pure difference, the experience of democracy should consist of the recognition of the multiplicity of social logics along with the necessity of their articulation. But this articulation should be constantly re-created and renegotiated, and there is no final point at which a balance will be definitely achieved. (p. 188)

A strong impediment to such a reconception of identity and difference (which continue to appear as polar opposites) is the parallel pair self and other. The hailing of subjects into ideological positions is always an incomplete and multiple way of terming what appear to us as single, physical individuals. The bodied self speaking in the discourse of college student is also apparently the same bodied self speaking as left radical, the same speaking as upper middle-class White male. The subjects are multiple and seemingly conflictual, but the single physical self denies this.

It is, in at least some part, this sense of physical presence that opposes students to author in texts such as THE IN MEMORIAM WEB and even KARL'S FORKING RESPONSE. The students, writing individually, are bound by a number of forces into a structure of greatly unequal power. The signifier of an individual name provides the stand-in for forces such as authorship and ownership, relegating the student names to commentary and observation. Instead of students working together or assuming multiple pseudonyms, they each write parasitically on the text of Tennyson's *In Memoriam*. If a project such as THE IN MEMORIAM WEB or KARL'S FORKING RESPONSE had instead been organized as a collaborative work constructed around a social or political goal, students could use the space of the text(s) to examine, deconstruct, and reconstruct relationships of authority and power.

The potential depersonalization of electronic textual communication, coupled with the multilinear structure of hypertext, might be used to help downplay the physical presence of writers and readers. In many hypertext programs, the electronic media work to depersonalize individual contributions to the text—fonts on screen are often the default fonts (or chosen from a small subset), the framing of the text is often consistent for all students, and so on. This is useful in the way anonymity may encourage participation by students who may not talk in class because they are wary of being prejudged by the markers of race, gender, age, or ethnicity (Cooper & Selfe, 1990; George, 1990; Hawisher, 1992; Thompson, 1988). The multilinearity of a hypertext discussion, unlike a linear online conference, can also provide a space that multiplies interpretations and positions rather than orders them in a single line or orchestrates them as a hierarchy of education and privilege.[9]

One recent approach to hypertext illustrates some of the potential for this articulation: the use of a synchronous conferencing program followed by the construction of hypertext webs based on that conference. In other words, conversants take the linear text of the online conference transcript and rewrite it as a hypertext. In the example discussed here, users engaged in a real-time discussion using DAEDALUS INTERCHANGE (1992), then reworked the text in STORYSPACE (1991). Participants begin with a linear online discussion of a topic. The text of this discussion, saved in a linear computer file, is then imported by the participants into a hypertext program such as STORYSPACE. Participants break the long, linear file into small segments of text (often one conversational contribution per node). The resulting collection of disjointed texts can be mapped in a variety of manners (multiple articulations of the same text) with connections or trails linking nodes chronologically (as in the linear text), by name of writer, by topic, by keyword, by argument, and so on. As the interconnected text develops, these threads cross and connect single, "isolated" entries into multiple, often contradictory, ways of conceiving the conversation and the identities of writers.

Online conferencing mixes characteristics of both literate and oral qualities of discourse: semipermanence but informality, rapid shifts between fragmented sentences and complex grammatical constructions common to

---

[9] It is certainly possible for a linear text to explicitly assert multiple truths, but the conventions of print and the line continue to implicitly assert their own hierarchy on contributions: who provides the initial contributions, who has the "last word," and so on. In some articulations of hypertext, these devices are still present but to a lesser degree than in linear online text. (Conversely, of course, it is possible for some articulations—such as the little machine—to be even more efficient at constructing hierarchies than print.)

print; public soliloquies and person-to-person exchanges. As such, the hypertextual discussion preexists with a weaker sense of the ideological carryover of print as fixed, unified, and final. Because the "text" is still literate, it retains some of its qualities as a textual object, but it also exists as a process more strongly than a print text is able to do. In addition, the conversation is clearly multivocal. Rather than being a seemingly isolated object in which other voices can be discovered with much work and the proper academic credentials, this conversation begins with a basic sense of intertextuality and (as illustrated later), quickly makes that even more complex. Perhaps most importantly, the combination of the social reality of the initial conversation and visible, graphical nature of the network can be used to illustrate the beginnings of a cognitive mapping (it is necessary here to continually point out that this map does not exhaust the reality of the conversation historically or in the future): The participants move both in the geography and over the geometry of the discourse(s) while they learn, as Bakhtin (1981) urged, to "deal with the life and behavior of discourse in a contradicting and multi-layered world" (p. 275).

An early example of this approach can be seen in a text generated by participants at the 1992 Computers and Writing Conference. A set of two linked sessions, moderated by Michael Joyce, Nancy Kaplan, Stuart Moulthrop, Jay Bolter, and Martha Petry, began with a linear online conference among 20 conference attendees.[10] Participants began discussion with the opening entry:

> Minutes into his first encounter with a real-time co-authoring tool, Jay Bolter was heard to exclaim, "THIS IS NOT WRITING!" We'd like to begin with this negative eureka-phenomenon, or discovery of absence. If you agree that what you are doing now is in some sense not-writing, then what do you think you're doing? Or do you think "writing" still goes on in real-time interchanges like this one, in hypertext writing systems, in multimedia environments...?

The linear discussion that followed—a nearly 6,000-word text that I quote at length later—was imported into STORYSPACE during the second session, broken into smaller nodes (Figure 6.1), and reconnected and reorganized through suggestions given by participants, including connections based on temporal (linear) order, participant names, and keywords (Figure 6.2).

Consider, for example, a single entry by participant Mark Lester, writ-

---

[10] In the text excerpted here, I have retained the original spelling and grammar. The frequent mistakes in typing, sentence fragments, and other characteristics not typically considered "proper English" are characteristic of informal online text, which retains qualities of both everyday oral speech and more formal text.

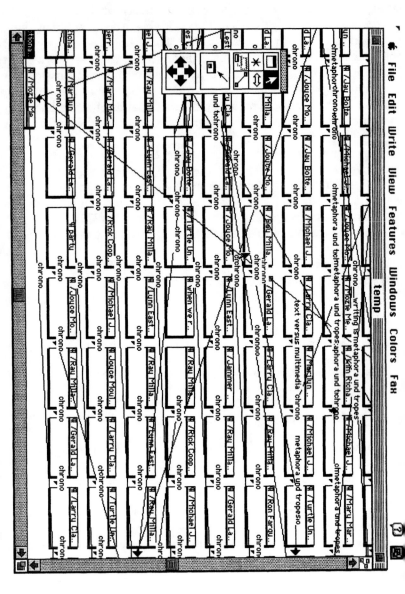

FIGURE 6.1. Screen from REAL-TIME HYPERTEXT (hierarchy flattened and most links removed).

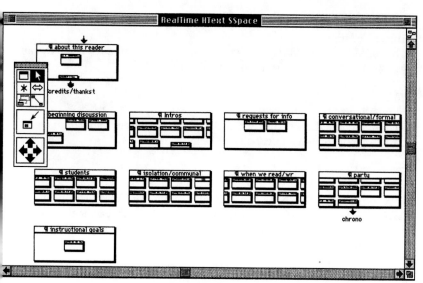

FIGURE 6.2. REAL-TIME HYPERTEXT after hierarchial structuring.

ten approximately halfway through the discussion. Lester's entry is interesting for a number of reasons: It is his first entry since the opening biographies provided by many of the participants; it is his only entry in the main body of the discourse. But Lester's entry belies that isolated nature by being both one of the longest entries in the discourse and heavily connected to other entries (both conceptually, in the linear text, and visibly, in the resulting hypertext). In order to construct the traditional linear argument (which appears to represent the "real" structure in that the conversation took place over time in a visually linear fashion), I provide here an extended chronological transcript, similar to what participants would see scrolling onto their screen during the conference.

72
Marilyn Nowell:
Larry: My basic writers love to talk in writing, fragments and all. If we can understand each other without gestures, tones, and body language in fragments and fragmented texts, why OR when shall we address unity of thought?

73
Michael Joyce:
Jay, I agree that there is no center of gravity, but there are increasingly heavy particles (or what Nancy K calls object-events) which become centers of constellated discourses, much like hypertext, no?

74
Turtle Under:
The veiled identity adds another creative dimension to writing. Not only can you work with ideas but you can explore voice.

75
Ray Milland:
The frightening thing is that SOMEBODY has to address "unity of thought" for this production in a fraction of an hour...

76
Lynn Easterling:
Joyce—no, absolutely NOT (stability and continuity)! Yes, I am in a very TRADITIONAL rhetoric program, but I am also the only candidate to work in the field of computer composition, specifically hypertext in the compostion classroom.

77
Joyce Moulkaplan:
Jay—That's right. No domination. Domination means CENTERs and MARGINs. Some of the point is to stop thinking in such terms. I do want discourse to change, to be more inclusive and less like a perpetual game of "king on the mountain." We've had centuries of that.

78
Mark Lester:
I have a lot of trouble seeing the value of hypertext. I seldom break my concentration when I am reading something I am interested in to look at the bottom of a page to read a footnote, let alone go to the end of a chapter for an endnote. I think good writing should be sufficiently audience sensitive to not require footnoting. Hypertext strikes me as a super-intrusive form of footnoting. If the reader needs to have some small special piece of information it should be incorporated into the text or at worst treated as an aside (like this).

A text is the author's best shot at communication. Breaking away from that communication to chase down a "hot" word (when I have no way of knowing what kind of information is hidden behind the "hot" word) is terribly intrusive on my comprehension of the text. To me, it is like trying to listen to a piece of music that is continually interrupted to give me information that I may or may not want to know. I suppose that one could argue that the reader can ignore a "hot" word, but by the same token one can argue that you can ignore a ringing phone—you can, but it is still intrusive.

79
Larry Clark:
Turtle Under,

Writing is not an isolated action. One of the benefits I see to this type of communication is that students can see IMMEDIATELY if their rhetorical strategies are effective by the types of replies (or lack of them) that they get back. In a way, it's a subtle form of collaborative writing.

80
Gerald Lacy:
Larry, I think what we are doing is basic to language/symbol; music and art, I think (?), work on another base??

81
Joyce Moulkaplan:
Ray—Unity? YOu want unity in less than an hour? I think that will take a bit longer. But fortunately, it's not unity but patterns that we're after (I think).

82
Lynn Easterling:
Is anyone working on an application with "Toolbook" by Asymetrix? I would like to know about your work with this package.

83
Jammer G:
Kim: I'm too literal. Someone said type a "handle" and so I did —always the good student. My real name is Jan Geesaman and I'm in the navy blue polka dot suit. I'm interested in your response to the interruptions between our conversation. If I were speaking to you, I would have already tried to say how I am responding to the interruption. Because I am typing this, seeing my words on the screen, I'm hesitating more. I'm finding it takes some time to get used to this mode of conversation/writing.

84
Ray Milland:
Mark Lester's right—this kind of "writing" is like a CONSTANTLY ringing telephone which you can't really ignore. If by "writing" you mean something clear, distinct, hard, and nugget-like, then Jay's apocryphal remark says it all—this is not writing.

85
Gerald Lacy:
We are realize, we are following several texts at once, and in effect, one text

86
Michael Joyce:
Mark, and if the music itself is intended (as serial composition, for instance) to constantly break you away from your individuated sense of an interpretive self?

The linear string of entries here shows one conventional organization, the chronological ordering of entries as they were made during the course of the discussion. During the remapping of the text in STORYSPACE, other organizations were constructed, overlapping paths laid out and hierarchies constructed in the text. The criss-crossing of these paths occurs at the nodes, places we might also help our students see as border zones:

> [B]order pedagogy points to the importance of offering students the opportunity to engage the multiple references and codes that position them within various structures of meaning and practice. In part, this means educating students to become media literate in a world of changing representations. It also means teaching them to read critically not only how cultural texts are regulated by various discursive codes but also how such texts express and represent different ideological interests and how they might be taken up differently by students. (Giroux, 1992b, p. 210)

Mark Lester's entry, for example, exists as and constructs a complex border zone. The particular discourses meeting here are alluded to by the thematic paths and codes in Figure 6.3 (showing paths in and out of entry 78) and Figure 6.4 (showing keywords tagging Entry 78 in order to map it at the confluence of other threads). The organization given by these other threads reveals different ways of writing Mark's discursive position. For example, the thread entitled "metaphor" maps the discourse with a differ-

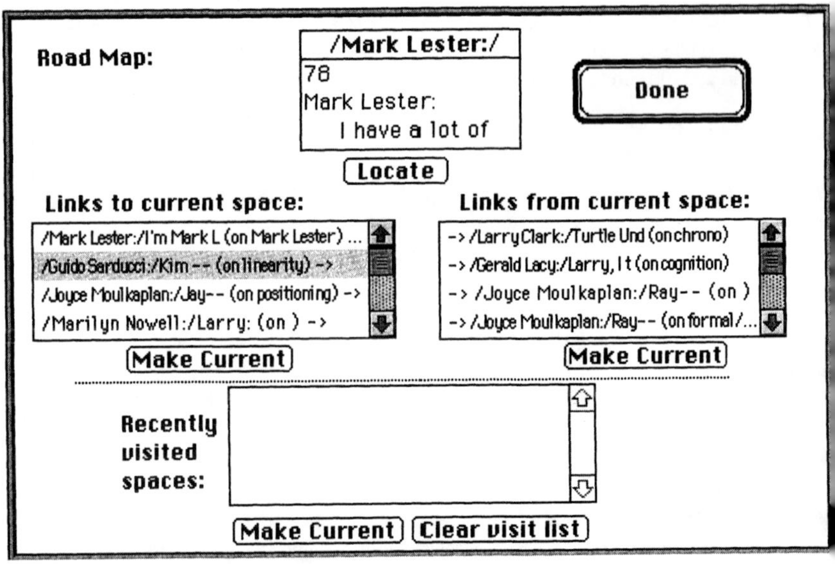

FIGURE 6.3. Links running in and out of Entry 78.

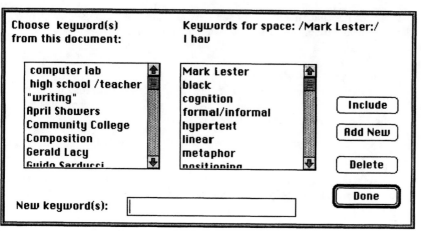

FIGURE 6.4. Partial list of keywords for full document and Entry 78.

ent structure,[11] one overlapping, contradicting, and reinforcing not only the chronological thread but other threads as well.

47
Mozie Med:
Do the words flow easier because the writer knows how to push the ideas from the brain to the keyboard? It IS writing, surely—and exchanging ideas is fun!

49
Michael Joyce:
Marilyn, does it remain free-form wandering if I respond to you. Aren't you seeking in that characterization to shape the discussion and the eventual "document" here

52
Guido Sarducci:
Kim—What if what we're doing is still "linear" in a sense—Jay's remark about aphorism and contextualization—but linear in the context of multiple lines, webs, complex geometries?

60
Jay Bolter:

---

[11] The other paths constructed are frequently temporally as well as topically ordered because STORYSPACE's default ordering uses a first-to-last mechanism. It is possible to restructure this ordering, although it was not done (perhaps because no one at the sessions noticed the structuring in the midst of the other ways of mapping).

It strikes me that this is a very self-conscious form of writing—rather like salon conversation, with everyone search for a bon mot.

73
Michael Joyce:
Jay, I agree that there is no center of gravity, but there are increasingly heavy particles (or what Nancy K calls object-events) which become centers of con-stellated discourses, much like hypertext, no?

74
Turtle Under:
The veiled identity adds another creative dimension to writing. Not only can you work with ideas but you can explore voice.

78
Mark Lester:
I have a lot of trouble seeing the value of hypertext. I seldom break my concentration when I am reading something I am interested in to look at the bottom of a page to read a footnote, let alone go to the end of a chapter for an endnote. I think good writing should be sufficiently audience sensitive to not require footnoting. Hypertext strikes me as a super-intrusive form of footnoting. If the reader needs to have some small special piece of information it should be incorporated into the text or at worst treated as an aside (like this).

A text is the author's best shot at communication. Breaking away from that communication to chase down a "hot" word (when I have no way of knowing what kind of information is hidden behind the "hot" word) is terribly intrusive on my comprehension of the text. To me, it is like trying to listen to a piece of music that is continually interrupted to give me information that I may or may not want to know. I suppose that one could argue that the reader can ignore a "hot" word, but by the same token one can argue that you can ignore a ringing phone—you can, but it is still intrusive.

80
Gerald Lacy:
Larry, I think what we are doing is basic to language/symbol; music and art, I think (?), work on another base??

Despite his expressed objections, Lester's "text" no longer constitutes "the author's best shot at communication" because this particular articulation in hypertext is not a single shot at a target (the Shannon & Weaver [1949] model discussed in Chapter 2), but a continual, multiple, conflictual, inde terminate process of social negotiation. What is structured in the temporal strand as a commentary on Joyce's (Entry 73) description of the Interchange session as a text without a single "center of gravity" (but, like hypertext, having several "heavy particles") becomes, in the metaphorical articulation of the border zone, a laundry list of metaphorical allusions: "best shot," "'hot' word," "ringing phone." Entry 78 brims with discursive excess: Like Crary, Lester argues against hypertext ("a super-intrusive form of footnoting") from within hypertext. As Douglas (1994) observed, even while we continue to read hypertexts with expectations of closure, we can come to understand that a single reading can "explain the versions of text I have experienced without exhausting the number of other versions and explanations I might experience on other readings" (p. 185).

But unlike Crary's attempt at resistance, Lester's argument is anchored (in a very loose sense[12]) by the linear flow of the INTERCHANGE discussion, which itself refers to (among other things) a material reality more clearly than many other types of texts. Where Crary undoubtedly wrote in the social context of a class of students who all talked to each other and perhaps critiqued drafts, the material text of Crary's response situates him in a traditional literary model: lone critic against canonized master. Furthermore, despite frequent assertions that hypertext disempowers the author, Crary here as student is clearly—even in his "own" text, KARL'S FORKING RESPONSE—much lower in the social hierarchy than Borges or Moulthrop, let alone the combined force of the two. Lester and the other participants, in addition, are not operating under the assumptions positioning writers of conventional literary critiques, but instead those of a hybrid space that encourages both literate and oral activities—an aspect often seen as encouraging writers to participate more fully in discussions.

The parallel activities of synchronous conferencing and collaborative hypertext writing serve to break down the extreme forms of opposition without denying the possibility of opposition; as Giroux (1992a) put it, "Border pedagogy decenters as it remaps" (p. 30). What is denied is a totalizing, geometrical perspective—the god's-eye view of the text (or the critic's view that somehow is capable of extracting the text from the complications of time and culture).

The number and complexity of discourses articulating all participants here are overwhelming—STORYSPACE does not provide a way of mapping these in a completely geometrical sense (one cannot get a grasp of the whole), but in a way that (only potentially) helps participants to live a combination of geography and geometry apart from universal truths but still in the social, which becomes the realm of contingent truths. Such uses resemble what Joyce (1995) described as a narrative geography "concerned with the connections among useful entities... with episodic recognition of

---

[12] The term *anchored* poses the problem of connoting a boat anchored to a pier—a movable object anchored to something immovable. The relation between text and experience, however, in the examples here is more a matter of mutual construction, perhaps like two or more boats loosely connected to each other rather than to a land-bound object.

successive interdependencies" rather than the "traditional Adamic view of dominion over the world" (p. 168).

Besides the chronological and metaphor paths intersecting at Entry 78, there are threads on cognition, the distinction between formal and informal discourse, hypertext, linearity, and positioning, each different ways of rewriting Entry 78 and, ultimately, Lester's discursive positions. Each path, in turn, can be deconstructed because nearly every entry on every path is similarly mapped and remapped. Lester's entry provides one centering for the map, but others always pull this center away (from each entry, writers and readers can skip to another thread or begin constructing and deconstructing their own). These forces, however, remain in tension rather than obliterating identities or constructing parasitic commentaries.

But we need to keep in mind that it is necessary, in this project, that we avoid thinking of individual paths through the text as somehow constituting discrete subsets of the full text. The path named *hypertext*, for example, should not be seen as a discrete collection of nodes that somehow fully exhausts the hypertext-related content of the text. This view would result in the idea that the content of the nodes was separable—not merely abstractly but actually—from the ways in which the text is read, the unfortunate position Giroux (1992a) identified where "pedagogy is… what is left after curriculum content is determined" (p. 98). The reading and writings are articulations, and we can identify content and curriculum as social forces, but we cannot actually separate them in practice. Instead, the hypertext thread should represent to teachers and students one necessarily incomplete way of representing positions in relation to the text and world. The hypertext is a stand-in for the cognitive mapping of each individual node against the totality of the text—a totality that is as ungraspable as the attempt to gain a full understanding of the text by "reading" the map in Figure 6.5, which was constructed by "flattening" the hierarchical display of Figure 6.2, retaining the numerous paths of the text. There are no single centers here (as in THE IN MEMORIAM WEB), but there are plateaus (unlike KARL'S FORKING RESPONSE) in which identities and discourses are continually deconstructed and reconstructed.

This type of hypertext (activity and object, history and space) attempts to disturb two key forces that work to hold in place the concepts of individual authorship (a notion that, at the frequent extreme it often takes in our culture, denies the social) and textual ownership that commonly articulate text in writing and literature class (coupled to authorship in order to make literature a commodity culture to be consumed by well-trained readers) There is no center object (the father text) to which either individual readers or the group as a whole must continually position themselves (even the chronological thread can be questioned or completely removed, something difficult to do in linear electronic discussions). But unlike traditional oral

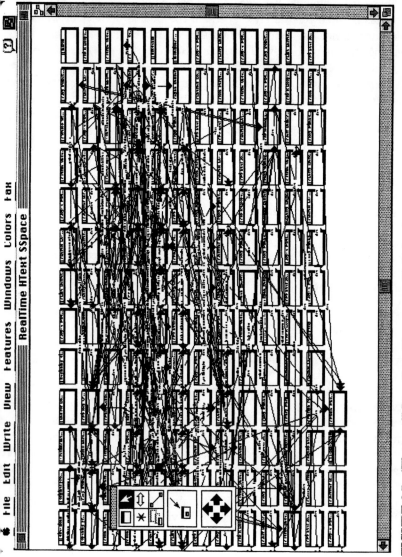

FIGURE 6.5. "Flattened" REAL-TIME HYPERTEXT with links shown.

conversations, the text does not vanish in its creation as the voices die away. The text exists as both process and product, the writers of the text being rewritten by both themselves and others. Identity is not so completely overthrown that it leaves participants with the sense that each of them has become completely dispersed; the bodied activity of writing to each other stands as a reinforcement that even though there might not be anything outside of the text (Derrida's [1976] *"il n'y a pas de hors-text"* [p. 158]), there is something other than text.

This general method plays out in different ways depending on characteristics such as group size and makeup, time span, and so on. The tactics of deconstructing the linear text and reconstructing it as a social artifact and process can provide writers and readers with ways to work against reductive readings and oversimplified concepts of subjectivity. Lester and the other participants both write and are written by multiple, overlapping, complementing discourses, and the discourses are rewritten by each and all of them. To recall Hall's (1989) observations about Althusser, this single node in the STORYSPACE text can help us to think "difference in unity":

> As you enter an ideological field and pick out any one nodal representation or idea, you immediately trigger off a whole chain of connotative associations.... The notion of *the* dominant ideology and *the* subordinated ideology is an inadequate way of representing the complex interplay of different discourses and formations in any modern developed society. Nor is the terrain of ideology constituted as a field of mutually exclusive and internally self-sustaining discursive chains. They contest one another, often drawing on a common, shared repertoire of concepts, re-articulating and disarticulating them within different systems of difference or equivalence. (p. 104)

Here we have a subtle but powerful way of provisionally distinguishing between THE IN MEMORIAM WEB and the INTERCHANGE/STORYSPACE session discussed earlier (as well as a way of approaching THE IN MEMORIAM WEB in a resistant manner). The text, the links through nodes, and the connections of links into thematized paths, do not name a truth of a work or attempt to discover Lester's (or anyone else's) single, unified position in the text, but exist as a way of deconstructing and reconstructing social forces being played out in and as the text. It is not that hypertext ever automatically deconstructs anything—to deny the various authorities operating in the construction of these particular texts is to succumb to the more powerful social discourses in which texts are written and read. "It's naive to deny the existence of authority," Giroux (1992a) wrote. "Instead one should investigate how it is exercised" (p. 157). What the INTERCHANGE/STORYSPACE text allows (but that THE IN MEMORIAM WEB somehow opposes) is the critique of such lines of authority.

I want to avoid giving the idea that deconstructing an

INTERCHANGE/STORYSPACE session is automatic, simple, or inevitable, but the need for it can be made manifest by the nature of the text in process under certain conditions. An even more useful text, I think, would be one that combined the characteristics of THE IN MEMORIAM WEB and the INTERCHANGE/STORYSPACE session discussed previously in a challenging way. The INTERCHANGE/STORYSPACE session as it plays out here is only a small part of a critical pedagogy of hypertext writing and reading—the tactics students learn in this forum must be played out in texts such as THE IN MEMORIAM WEB.

Students can work with not only the forces at work during the production of the original text (important in itself because, as Belsey [1980] noted, these traces are traditionally hidden during the subsequent textual production) but forces in the past, present, and future. At this point, writers might be able to decenter Tennyson's work by shifting the focus of the hypertext from the production of a single author to the general act of textual production. Teachers could work to strengthen that idea by playing it out across numerous examples, by helping students begin a second stage of the work, a discussion of their own commentaries in THE IN MEMORIAM WEB. The current text is clearly centered around Tennyson's text, with students being encouraged to write individual responses toward the authoritative texts.

This task requires that we and our students rethink the ideas of quotation and citation. As Bialostosky (1991) wrote:

> Most handbooks on argumentation treat the quotation as a technical citation in support of the author's claims in genres like the research paper, but I suggest that quotation is the very act in which one voice creatively absorbs another and defines itself in relation to the second voice. When we interrupt the quoted text, interrogate it, clarify its point, or expose its ambiguities, we make an opening for our own utterances and give shape to our own rules in the conversation. (p. 18)

Besides collaborative writing—which can be used tactically to increase the force of student writing by situating a lived social relation against the canonized text—students should also be encouraged to work out the social and political relations being constructed within their own work and its relations to Tennyson's (ever-blurring) *In Memoriam*. At first, such work appears (as it does in its infancy in THE IN MEMORIAM WEB) as a thin cloud around the father text. As the volume of commentary begins to gather, we might begin to see the possibility of helping the students (and ourselves) rethink the function and place of commentary as a self-reflective, social, political way of mapping livings. Rather than students being encouraged to comment on source texts, they should also learn to comment on their own texts and those of other writers.

Similarly, we might work in our classrooms at making textual criticism in hypertext (such as Crary attempted) a transitional method toward a more empowering terrain for writing, reading, and thinking—as Moulthrop and Kaplan (1994) themselves hinted at the end of their article on KARL'S FORKING RESPONSE. Mapping Crary's text into a broader social matrix might work to avoid the flattening and absorption of his text into Borges/Moulthrop's. Other students, other readers commenting not merely on the father text but asserting their own texts and discourses collaboratively might provide a counterbalance—a material, lived reality—to help Crary maintain the sense of resistance by constructing a collective social project.

Such a potential exists in the World Wide Web because it provides, at least hypothetically, a broad social context in which students can write to and with others. Although students have always been able to write essays for distribution among their peers (even if primarily written for the teacher), the means of distribution between student writer and the "authors" they read clearly separates the two types of text. The World Wide Web provides an environment in which students can be offered the means of both production and distribution. The Web rearticulates hypertext in important ways by returning to the emphasis on public discourse in Nelson's early writing. These spaces are open to students just as much as (if not more than) they are to faculty members and corporate managers. In the classes where I help students learn ways to write texts on the World Wide Web, they are able to rely on their classmates for technical assistance (who sometimes know the topic in greater detail than I). And although in every discipline there are a handful of intellectual stars who gain notice while still graduate students, the subdiscipline of computers and writing has been enriched by a large number of graduate student efforts. Some of the most widely visited and discussed spaces on the World Wide Web—John December's *Computer-Mediated Communication Journal* (Figure 6.6) and Greg Siering and Tari Fanderclai's *Tuesday Cafe* (Figure 6.7), to name only two, were created by graduate students when their projects first gained wide attention and influence.

This rearticulation is only a partial way of addressing the problem, to be sure. In the first place, current versions of hypertext mark-up language (HTML) make open collaboration difficult because they identify text fragments with single authors (each text fragments is closed to other writers, even those who want to add a link pointing to commentary on that text). Perhaps more importantly, the Web is only one environment of production and distribution. Powerful authors on the Web may also be powerful authors in other areas, such as print, politics, industry, or film. Finally, as many of us have found out in our struggles for institutional support for computing services, it is often difficult to gain and maintain access to the

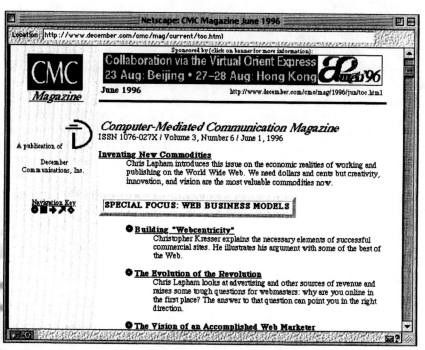

FIGURE 6.6. Screens from *Computer-Mediated Communication Journal,* edited by John December.

technology and expertise necessary to write and publish documents on the World Wide Web. At my own institution, like many others, ample access is offered to the tools to browse the Web (Netscape, Mosaic, Lynx), but little resources are offered for authoring documents for the Web, a situation that perpetuates the economy of scarcity surrounding traditional ideas of Great Books. And students in English and other nontechnical disciplines can work with a graphical browser only in public-access labs, whereas students in many technical disciplines can dial up a graphical interface from their homes with Point to Point Protocol (PPP) and Serial Line Internet Protocol (SLIP) accounts (something even *faculty* in English and professional communication are denied—I tell myself that this is an instructive inversion of the typical faculty–student power structure). Finally, the increasing privatization of Internet and World Wide Web services, coupled with frequent budgetary restrictions for public education, may make even the types of access some of us now enjoy the target of budget cuts. The same technical features that make the World Wide Web relatively open to marginalized groups such as student writers are also the technical features that administrators and legislators point to as the problems with the World Wide Web.

We need to defend against these impending problems by rearticulating literacy as well. The acts of writing and reading must be resocialized here, made to appear not as a natural extension of the traditional activities of literary scholarship but also a way of reenvisioning the functions of literacy at a number of levels. As genres blur in this commentary (the distinction between literature and criticism breaking down) they might also begin to blur across into some of the other genres I have taken up: functional documentation and online research spaces, two areas to which I return later. Instead of using hypertext to reinforce the current divisions constructed in these genres—divisions that isolate the discourses, make them less open to change, and more likely to be cut out in financial decisions about who really needs access to wide-area networks like the Web—we can be working to problematize for our students (and ourselves) the naturalness of these genres by juxtaposing and perhaps even mixing our uses of them. Rather than allowing the discourse to easily position writers and readers in given positions, hypertext might be constructed as a forum for enacting a broad form of critical literacy by making the use of genre an unnatural act.

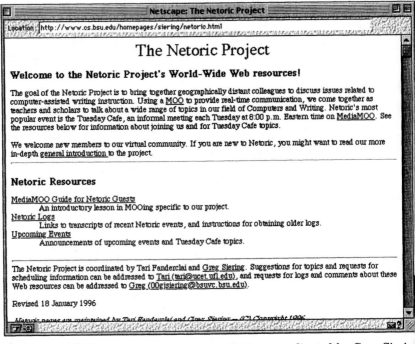

FIGURE 6.7. Home page for the Netoric Project, coordinated by Greg Siering and Tari Fanderclai.

REARTICULATING ECONOMIES OF RESEARCH SPACE

What if... we suppose that information is *not* inherently valuable? What if, that is, only a profound social reorganization can permit information to become valuable? What sort of historical changes would be required for such a sweeping and dramatic revaluation?

—Dan Schiller (1988, p. 32)

The development of information space has, for the most part, been an economic venture: The virtual and personal becomes objectified, landscaped (as in the private or conquerable property), and (paradoxically) made tangible and financially accountable. These forces are lived when people use such systems, when they take up given positions within this genre. Both teachers and students are increasingly living partially within these spaces, but they are not frequently thinking critically about how and why information becomes spatial. The two forces of the commodity space articulation take part in the construction and maintenance of a complex array of ideological forces supporting certain specific social configurations and concepts (limited versions of computer literacy, technological progress, physical isolation of workers, etc.). These forces also hide other important issues: If information is (both figuratively and literally) a piece of property, it can be exclusively owned; but in articulating this commodity to all of the traditional notions of the rights of property owners—against trespass, to be leased, and so on—the commodity space articulation of hypertext discourages questions such as what trespassing or ownership actually mean in a virtual space, or how colonizing an information space might parallel or differ from the repressive nature of earlier colonizations of more terrestrial realms (Africa, South America, etc.), or how moving around in the market of a virtual space is different from or like physically walking around in a shopping mall. Unless we begin helping our students think about these issues, they (and we) are likely to be positioned in an environment that perpetuates many of the repressive power distributions currently plaguing our society—unequal distributions of wealth, problems of access, social representations, and so forth.

One dominant force encouraging us and our students to think of information as spatial is the way in which our culture (and subcultures) conceive of space and landscape in general and the importance that the possession and circulation of space have taken on. Postmodern architecture illustrates well the ways in which we have begun—often without realizing it—to live in a new type of social and political space. The complexities of fragmented, postmodern spaces such as the Los Angeles Westin Bonaventure Hotel, Jameson (1991) wrote "[make] it impossible for us to use the language of volume or volumes any longer, since these are impossible to seize" (p. 43). For Soja (1989) as well, the Bonaventure offers an important example of postmodern living:

> [T]he Bonaventure has become a concentrated representation of the restructured spatiality of the late capitalist city: fragmented and fragmenting, homogeneous and homogenizing, divertingly packaged, yet curiously incomprehensible, seemingly open in presenting itself to view by constantly pressing to enclose, to compartmentalize, to circumscribe, to incarcerate. Everything imaginable appears to be available in this micro-urb, but real places are difficult to find. (p. 243)

This fragmentation encourages circulation—of people or commodities (or, people as commodities). Space is an asset, an item of value (often, but not necessarily, divorced from use value) rather than an environment. Information can then be more easily tracked, accumulated, sold, and billed for. What would an environmentalist perspective on information space be? Perhaps not very different, in that the environment is often considered a resource to be used, sold, developed, and managed, making Schiller's (1988) suggestions about information as resource potentially useful but also potentially complicitous with the same forces we want to resist. (Although there is a much more vocal debate about the environment than there is about information spaces.) Whereas environmental development frequently leaves behind physical evidence of ecological violence, the fluidity and intangibility of hyperspace (coupled with the seemingly objective array of information constituting these spaces) may make evidence of wrongdoing more difficult to see, let alone stop or reform.

Although certainly it seems that students in our classes (and ourselves as scholars) can now access (or access more easily) larger amounts of information in these spaces than in the physical spaces of campus library, an uncritical or overly optimistic perspective on information spaces is easily coopted by stronger social forces (Robins & Webster, 1988). The capitalism of current information spaces is something that Lash and Urry termed "disorganized capitalism" in order to distinguish it from the older, more familiar "organized" form: Centralized, planned state capitalism has disintegrated into a capitalism synonymous with postmodernism—fragmented and decentered, capital incessantly circulating. This system of consumption, among other things, centers on images rather than signs, the increasing degree of Baudrillardian "spectacle" over meaning, and the blurring of the divisions between high and low culture: "[E]veryday life in consumer (disorganized) capitalism predisposes an audience to the reception of post-modern cultural forms" (Lash & Urry, 1987, p. 292); virtual spaces begin making text something closer to image than it was. In Saussure's (1959) semiotics, the signifier–signified split parallels the use–exchange value split, both being artificial divisions that allow circulation and exchange of, respectively, symbols and money. Baudrillard (1988a), however, argued that the split inside both sign and commodity is artificial, that use value and signifieds are nonexistent and only alibis for capitalist exchange; consumption of signifieds with no referent, inattentive and distracted. Baudrillard (1983, 1988b, 1990) moved away from capital as an organizing cultural notion, situating consumption and exchange purely at the level of signs.

Although Baudrillard's insistence on the death of the real is problematic in our project of constructing a critical and cultural pedagogy for hypertext, it does point out some of the difficulties of the current social situation. The increasingly fragmented, heterogeneous, and multiple world in which we currently live makes us more receptive to disorganized postmodern capitalism, one of the most powerful forces articulating hypertext as a space that can be colonized and exchanged. No longer are colonies the backward, uncomfortable, mosquito-ridden sites of potentially embarrassingly public injustice. The computer makes colonialism, as Haraway might say, clean and light. The movement of spatializing information works to break traditional anchors of meaning and association; capitalist forces are then more easily able to reanchor the fluid information flows. As Deleuze and Guattari (1987) put it:

> Circulation constitutes capital as a new subjectivity commensurate with society in its entirety... [T]his new social subjectivity can form only to the extent that the decoded flows overspill their conjunctions and attain a level of decoding that the state apparatuses are no longer able to reclaim. (p. 453)

In some cases, such information spaces may offer a visible form of release (deterritorialization) quickly coupled to an invisible form of repression (capture): The freedom of movement across an immense space hides the implicit structure of that space.

Currently, the postmodern disruption between word and world is articulated—reterritorialized—back into an economically valuable space or capital. The pre-existing social situation codes the new fluid nodes into relations of repression or absorption. Information becomes like money, divorced from reality, nonproductive except as circulation and (temporary) accumulation (Wall Street as the pure text).

But despite the drawbacks of spatializing information, there also exist possibilities for social change. The implicit divorce (decontextualization) between the relations of information and the relations between physical objects acts as an important deterritorialization, one that teachers and students might instead appropriate at the key point between disarticulation and rearticulation. Constructing information as a space can be seen as working in the interests of currently dominant social forces, in particular those of late capitalism. (Recognition of this case, as most teachers have found, never guarantees that students will also begin to work in different ways to rearticulate their activities.)

From a pedagogical perspective, we can start thinking about ways in which our own methods support the idea of information as a commodity. Although hypertext theorists such as Landow and Bolter maintain that the medium allows writers and readers to make connections across public, collaborative networks of text, our teaching strategies still negate this possibility when they emphasize tasks such as writing individual essays.

Researchers using ProQuest, for example, the full-text online space I discussed in Chapter 3, search index maps for potentially valuable locations, travel to those locations (either in the virtual space, or in the physical stacks) to scout out their resources, and evaluate where they might fit into our overall projects. Then, if necessary, they copy information from the relatively public, online space to their own private spaces (either as a printed facsimile, notes, or potentially even on disk).

Because the space is modeled after the traditional idea of the library, it probably does not seem odd to users that they "enter" a virtual space and bring back, across the gap they perceive between self and Other, commodified pieces of information. Although we can in many ways term this a social activity (because the navigation in a sense requires the research to move into a social space, a shared, virtual library), that sense of social is founded on a Cartesian notion of mind and world: The individual mind interacts through the senses and, in that mind's gifted fashion, constructs new thoughts. The commodity-space workers are valued by the degree to which they can develop (move beyond) the resources they have colonized in hyperspace. The strong articulation of information to capitalism requires both that "ownership" of text (or "rental" or "use-rights") remain a constant and that the text commodity continually circulate as a social activity (Slack, 1984a). Discussing the resurgence of spatial thought in contemporary philosophy, Smith (1993) warned that metaphorical space often "simplistically repeats the asymmetries of power inherent in traditional social theory" (p. 98).

Quotations and citations in this articulation often connote not only positive terms like intertextuality and social construction but also traditional notions such as possession and legitimation; the quote is almost a bounty taken by a strong, capable reader and consumer. The very best student consumers become producers of this capital. This conception of research and writing is maintained and reinforced by the many online research spaces that force readers to download information from the original space and place it into their own authored texts. Delany wrote enthusiastically of the development of "personal docuverses," individual versions of the dynamic and social docuverses Nelson envisioned for hypertext in the 1960s. In an essay in the same volume, Virbel (1993) described proposed "reading sta tions" for the future Bibliothèque de France, listing the first priority for the online system as the capacity to "permit each reader *to build a personal corpus*. Building a personal corpus involves three issues—access, acquisition, and archiving in mass storage" (p. 33, italics in original). Virbel later covered topics such as publication of material, but these facilities (as with contemporary research and publishing) encourage authors to possess the text in their own spaces before releasing it in new form.

If we are interested in constructing a more social research space, we can attempt to reinforce an idea inherent in early conceptions of hypertext, especially in Nelson's notion of the "docuverse," the public space containing all the world's text, open to any person for writing and reading (Nelson, 1982, 1987b). As Bolter (1991b) noted, there are a number of social, technological, and political impediments to actually achieving the goal of placing every existing document in a single space—but we can still use the general idea of the docuverse to inform tactics for thinking about and working with about text in our classes.

These spaces can be as local as a collaborative group's critical interpretations of an essay within a program like STORYSPACE, or as broad as discussions on the World Wide Web. The technology and context must support at least two key aspects: First, it must allow writers and readers to work within the space of the texts (rather than downloading them, preserving the purity of the master text). Second, it must encourage more than one person to write within that space (in order to avoid pitting the weight of a published author against a single reader). Although the World Wide Web makes the first somewhat difficult for reasons discussed previously, it works very well at multiplying opportunities for collaboration; conversely, STORYSPACE makes it easier for an individual to write within a "public" space, but the documents are not as easily shared across the World Wide Web. (The two overlap, with STORYSPACE, like many current word processors, offering capabilities to export HTML files and Web browsers having the ability to read local files.)

In these spaces, users do not construct completely new texts (although this certainly would be allowed), but are encouraged to begin constructing connections among preexisting nodes, and across and between evolving networks. This work can be used as a way to break down genre in the senses described earlier. For example, students in THE IN MEMORIAM WEB might be encouraged to comment not only on source material but also on their own work and the work of others (which also might help to break down the currently strict division between "self" text and "other's" text). We can see a prototypical version of this in World Wide Web home pages, frequently composed not only of "original" text but also (and often primarily) collections of pointers to other material (Figure 6.8).

In addition, the act of linking, when it is given more importance than it

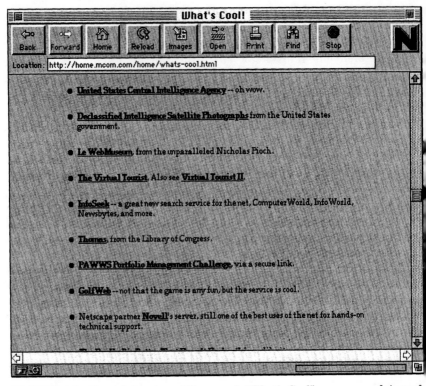

FIGURE 6.8. Partial showing of NETSCAPE'S "What's Cool" page, an evolving collection of pointers to other interesting material.

currently seems to have, restructures the way in which concepts such as text and research are constructed. In a Lyotardian sense, writers are not valued for their creative genius so much as their ability to combine and connect information in useful ways. Strong similarities exist between Nelson's (1987b) still-hypothetical docuverse and Lyotard's (1984) games of pure information. Consider, for example, the comments of an employee at a high-tech bank, recounted by Zuboff (1988):

> We could buy information and build integration of information from several sources and give it to the client. We could find out how they dream. Give them information about real estate to buy a house... and then tell them we'll provide the loan for the house, too... and insurance... then we've got him hooked. (p. 161)

But as the banker pointed out, there is not yet a single sphere in which we can access all information (although the World Wide Web may be moving in that direction). There are, at this point, only limited versions of Nelson' utopian docuverse. THE IN MEMORIAM WEB of Chapter 5 gives us one example of the general structure of such a space, although this particular web is structured along the lines of traditional literary scholarship and currently encourages writers and readers to link their contributions back to *In Memoriam* (the "master" text) in a hierarchical manner more than across the network of text. More promising are potential uses of the Internet and World Wide Web discussed earlier, and work on collaborative systems such as ABC at the University of North Carolina, Chapel Hill (Shackelford, 1991; Shackelford, Smith, & Smith, 1993; Smith & Smith, 1991), MCC's GIBIS (Conklin & Begeman, 1987) and RIBIS (Rein & Ellis, 1991), and some uses of Xerox/Venue's NOTECARDS (Irish & Trigg, 1989; Trigg, Suchman, & Halasz, 1986). But the current context of many these systems is one of decision making, with the hypertext existing as a temporary aid in group discussion. In Figure 6.9, for example, writers in rIBIS, a synchronous collaborative hypertext environment, work out issues in the design of a particular software package.

These systems, then, do not directly address large-scale issues such as the design of Nelson's docuverse. What they do offer is a way to rethink models of online research space. We might instead (or in addition) model

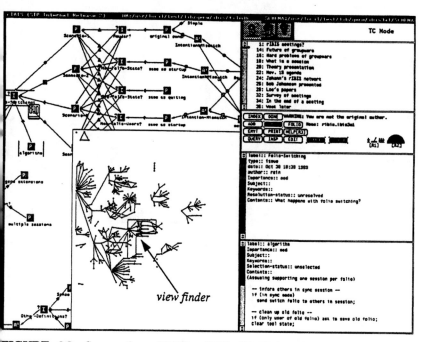

view finder

FIGURE 6.9. Screen from MCC's RIBIS ("Real-time Issues-Based Inquiry System"), a collaborative hypertext program.

a library that departs from the physical structure and toward an intertextual one, not merely the library metaindexes on the World Wide Web—which are not much more than large versions of current online card catalogs—but spaces encouraging the construction of associative connections between source materials on the net itself. Current versions of HTML, the document description language in which most Web documents are written, does not provide facilities for crucial elements for collaboration, such as the ability to add a link inside another author's text; on the Web, each writer owns the space of their text. Although the Web supports

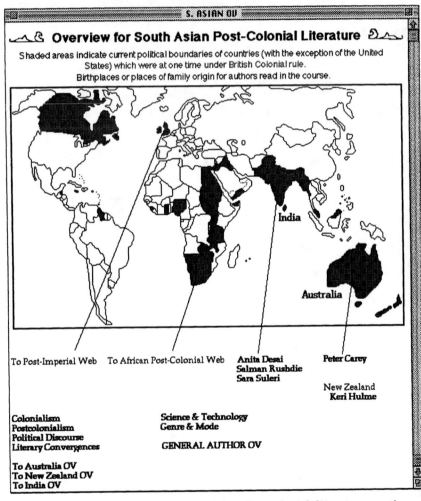

FIGURE 6.10. Overview of South Asian Postcolonial literature section of CONTEXT34.

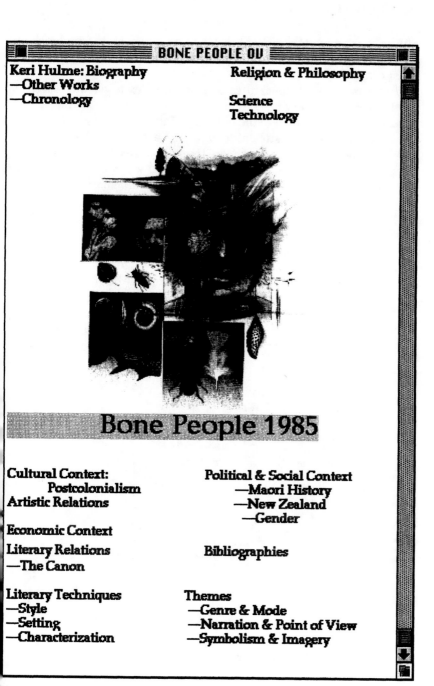

BONE PEOPLE OU

Keri Hulme: Biography
—Other Works
—Chronology

Religion & Philosophy

Science
Technology

Bone People 1985

Cultural Context:
    Postcolonialism
Artistic Relations

Political & Social Context
—Maori History
—New Zealand
—Gender

Economic Context

Literary Relations
—The Canon

Bibliographies

Literary Techniques
—Style
—Setting
—Characterization

Themes
—Genre & Mode
—Narration & Point of View
—Symbolism & Imagery

FIGURE 6.11 "Bone People" overview in CONTEXT34.

a futuristic version of document distribution, much of its foundation still supports ideas of textual authorship having roots in romanticism and capitalist ownership of property.

Rather than using the card catalog as an index to another space, we should make the library itself intertextual and open. Landow himself provided some of the solution to the difficulty of the weight of the classical literary text subordinating student texts when he discussed classes in which other types of source texts—and more than one source text—were used. In the INTERMEDIA document CONTEXT34, students wrote and read within a web built up during a course taught by Landow on autobiography and postcolonial fiction (Figure 6.10).

The series of screens shown in Figures 6.11 through 6.14 follow a thread moving through the overview of Keri Hulme's work, one of a number of authors covered by CONTEXT34. The "Religion and Philosophy" heading in Figure 6.11 is connected to eight different nodes (Figure 6.12): The initials following the thread titles indicate student texts (the number of which appears to be much higher than in THE IN MEMORIAM WEB). This node is

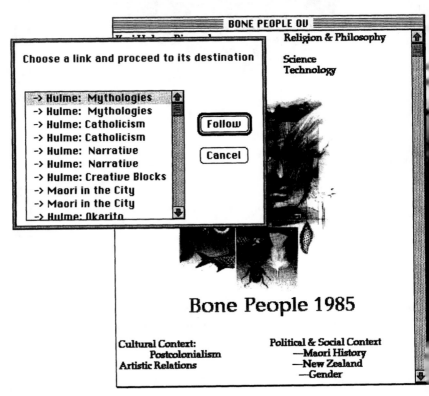

FIGURE 6.12. Partial list of links from Bone People overview.

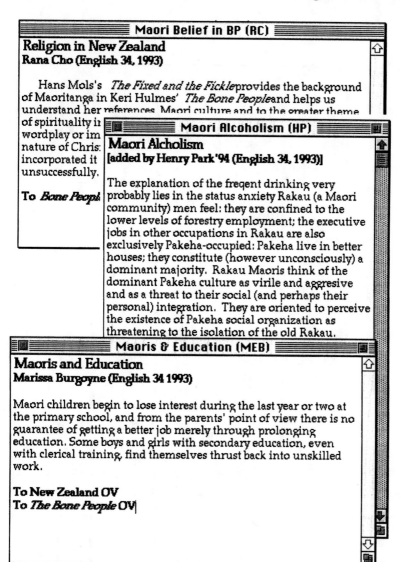

FIGURE 6.13. Nodes from CONTEXT34.

connected to work by, among others, Rana Cho, Henry Park, and Marissa Burgoyne (Figure 6.13).

CONTEXT34 appears, at first glance, to be still largely on the side of conventional literary criticism, with students writing shorter versions of traditional, individual research essays that are connected electronically to their more authoritative source texts (rather than the virtual citation exist-

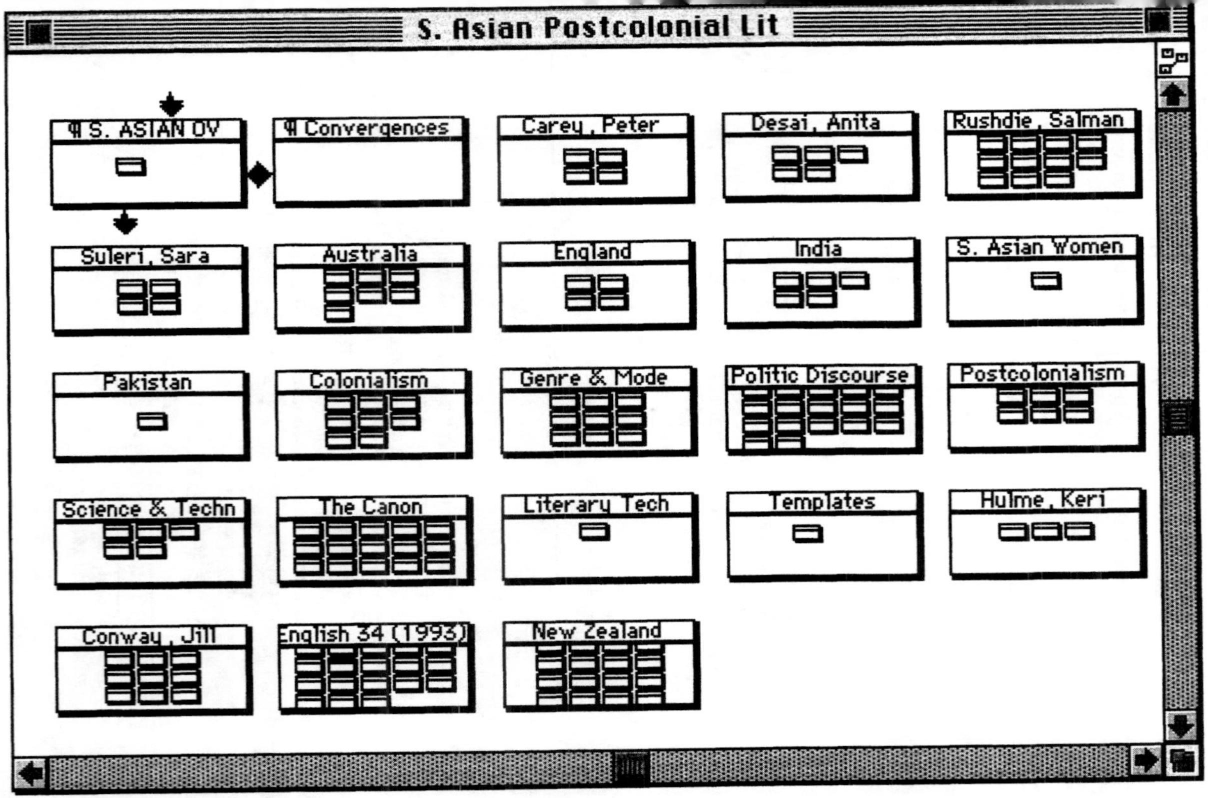

FIGURE 6.14. Hierarchial division of text spaces in South Asian Postcolonial literature overview.

ing in print-based citations). In addition, at one level the text is organized in a way that clearly separates student texts out from the rest of the web (Figure 6.14). Still, the existence of this web and the fact that students write into and across the web rather than in isolation from it points toward more radical disarticulations of the literature commodity paradigm. The act of citation here is one of association or recognition rather than possession or appropriation—seeing rather than taking. We should not, after all, ask students to completely deny existing methods of academic literary traditions—if we were successful in converting student writers to this belief, they run the danger of alienating themselves from the social structures we might want them to work within toward change; if we fail at converting students, we alienate ourselves from them. So CONTEXT34 appears to be a useful border territory in which students might be urged to write autoethnographic texts that display characteristics of individual authorship as well as social construction and postmodern dispersal.

However, we have to remain aware of the shortcomings of this work, especially in the ways it continues to encourage the conception of the author as a relatively isolated individual (even when a text is authored by numerous writers, the individual nodes retain individual authorship and

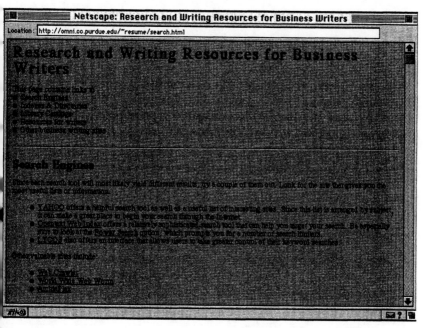

FIGURE 6.15. Typical home page on the World Wide Web, containing links to other pages.

students such as Rana Cho are clearly identified by the course-belonging-ness of "English34"). As Landow (1992c) explained the origins of this web, CONTEXT34 began as a text dedicated to a single postcolonial author, Wole Soyinka (an origin somewhat reminiscent of THE IN MEMORIAM WEB or THE DICKENS WEB):

> The success of this ongoing experiment [the writing of the Soyinka web] has recently led me to expand the Soyinka web into CONTEXT34, a set of more than five hundred largely student-created documents that support the teaching of a new course on postcolonial fiction and autobiography in English. Work done by students in English 32 and other courses provided, I realized, the basis for a richer hypertext corpus. After creating graphic overviews for the thirteen authors in the course and for relevant topics such as Nigeria and women in India, Pakistan, and Bangladesh, I proceeded to edit and then link a range of student documents to these overviews and to one another. The sheer practicality of a hypertext system like INTERMEDIA for teachers appears in the fact that I managed to create CONTEXT34 between the end of the first semester and the beginning of the second. (pp. 146–149)

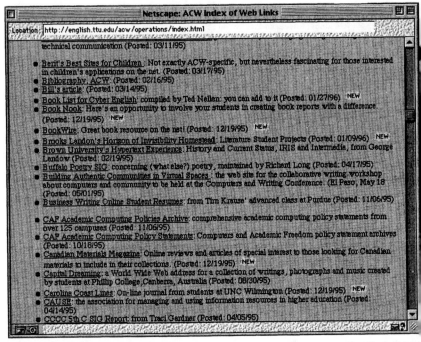

FIGURE 6.16. Clearinghouse for online resources at the Alliance for Computers and Writing's World Wide Web home page.

FIGURE 6.17. Screen from Kaplan's "Electronic Literacies" hypertext essay on the World Wide Web.

Landow here acted as the compiler and editor of the text, which came to be identified as a whole with him and only at the microlevel with the student authors—this situation potentially serves to reinforce the hierarchies of author or teacher to student. (This situation mirrors the current state of collaborative work on the World Wide Web, where a single "owner" must approve and actually implement the addition of citations into the body of the work proper.) In addition to writing conventional essays, students might be encouraged to work with juxtapositions of material. Rather than turning in essays, students writing on the World Wide Web tell their reviewers, readers, instructors, and collaborators the location on the web of the maps they have constructed. These maps construct new information spaces through association with other textual fragments.

In order to move beyond outdated notions of the author, however, writing teachers will have to begin articulating new projects for student writers, new value systems for the task of writing, which become less a question of "What can you produce?" than of "How can you arrange these texts?" and, as Deleuze and Guattari (1987) might put it, "What other machine can this machine be connected to?" In addressing these questions, students can come to understand the ways in which representations are interested constructions, none of which can ever completely and authoritatively map social reality. Early versions of such work are pervasive in the collections of links found on home pages (Figure 6.15). More ambitious projects—often in the form of clearinghouses for disciplines such as the Alliance for Computers and Writing's (ACW) home page (Figure 6.16) and Nancy Kaplan's groundbreaking HTML essay on the late age of print (Figure 6.17)—provide some indications of directions in which we might head. These texts blur the distinction between bibliography and body text in useful ways, moving beyond the common linear and hierarchical lists of universal resource locaters (URLs) (although these still have a place) and toward a postmodern orchestration of fragments.

In addition, by occupying these spaces rather than seeing them as storehouses from which information is retrieved, online research spaces are rearticulated in a way that weakens the commodification of these spaces. Although we cannot (and probably do not want to) remove the potential for postcapitalist enterprise from the World Wide Web, we have to recognize the necessity to mediate between the incessant circulation of postmodern capitalism and the chilling stasis of modernist authorship.

CONTAGION: REARTICULATING THE LITTLE MACHINE

Considering the politics of even "low-level" texts (an inaccurate but common notion) such as functional hypertexts is both vital and, compared to the other articulations just discussed, extremely difficult. These texts have become so common that they are largely invisible, seen as so straightforward that they are removed from ideological concerns. But the functional text in many ways defines for us how to use the technology—it tells us how to write, how to read, and how to position ourselves in relation to the technology, the text, and society. More importantly, once we agree to the rules of this discourse, it tells us these things in more or less unarguable terms; it is very difficult to reintroduce concepts such as ethics and ecology in an articulation that accepts technological efficiency as its primary goal (cf. Feenberg, 1991; Slack, 1989). As I argued in Chapter 3, the difficulty of politicizing functional texts lies largely in the way that the discourses in which these texts are both constructed and used often disregards any terms not directly associated with technical efficiency. The value of functional documents (paper or online) in these discourses lies primarily in where they fall in the range of lesser to greater technical efficiency (speed, ease of use). So where our tactical approach to deconstructing and reconstructing the already dialogical writing of Chapter 5 consisted of multiplying the voices beyond the "I" of each node, making functional hypertexts or online databases explicitly political and social requires a preliminary series of maneuvers.

Our task here, as I mentioned earlier, is made more difficult because the social and the political are not frequently considered a useful aspect of functional documents (not to mention the corporate settings in which these documents are frequently used). Politics are considered by many to be independent of and extraneous to technology development and use. We can begin by questioning how and why the machine is constructed as it is, whose interests it serves, by seeing what escapes the dominant structure, by attempting to tease out a different, conflicting articulation. As Massumi (1992) pointed out, Deleuze and Guattari's (1987) broad concept of "machines" can be articulated in two, radically different manners:

> The MECHANICAL refers to a structural interrelating of discrete parts working harmoniously together to perform work…. By MACHINIC [Deleuze and Guattari] mean functioning immanently and pragmatically, by contagion rather than by comparison, unsubordinated either to the laws of resemblance or efficiency. Living bodies and technological apparatuses are machinic when they are in becoming,… mechanical when they are functioning in a state of stable equilibrium. (p. 192)

Keeping in mind that it is the mechanical articulation that now exerts some of the strongest forces structuring hypertext use, we can work at highlighting the side of machinic operations, encouraging contagion rather than equilibrium. Hypertext affords (but does not always encourage) the possibility of multiplicity, activity, and empowerment for those working within situations of unequal power. Despite the pessimism of social theorists such as Ellul (1964) and Marcuse (1964), machinery does not necessarily have to be articulated into positions of efficiency and conservatism—this is only a currently strong and tenacious force.

Although one of the primary goals of technical communication appears to be the continual increase of technical efficiency—that is, the eventual construction of a transparent medium—this goal can never be completed. A single discourse can never completely close off other voices. The term *single* is in fact misleading: One might more accurately think of discourses as different ways of making and moving along infinitely fine webs of living.

Two points of tension in the broad social environments in which functional hypertext is frequently used can be brought to bear on the current articulation of functional hypertext in a productive way: (a) the initial
conception of hypertext as a revolutionary new way of thinking (rather
than a neutral or transparent technology) remains partially active in current definitions of hypertext, even though it is not reinforced by automated texts; and (b) the growing awareness in corporate and factory settings
of the benefits of collaborative work may be used to obstruct the fragmentation and isolation in simpler forms of automation.

In many cases, the isolation of individual workers while they are learning software packages and operating systems provides increased force to
this mental Taylorization. Zuboff (1988), for example, recounted the story
of automation—and resistance—in one recently computerized office:

> One afternoon, after several weeks of participant observation and discus-
> sions with clerks and supervisors, I was returning to the office from a lunch
> with a group of employees when two of them beckoned me over to their
> desks, indicating that they had something to show me. They seated them-
> selves at their workstations on either side of a tall gray partition. Then they
> pointed out a small rupture in the orderly, high-tech appearance of their
> work space: the metal seam in the partition that separated their desks had
> been pried open.
>
> With the look of mischievous co-conspirators, they confided that they had
> inflicted this surgery upon the wall between them. Why? The small opening
> now made it possible to peek through and see if the other worker was at her
> seat, without having to stand up and peer over or around the wall. Through
> that aperture questions could be asked, advice could be given, and dinner
> menus could be planned. (p. 125)

But unlike the office, the writing class is frequently constructed as a
more open environment, where students and teachers learn software
together in the midst of discussions that, even if they are often more
practical than political, provide a shared social space that can be politicized by introducing questions of ethics, rights, technology in society,
and so forth.[13] Learning to use the computer in this environment can
become a reflective social activity, helping students restructure their
uses of text outside of the classroom. Discussing the use of computer-
based conferencing in the writing class, Cooper and Selfe (1990)

---

[13] See Cooper and Selfe (1990), Selfe and Eilola (1988), and Sullivan (1991b), as well as
discussions of such issues in technical communication classrooms, which have also traditionally attempted to present themselves as apolitical and practical (Johnson-Eilola & Selber, in
press; Katz, 1992; Selber, 1995a; Sullivan, 1990).

described how, when constructed in a discourse of critique and egalitarian discussion, electronic spaces

> can encourage [students'] attempts to re-construct and re-think existing social structures and visions. If we can't eliminate the effect of racism, sexism, and classism in our traditional classrooms because of social inertia, we may be able to set aside smaller electronic spaces in which such problems can find expression and be debated.... [S]tudents can discover or evolve among themselves different patterns of power and linguistic exchange to facilitate these discussions, patterns which may run directly counter to those that have become habitual in our classrooms. (p. 867)

But where students in the classes described by Cooper and Selfe discussed issues such as Marcuse's (1964) *One-Dimensional Man* or the work of professional technical communicators, class discussion can also involve the ways in which the writers learn to use the technology itself (something that online conference writers frequently do, but in largely invisible or unappreciated "underlife" activities as defined by Brooke [1987] in traditional classrooms).

What a hypertextual structure and process can bring to this discussion is the ability to cross discursive boundaries in an attempt to articulate the discrete, largely isolated and invisible activities of using a functional document to learn a system with the intersubjective activities of discussion and group critique. This boundary crossing can be strengthened by the general blurring of genres and activities I have discussed in terms of rearticulating other forms of hypertext previously.

For the user of most current systems of functional hypertext, both writing and reading are inherently private affairs of information transferral. The writers of such technical hypertext are not normally considered authors of messages, but documentors or, at best, translators (Slack et al., 1993). Articulating hypertext to earlier conceptions of books as little machines enforces this view by relating the mechanical operations of hypertext and reading to the virtual machine of the computer. The information is always "right there," but it needs to be moved around in order for the machine to function effectively—moved, that is, from its location in one portion of the machine (storage) to another portion (the user, who is actually used as a part of the machine). Such a conception attempts to isolate each user from other users and to separate functional parts of the user's life from "nonfunctional" parts in order for the machine to operate without impediments. The ideology of mechanics and technology constructs users who recognize themselves by their "natural" place in the machine system—they are positioned as receptacles of information. Frequently, this positioning also limits workers' activities by removing the "temptation" for distraction (e.g., the clerks, secretaries, and shopkeepers in the automated workplaces studied by Hirschhorn, 1984; Shaiken, 1986; and Zuboff, 1988). In this way, elements of the user needed for the machine to function efficiently (fingers at the keyboard, eyes on the CRT or on material to be transcribed) are mobilized whereas extraneous elements are immobilized or conceptually removed or refigured (legs immobilized, social relationships removed, etc.).

But how does one mark a division between necessary activity and distraction? Such categories rely heavily on the idea that the social situations in which people work are amenable to mechanical description—and to some degree, they are (as evidenced by the at least relative success such management structures have). But the idea that such strategies work does not mean that they are ethical or even the most productive. Although the limitation of movement (cognitive or physical) may result in more easily predictable results for a company, such situations may be in themselves limiting by not opening up operations to new ways of thinking (a fact not lost on the new wave of posthierarchical management enthusiasts).

The issue here is also one of class: Upper level workers are much more likely to have access to articulations of hypertext that encourage "free-form" thinking and communication, that allow both reading and writing within the same textual space, and that encourage collaboration. Programs such as LOTUS NOTES are commonly used by engineers to track complicated, collaborative projects.[14] Lower level workers, however, experience an articulation of hypertext relying on automation and reproducibility: The same functional text must be able to provoke the same general response in every user that calls on it. Workers are expected to read the text passively, quickly, and in isolation; then, they are expected to act on the information they have received in order to get back to their real work. Whereas for management the "real work" is often something creative and social (in one way or another), for lower status workers the "real work" is frequently repetitive and solitary. (In fact, in offices where the online help system is not advanced to the point of automation, asking a colleague for help may represent crucial social interaction.)

Taylorism, however, always falls short of its goal of completely specifying and optimizing activities. Unlike easily reproducible mechanical parts of identical properties, people bring with them a broad range of abilities, attitudes, behaviors, and social relationships that resist integration into the machine. The idea of information space discussed in the previous section, for example, positions users as explorers rather than receptacles—this contra-

---

[14] I should not be too quick to grant sole agency to the program, however. We could also easily envision such programs applied in the context of "low-end" work as a way for managers to track responsibility and production rates. Context is crucial in the construction of power in technology use.

diction can be used as a way of subverting each of the forces alone. As online spaces and discourses become more integrated, users might, if encouraged, begin to realize the indeterminacy and interconnectivity of their own subjective and social positions as they traverse, collaborate, and construct these spaces. De Certeau's theorization of tactics and Hall's emphasis on struggles over articulation rely on the gaps and contradictions within and between discourses. Workers in technologically optimized situations invariably find ways to subvert control and optimization when it comes at the expense of personal responsibility, status, and fulfillment—two discourses that each struggle to position the subject in contradictory ways.

The discourse of efficiency itself is composed of many interconnected meanings, of which simple technical efficiency is only one (albeit a common and powerful one). Users of functional hypertexts or other computerized office technologies cannot be completely isolated from other workers or even other tasks. The automation of functional hypertext was intended to give workers time to complete work that is less open to automation. It is these other tasks that might provide a force counteracting that of simple efficiency; even in the most automated hypertexts, other texts and even completely different genres of text can exist in the margins, ready to be taken up by the reader in ways that resocialize the automated task.

The difficulty with acting positively within these margins is that localized resistance is not political, in Laclau and Mouffe's (1985) useful sense of the term as being involved with social reform rather than "making do" (p. 153), which seems more directed toward survival. Both are obviously important, but tactics that remain completely unconnected to strategies—something that can be taken as a form of cognitive mapping—remains easily appropriated by the late capitalist system. If students and workers are to succeed in changing sometimes oppressive social structures, they must learn to not only tactically appropriate or work outside the rules, but to make their work meaningful in the broader sense of collective acts of resistance and revision.

There are numerous ways, however, in which the individual text can be more fully connected to social and political discourses, both corporate and educational. In the face of the failure of Taylorism (commonly now seen as overmanagement), corporations have come to recognize the benefits of workgroups and other collaborative ventures, if for no other reason than the demonstrated increase in output and/or quality associated with collaboration (Drucker, 1988; Ede & Lunsford, 1990; Johnson-Lenz & Johnson-Lenz, 1992; Kanter, 1989; Selber, McGavin, Klein, & Johnson-Eilola, 1995; Spilka, 1989; Sullivan, 1991a). Although innovation has often been articulated by management as a way to increase efficiency and productivity (the inefficiency of some small tasks being sacrificed to increased overall efficiency), these organizations also hold the potential for a radically different articulation—one of community and resistance to control. Important studies of collaboration as a political activity of both consensus and dissensus (George, 1989; Trimbur, 1989; Trimbur & Braun, 1992) can help to productively complicate the notion that collaboration represents only a more technically efficient way of thinking.

Recalling that the initial visions of hypertext emphasized the transgression of boundaries between specializations and discrete texts, we can begin to articulate hypertext to a different relationship—one of explicitly social communication.[15] The boundaries to be crossed now are both physical and virtual, centered around individual computers. In a new, more explicitly social articulation—which is at this point more of a possibility than a reality—the mental location of the worker begins to move outward from the little machine of the online operational manual to a discussion among different workers. From a management standpoint, socializing even functional documents may appear beneficial (Selfe, Selber, McGavin, Johnson-Eilola, Brown, 1992; Selfe & Eilola, 1988), as users begin to help one another work more effectively (in effect, articulating "efficiency" to a related but slightly different set of forces). An online help text such as the HyperCard Help Stack can begin to contain not only functional operating instructions but also corrections, additions, interpretations, and questions added by other users—the simple technical efficiency articulation for functional hypertext can be weakened (without being completely removed); the texts can become forums for collective construction, appropriation, and critical resistance. Such possibilities increase with the rapidly growing use of local and wide area networks and the corresponding integration of e-mail-like capabilities into general productivity programs such as word processors. This collaboration can be as complex as the integration of a full-fledged messaging or conferencing system into the same environment as the functional documentation, or as simple as the provision for users to add electronic notes to existing functional documents (see Selfe et al., 1992). Netscape Corporation's Help system (Figure 6.18) begins this socialization by connecting the online help in the Netscape browser to Netscape's World Wide Web home page, which offers, among other things, pointers to tutorials on HTML specifications. Such systems, however, are still limited to areas in which accessing material across wide area networks seems "natural." Figure 6.19 illustrates a mockup of such a system in a traditionally "individual" program, giving users the ability to request help from and offer advice to other users in a hypothetical version of FreeHand's (1994) online

---

[15] The term *social communication* is, on the surface level, redundant in that all communication is social. Some of the more repressive aspects of the forms of hypertext I discuss here however, rely on the unspoken assumption that information is communicated from one isolated individual to another—that is, communication is only social in a very limited sense.

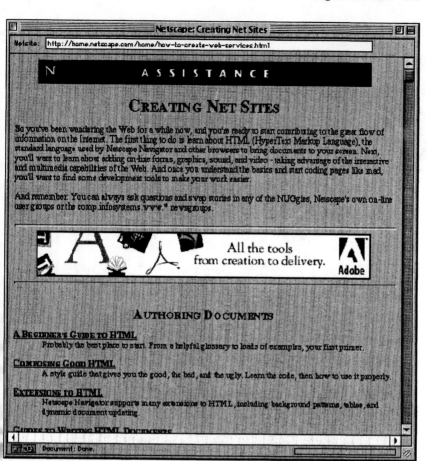

FIGURE 6.18. Online help for NETSCAPE NAVIGATOR, linking users to resources by other users on the World Wide Web.

help. The addition of options for users to call up tutorials while they are reading online help (common in many programs) also authorizes the idea of collaboration and discussion explicitly connected to reading reference or instructional material.

But the emphasis on control inherent in most articulations of online help views discussions as sloppy, chancy affairs (and so they are). In the ideology of most technical communication, questions should not be acknowledged (let alone encouraged) if they resist simple, easy answers. So tutorials in online help rely on canned (often inappropriate) responses about topics such as writing and design even though in many cases individual users could easily be connected to other users of the same program. Microsoft was quick to add

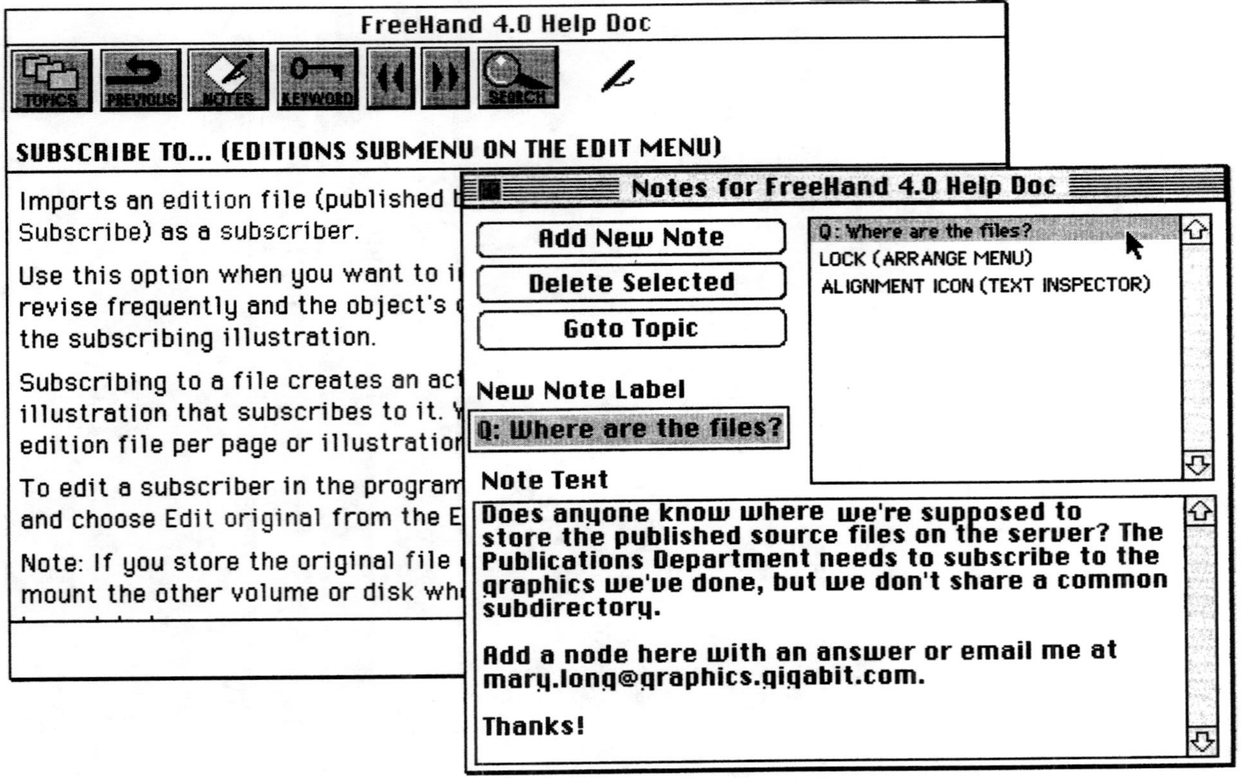

FreeHand 4.0 Help Doc

SUBSCRIBE TO... (EDITIONS SUBMENU ON THE EDIT MENU)

Imports an edition file (published t
Subscribe) as a subscriber.

Use this option when you want to i
revise frequently and the object's
the subscribing illustration.

Subscribing to a file creates an ac
illustration that subscribes to it. W
edition file per page or illustratio

To edit a subscriber in the progra
and choose Edit original from the E

Note: If you store the original file
mount the other volume or disk wh

Notes for FreeHand 4.0 Help Doc

Add New Note
Delete Selected
Goto Topic

New Note Label

Q: Where are the files?

Notes for FreeHand 4.0 Help Doc

Q: Where are the files?
LOCK (ARRANGE MENU)
ALIGNMENT ICON (TEXT INSPECTOR)

Note Text

Does anyone know where we're supposed to
store the published source files on the server? The
Publications Department needs to subscribe to the
graphics we've done, but we don't share a common
subdirectory.

Add a node here with an answer or email me at
mary.long@graphics.gigabit.com.

Thanks!

FIGURE 6.19. Adaptation of FREEHAND online help illustrating open help system showing potential for collaborative functional hypertext.

facilities for reading and writing HTML documents to *Word for Windows*, and to integrate *Microsoft Network* into *Windows 95*, but so far has avoided the idea of linking users to each other through these networks except through the "external" path of online users' groups.

In many cases, this type of writing does not automatically lead to social and political critique (the discussion in Selfe et al., 1992, e.g., might be situated as a way to make the use of online documents more technically efficient in specialized situations). This discussion must be explicitly encouraged by teachers because it will probably not occur spontaneously, at least in the beginning. Although spending class time critiquing the ideology of online help systems might seem to some teachers an unnecessary politicization of the writing class (see, e.g., Hairston, 1992; Ruszkiewicz, 1992), we must admit that the ways in which a writer is taught to operate within a virtual writing and research environment hold a great deal of influence over the ways in which that writer lives and thinks.

Obviously, this is not a simple, automatic solution. In the first place, visibly resistant acts in corporate sites can quickly result in either the removal of the collaborative provisions in the technology or even the monitoring of ostensibly private worker-to-worker conversations by management (see Grudin, 1990; Janangelo, 1991; Zuboff, 1988). The collaborative component, in itself, does not necessarily lead to critique. Discussing the results of one study of collaborative computer technologies by Huff, Sproull, and Kielser (1989), Sproull and Kiesler (1991) pointed out that the frequency of electronic mail use is sometimes highly coordinated to employee commitment for workers. In this study of city employees, researchers found that:

> [T]he more they used it, the more committed they were to their employer—measured by how willing they were to work beyond the requirements and hours of their jobs, how attached they felt to the city government, and how strongly they planned to continue working for the city. (p. 85)

So although employees may be offered the possibility for collaboration, it may end in benefiting primarily the employer. Employee commitment can be important for both company and worker, but both parties must carefully evaluate who is profiting, by what means, and to what ends. As Zuboff pointed out, computerization and automation often involve increased responsibilities for lower level workers without corresponding increases in pay or status. And in many cases, lower level workers are temporary, unable to remain in one context long enough to master functional skills.[16]

---

[16] Workers in these situations do not stay in the same situation long enough to master functional tasks. Because of the way in which productivity is defined and tracked, learning broader skills or learning ways to improve on those skills is impossible.

Most importantly in terms of functional hypertext, managers insistent on increasing efficiency will be unlikely to encourage users (or even allow them the possibility) to add "dysfunctional" material to an online help system. But as Shaiken (1986) illustrated in his ethnographies of machine-shop automation, once workers sense the possibility of increased power, management has a much more difficult time resisting the demand for change; workers also quickly develop and share ways of working around (and within) the system.

This critique of the technical sphere can also take place as a classroom activity. By beginning these activities in our classrooms—which still value efficiency but also frequently encourage resistance, or at least critique—we might provide this sense of possibility, giving students tactics to use in other environments: socialize, blur boundaries and genres, and politicize the production and circulation of knowledge and information. Although it is often difficult to remember in such highly technological settings, these discussions can be verbal, face-to-face class discussions that augment, parallel, and perhaps rearticulate technology use by students and teachers.[17] Exposing a contradiction by no means effects change of itself; but thinking about those contradictions can be part of an overall plan toward reformist social action. Even when hypertext is portrayed or used in mechanical ways, the hypertext user's subject position is not completely constituted as mechanical in the classical sense—the map dynamically generates relationships and exerts social forces while serving interests. Users may be sutured in a psychoanalytic and cinematic sense into a virtual reality, but the stitches can only ever be partial (Johnson-Eilola, 1993a; Ulmer, 1992). As Heath (1977–1978/1981) explained:

> [T]he "I" is a division that joins all the same, the stand-in is the lack in the structure but nevertheless, simultaneously, the possibility of a coherence, of the *filling in*. At the end of the suturing function is the ego, the *me*: "it's me!", the little linguistic scenario of the ego—that *I* am the only one who can say, can say in so far as I am *one*. (p. 87)

Every node in a hypertext can function both as a *presence* and a productive *absence*, assuming meaning not by what it holds but by its relationship to

---

[17] Technology frequently assumes such a strong hold over users that they forget about activities that might be better placed outside of the technology. Users of desktop publishing programs in the computer lab where I used to work frequently spent hours in "fatbits mode" ("fatbits" is the close-up view common to Macintosh graphics programs) nudging artwork back and forth one pixel at a time or struggling to draw a figure freehand with a mouse—it rarely occurs to many of the users to pick up a pen and draw the figure on a printout, or to use scissors and glue to paste something onto a page and then photocopy it to blend the two pieces together.

other nodes in the text and to the larger cultural, linguistic text. Viewers and readers are hailed here in the Althusserian sense of the term, positioned as subjects in the ideological act of *suture*. Although a suture is a way of covering over a gap it does not in itself impair the degree to which ideology operates effectively; Heath (1977–1979/1981) noted the ways in which making the technological frame of cinema partially explicit acts to heighten the viewer's desire for closure. It becomes necessary, as Hall noted in reworking Althusser's use of Lacan, that we insist on the role of human action in these activities, that we work to help make readers and viewers also producers and writers through the critical analyses of technology use—not that they attempt to merely abandon it, but look for ways to appropriate it. Just as we now encourage students to carefully analyze, for example, the ways in which they address their readers in terms of voice (active or passive) or tone (friendly, impersonal, etc.) in order to become better writers, we should also encourage our students to begin looking at the ways in which texts position readers.

Current discussions already provide some grounds for this type of work, which we can use to add force to the more political, social articulations of technology. In his technical writing textbook, Anderson (1991), for example, itemized the subject positions available to readers of technical reports: investor, decision maker, reviewer. Although Anderson does not explicitly make the connection between his advice that writers cause social action and his categories of readers (making those categories seem preexisting to the reader's construction of and by the text), we can begin helping our students map their "isolated" texts against broader social and political networks. The discourse of the machine never constructs only a tracing of reality, but is always (recursively) rewritten by other, potentially contradictory, discourses and maps. By coupling the intertextual, intersubjective tendencies of online text with the increased managerial interest in collaborative work, the articulation of hypertext to the mechanical conception of the little machine might conceivably be weakened.

THE CLASSROOM AND THE WORLD

Although a new civilization cannot be extracted out of nostalgia for the old, nostalgia is a significant symbolic articulation of interests that are ignored today. These interests point not backward but *forward to nature*, toward a *totality* consciously composed in terms of a wide range of human needs and concerns. This conception of totality as the goal of a process or mediation rather than as an organic presupposition suggests a reply to some common objections to radical arguments for social reconstruction.

We cannot recover what reification has lost by regressing to pretechnological conditions, to some prior unity irrelevant to the contemporary world. The solution is neither a return to the primitive, qualitative, and natural, nor a leap into a "new age" and a whole "new technology." On the contrary, the critical concept of totality aids in identifying the *contingency* of the existing technological system, the points at which it can be invested with new values and bent to new purposes. Those points are to be found where the fragmentation of the established systems maintain an alienated power.

—Andrew Feenberg (1991, p. 196)

The map articulates the world, but it is not the Borgesian simulacrum that Baudrillard (1983) rehearsed in *Simulations* "where the cartographers of the Empire draw up a map so detailed that it ends up exactly covering the territory" (p. 1). The benefits of cognitive mapping are in the consistent failure to fully cover the Empire. As Feenberg noted, the totality does not identify determinacy, it connotes contingency.

In order to appropriate and construct power in these virtual spaces, we must *inhabit* and *politicize* them (Selfe, 1992). We need to construct a spatial rhythm of affirmation and resistance:

> [B]order pedagogy points to the need to establish conditions of learning that define literacy inside rather than outside the categories of power as social and historical constructions, to engage texts in terms of their presences and absences, and to read texts oppositionally. This means teaching students to resist particular readings while simultaneously learning how to write their own narratives. (Giroux, 1992a, p. 176)

Although this inhabitation might sometimes assume the image of a late-capitalistic or postmodern dehistorization in favor of flat space (the large databases of the Chapter 4 finding shared elements with the FORKING PATHS of Chapter 5), the explicit move to also always politicize and socialize requires us to consistently construct and then problematize social histories. This is true not only in the usual sense of the historical as what has happened previously, but also, perhaps more importantly, in the sense of affirming and critiquing multiple, local, and utopian narratives, of writing the past, the present, and the future simultaneously at a both global and local scale: cognitive mapping. Borders and contact zones seem, at face value, to exist as nonpermeable contacts between two cultures. But, as both Giroux and Pratt developed the concept, they are also the intersections of multiple discourses in what are traditionally seen as homogeneous cultures. "[O]ne would want to avoid, in the case of a linguistics of contact," Pratt (1987) warned, "a utopian impulse to joyfully display all humanity in tolerant and harmonious contact across all lines of difference, or a dystopian impulse to bemoan a world homogenised by western media or run only by misunderstanding and bad intentions" (p. 61). Mapping does not merely ly represent what is already there but articulates new relations and deconstructs old; living in contact zones or crossing borders remakes those spaces. The subcultures frequently living in those spaces exist by appropriating and transforming master narratives (punk, reggae, etc.):

> Subcultures represent "noise" (as opposed to sound): interference in the orderly sequence which leads from real events and phenomena to their representation in the media.... an actual mechanism of semantic disorder: a kind of temporary blockage in the system of representation. (Hebdige, 1979, p. 90)

This blockage is not always (or even frequently) successful at disrupting the dominant order, as Hebdige (1979) warned; subculture "communicates through commodities even if the meanings attached to those commodities are purposefully distorted or overthrown" (p. 95). Similarly, our pedagogy will only infrequently succeed, and even when it does, those successes are partial and temporary.

Sustained resistance and social change require more (or perhaps less) than overthrowing a dominant order. Laclau and Mouffe (1985) offered a useful definition of "political" that may help us make hypertext an arena for social change. For Laclau and Mouffe, to work politically means to engage in "a type of action whose objective is the transformation of a social relation which constructs a subject in a relationship of subordination" (p. 153). Representing hypertext as an open, egalitarian forum—one that equalizes despite (or in ignorance of) existing social inequalities, may open up students to an even greater degree of oppression. If flattening the text does not map positive social space for student activities, we are denying discourses of resistance or affirmation to students. Assuming that they are consenting rather than coerced, flattened texts can encourage either totalization through an imposition of a unity of now-identical subjects (as in fascism) or, contrarily, through the disappearance of the political itself (as in ludic postmodernism; cf. Laclau & Mouffe, 1985, pp. 187–188). Even Eagleton (1991) was in relative agreement with Baudrillard (1983) on this despite Eagleton's explicit misgivings about Baudrillard's general tone:

> Capitalist society is a battleground of competing interests, and cloaks this incessant violence in the guise of disinterested ideas. Those postmodernists who quite properly see through this illusion often end up pitting against it a "radical" version of the very marketplace it conceals. In espousing a rich plurality of contending viewpoints and idioms as a good in itself, they turn an idealized version of the market-place reality against the monistic certitudes which help to hold it in place. It is then no wonder that their "radical" politics are a little strained and bleak, or at the worst (one thinks of Jean Baudrillard and Jean-François Lyotard) entirely vacuous. (Eagleton, 1991, p. 166)

For these reasons, if we allow hypertext to represent a mythical level playing field or free market, we would be merely neutralizing one aspect of unequal power relationships—the physical structure of the text(s)—while the other components of the dominant articulation orchestrate and coopt what has been fragmented (strip mining succeeds vein mining); the culture of the book overdetermines how we read the book. Deconstruction should involve more than a rupture of the technology; it should also help us redefine how we write and read and how we think about literacy and culture. If the choice for our students is either to accept the (more or less) authoritative voice of the book, or to accept no authority at all (the ideology of some forms of hypertext), then students (and, indeed, most of us) will find that we are subsumed back into the text, thinking of our own responses as parasitic to and/or composed from either the "original" text (as in geometrical intertexts) or as subsumed into the geographical father text. The flat text ruptures structure, but dominant social forces are quick and effective at recoding. Hypertext makes the subject complicitous in the continual deconstruction and reconstruction of self and text, but, given current orientations, hypertext is also "good at hiding the degree to which it constitutes the 'self-constituting subject'" (Slack, 1992). Capitalist society works through fostering the idea that subjects understand their own (multiple) positions as somehow absolutely autonomous and self-governing (Belsey, 1980; Eagleton, 1991; Gramsci, 1971; Mouffe, 1979)—the primary concept on which much theory and practice of hypertext is founded.

This vacuum is a consequence of our own attempts at deconstructing power systems, because we have created social situations that encourage this deconstruction. The force of a hypertext that deconstructs a canonized work also tends to deconstruct many other institutionally sanctioned ideas, such as the identity of the reader. The "death of the author" has not, as Barthes (1977a) prophesied, enabled merely the "birth of the reader," but also a potentially undifferentiated, flattened plane of complete equivalence (difference) that unsuccessfully attempts to separate itself from the world. Despite the frequent claims made for hypertext's ability to transform activities in ways that empower readers in one way or another, true democratic reform must take place as part of a larger discourse. As Laclau and Mouffe (1985) explained:

> "Serf", "slave", and so on, do not designate in themselves antagonistic positions; it is only in the terms of a different discursive formation, such as "the rights inherent to every human being", that the differential positivity of these categories can be subverted and the subordination constructed as oppression. (p. 154)

In order for hypertext to become the site for reconfiguring the social power of writers and readers in general, the technology and its range o specific uses must be articulated in terms of a broad social politics of text. Unfortunately, this has not occurred: Many specific uses of hypertext are constructed as apparent forums affording a mythical, individualistic reader control while in fact situating their users in a hegemonic arrangement to larger social forces such as workplace, marketplace, and literature. The numerous articulations of hypertexts are made to appear as if they grow naturally out of some neutral background: Hypertext is the better book, or the better library, or the book's response to deconstruction, or a shrine to Great Authors, or the denial of that unhip, modernist baggage called "I." Such ideas of hypertext are not "false" ideas in the vulgar Marxist sense of ideological blinders that can be removed in order to see the "true" hypertext. The articulations of hypertext as book, library, or deconstruction are very real. But currently too little attention is paid to the interests being served by those constructions; that they are real does not make them right.

The denial of political connections between the types of hypertext use discussed here acts as a method of hailing subjects in relation to specific functions. This fragmentation was of course recognized in various forms historically by hypertext theorists and practitioners: Bush's memex and Nelson's Xanadu both took as explicit goals the obliteration of disciplinary boundaries. But Bush's vision remained tied to the class of scientists as cultural elite and a text based on an unattainable symbolic logic. Nelson's vision, perhaps the most revolutionary, remains tied to the liberal idea that free access automatically results in democracy and that participation relies primarily on explicit ties between information and capital. This is the potential and the danger of spaces such as the World Wide Web: They encourage people to think of them as all-inclusive, a useful idea for humanists because we are still frequently locked out of such technological spaces (perpetuating the idea that print literacy is somehow nontechnological). But at the same time, it is also easy to forget that even if some of us do gain admittance to those spaces, many, many more do not. And even those of us who do have access find that institutional constraints of one type or another validate one type of use but not others. We need to simultaneously agree with the notion that the Web contains everything even as we contradictorily point out that it does not. The first position comes, contradictorily, to justify the second.

Access, as Lyotard (1984) noted, becomes a key issue but it can sometimes hide other, equally vital concerns. In a sense, hypertext most frequently enacts functional literacy (how to read) and cultural literacy (what to read) but normally falls short of critical literacy (social critique). Or, to take Scholes' (1985) distinctions in *Textual Power*, we have *reading* and *interpretation*, but rarely *criticism*: "In *reading* we produce *text within text*; in *interpreting* we produce *text upon text*; and in *criticizing* we produce *text against text*" (p. 24, italics in original).

In an idealized hypertext world, such as Nelson's docuverse, access to text would not necessarily do anything but replicate existing social structures: Without explicit and strong social forces disarticulating hypertext at least partially away from its print text parallels, the medium only repeats the uses of print.

Coming at the issue from another perspective, Brantlinger (1990) argued that cultural theorists must overcome academic boundaries:

> One aim of cultural studies should thus be the counterdisciplinary one of breaking down intellectual barriers to culture and forging new patterns of intellectual and political critique both within and outside the university. A renewed cultural criticism ought to look beyond the isolated text to the creation of oppositional forms that are simultaneously academic and public, literary and political. Culture in this context means both literature and politics, or the recognition that the two are inseparable. (p. 21)

As Massumi (1992) said, "[a] structure is defined by what escapes it" (p. 57). In hypertext discourses, what escapes is often the social milieu in which the technology is developed, used, and remade. Critical theories and pedagogies of hypertext must begin mapping these uses, users, and discourses against each other—the endless task of cognitively mapping local to global that is only ever struggle, never resolution. Precisely because hypertext occurs across these various discourses, we may be able to articulate our concerns about power and politics to those discourses. Hypertext represents opportunities, but we must be active in the construction of them by articulating the medium as a method for breaking down genres, of socializing and politicizing not only the production and reception of texts, but also the reproduction of meaning in text, as Jameson (1992) argued for postmodern theories of multinational capitalism in general.

This conception of hypertext writing and reading bears a not accidental resemblance to what Hall (1989) envisioned in a critical theory of communication:

> The transitions from the dominant to the critical paradigm can be marked briefly. They have to do with competing ways of conceiving of all the elements of a communicative practice. The conception of a particular content that can be isolated in behavioral terms and measured in terms of its isolated effects has to be replaced by a quite different conception, an understanding of each element's cultural aspect, its semiotic or discursive character; an awareness that the media function in and through the domain of meaning.... Meaning is polysemic in its intrinsic nature; it remains inextricably context bound. It is caught in and constituted by the struggle to "pre-fer" one among many meanings as the dominant. That dominance is not already inscribed in structures and events but is constructed through the continuous struggle over a specific type of practice—representational practices. These are the objects of

the study of communication. Those representational practices, codes, and systems alone allow meaning to be conferred upon the world. (p. 47)

A critical practice of hypertext then relies on at least two primary impulses: (a) the movement to politicize the production and consumption of cultural meanings, and (b) the socialization of all forms of hypertext in a recognition of and attempt to overcome the disciplinary and occupational boundaries that serve to rationalize hegemonic relationships. Simply put, hypertext writers and readers must consider their acts as political in the broadest sense, and cannot take for granted the assertion that functional hypertext, for example, is somehow less political than a postmodern literary hypertext, or that an enormous information space makes true an equation between equal access and equal rights.

As I argued earlier, compositionists occupy an important space in the construction of a critical literacy of hypertext: We teach a broad range of students what is considered a "basic skill," but that skill holds extremely broad implications. We are currently in a valuable middle ground, between high theory and everyday practice, but we need to continue to map these extremes against each other in hypertext writing and reading as a way of rearticulating technologies and societies. We need to make more explicitly political the work of deconstruction and postmodernism, also rethinking our relationships to the fundamental activities of writing, especially the ways in which we and our students learn our relationships to the technology. Technical communication and functional documentation are too frequently considered by composition (let alone literary theorists) as overly pragmatic and dull, whereas literary theory and cultural studies are often seen by technical communication teachers as esoteric and unrelated to day-to-day concerns. We must work to articulate the concerns of these subfields to each other by highlighting the productive relationships I have tried to make here.

Composition teachers and theorists have long been concerned with empowering students to become more capable language users. Our relations to technology, however, have often neglected the complexities of social power. Hypertext does not solve this problem; in many ways, it makes the issues even more complex. There is the potential for empowerment here, but it is certainly not automatic or guaranteed. If we do not adequately theorize the social and political contexts in which we write and are written by hypertext, we and our students allow ourselves to be positioned by existing forces. If we do not revise our pedagogies to take into account and construct new ways of writing and thinking—many computer-based composition classes still use word-processing programs as glorified typewriters—we will only perpetuate old ways of living in the world. In our theories and our pedagogies, we need to simultaneously politicize and socialize text, connect texts across disciplinary and occupational boundaries. Imperfect angels, nostalgic for a past that never was, we might instead learn to live as cyborgs. In mapping hypertext use we do not create a new world from nothing, but we do create discourses in which old worlds might be transformed.

References

Allen, Jo. (1992). Bridge over troubled waters? Connecting research in composition and business/technical communication. *Technical Communication Quarterly, 1*(4), 5–26.

Althusser, Louis. (1970). Contradiction and overdetermination: Notes for an investigation. In B. Brewster (Trans.), *For Marx* (pp. 88–128). New York: Vintage.

Althusser, Louis. (1971). Ideology and ideological state apparatuses (Notes towards an investigation). In B. Brewster (Trans.), *Lenin and philosophy and other essays* (pp. 127–186). New York: Monthly Review Press.

Amato, Joe. (1991). [Review of the book *Writing space.*] *Computers and Composition, 9*(1), 111–118.

Amato, Joe. (1992). Science-literature inquiry as pedagogical practice: Technical writing, hypertext, and a few theories. *Computers and Composition, 9*(2), 41–70.

Anderson, Paul V. (1991). *Technical writing: A reader-centered approach* (2nd ed.). Fort Worth TX: Harcourt Brace Jovanovich.

Anzaldúa, Gloria. (1987). *Borderlands / La frontera: The new mestiza*. San Francisco: Aunt Lute Books.

Aronowitz, Stanley & Giroux, Henry A. (1985). *Education under siege: The conservative, liberal and radical debate over schooling*. South Hadley, MA: Bergin & Garvey.

Bakhtin, M.M. (1981). *The dialogic imagination* (Michael Holquist, Ed., & Caryl Emerson & Michael Holquist, Trans.). Austin: University of Texas Press.

Barnett, George A. & Hughes, Carol. (1985). Communication theory and technical communication. In Michael G. Moran & Debra Journet (Eds.), *Research in technical communication: A bibliographic sourcebook* (pp. 39–83). Westport, CT: Greenwood.

Barthes, Roland. (1977a). The death of the author. In S. Heath (Ed. & Trans.), *Image-music-text* (pp. 142–148). New York: Hill & Wang.

Barthes, Roland. (1977b). From work to text. In S. Heath (Ed. & Trans.), *Image-music-text* (pp. 155–164). New York: Hill & Wang.

Bartholomae, David. (1985). Inventing the university. In M. Rose (Ed.), *When a writer can't write* (pp. 134–165). New York: Guilford.

Baudrillard, Jean. (1983). *Simulations* (Paul Foss, Paul Patton, & Philip Beitchman, Trans.). New York: Semiotext(e).

Baudrillard, Jean. (1988a). For a critique of the political economy of the sign. In M. Poster (Ed.), *Jean Baudrillard: Selected writings* (pp. 57–97). Stanford, CA: Stanford University Press.

Baudrillard, Jean. (1988b). *Xerox and infinity* (Agitac, Trans.). Paris: Touchepas.

Baudrillard, Jean. (1990). *Fatal strategies* (P. Beitchman & W.G.J. Niesluchowski, Trans.; J. Fleming, Ed.). New York: Semiotext(e).

Bazerman, Charles. (1988). *Shaping written knowledge: The genre and activity of the experimental article in science.* Madison: University of Wisconsin Press.

Beck, J. Robert & Spicer, Donald Z. (1988, February). Hypermedia in academia. *Academic Computing*, 22–25, 49–50.

Beeman, William O., Anderson, Kenneth T., Bader, Gail, Larkin, James, McClard, Anne P., McQuillan, P., & Shields, Mark. (1987). Hypertext and pluralism: From lineal to non-lineal thinking. *Hypertext '87 Papers*, (pp. 57–88). New York: Association for Computing Machinery.

Begoray, John A. (1990). An introduction to hypermedia issues, systems, and applications areas. *International Journal of Man–Machine Studies, 33*, 121–147.

Belsey, Catherine. (1980). *Critical practice.* London: Methuen.

Benedikt, Michael. (Ed.). (1992). *Cyberspace: First steps.* Cambridge, MA: MIT Press.

Berkenkotter, Carol. (1991). Paradigm debates, turf wars, and the conduct of sociocognitive inquiry in composition. *College Composition and Communication, 42*, 151–169.

Berkenkotter, Carol, Huckin, Thomas N. & Ackerman, John. (1988). Conventions, conversations, and the writer: Case study of a student in a rhetoric Ph.D. program. *Research in the Teaching of English, 50*, 9–44.

Berlin, James A. (1984). *Writing instruction in nineteenth-century colleges.* Carbondale: Southern Illinois University Press.

Berlin, James A. (1988). Rhetoric and ideology in the writing class. *College English, 50*, 477–494.

Berlin, James A. (1992). Poststructuralism, cultural studies, and the composition classroom: Postmodern theory in practice. *Rhetoric Review, 11*(1), 16–33.

Bialostosky, Don H. (1991). Liberal education, writing, and the dialogic self. In P. Harkin & J. Schilb (Eds.), *Contending with words: Composition and rhetoric in a postmodern age* (pp. 11–22). New York: Modern Language Association.

Bizzell, Patricia. (1990). Beyond anti-foundationalism to rhetorical authority Problems defining "cultural literacy." *College English, 52*, 661–675.

Bolter, Jay D. (1991a). WRITING SPACE: THE COMPUTER, HYPERTEXT, AND THE HISTORY OF WRITING [computer software]. Hillsdale, NJ: Erlbaum.

Bolter, Jay D. (1991b). *Writing space: The computer, hypertext, and the history of writing.* Hillsdale, NJ: Erlbaum.

Bolter, Jay D. (1993). Alone and together in the electronic bazaar. *Computers and Composition, 10*(2), 5–18.

Borges, Jorge L. (1962). The garden of forking paths. In Donald A. Yates & James E. Inby (Eds.), *Labyrinths: Selected stories and other writings* (Donald A. Yates Trans.). New York: New Directions.

Brantlinger, Patrick. (1990). *Crusoe's footprints: Cultural studies in Britain and America.* New York: Routledge.

Braverman, Harry. (1974). *Labor and monopoly capital: The degradation of work in the twentieth century.* New York: Monthly Review Press.

Brooke, Robert. (1987). Underlife and writing instruction. *College Composition and Communication, 38*, 141–153.

Bruffee, Kenneth A. (1973). Collaborative learning: Some practical methods. *College English, 34,* 634–643.

Burton, Richard. (1961). *The lake regions of Central Africa: A picture of exploration* (Vol. II). New York: Horizon Press. (Original work published 1860)

Bush, Vannevar. (1987). As we may think. In T.H. Nelson (Ed.), *Literary machines* (87.1 Ed., pp. 1/39-1/54). (Original work published 1945)

Capossela, Toni-Lee. (1991). Students as sociolinguists: Getting real research from freshman writers. *College Composition and Communication, 42,* 75–79.

Charney, Davida. (1987). Comprehending non-linear text: The role of discourse cues and reading strategies. *Hypertext '87 papers* (pp. 109–20). New York: Association for Computing Machinery.

Charney, Davida. (1994). The impact of hypertext on the processes of reading and writing. In Cynthia L. Selfe & Susan Hilligoss (Eds.), *Literacy and computers: The complications of teaching and learning with technology* (pp. 238–263). New York: Modern Language Association.

A Chicago Expanded Book [Computer program manual]. (1993). [Printed promotional instruction brochure accompanying Lanham, Richard. (1994). *The electronic word: Democracy, technology, and the arts* [Computer program]. Chicago: University of Chicago Press.

Clifford, John. (1991). The subject in discourse. In Patricia Harkin & John Schilb (Eds.), *Contending with words: Composition and rhetoric in a postmodern age* (pp. 38–51). New York: Modern Language Association.

Cohen, Raines. (1993, February 1). HYPERCARD goes home, to link with AppleScript. *MacWEEK, 7*(5), pp. 1, 111.

Conklin, Jeff. (1986). Hypertext: Introduction and survey. *IEEE Computer, 20*(9), 18–41.

Conklin, Jeff, & Begeman, Michael. (1987). gIBIS: A hypertext tool for team design deliberation. *Hypertext '87 papers* (pp. 247–251). New York: Association for Computing Machinery.

Connor, Steven. (1989). *Postmodernist culture: An introduction to theories of the contemporary.* Cambridge, MA: Basil Blackwell.

Connors, Robert J. (1982). The rise of technical writing instruction in America. *Journal of Technical Writing and Communication, 12,* 329–352.

Cook, William W. (1993). Writing in the spaces left. *College Composition and Communication, 44,* 9–25.

Cooper, Marilyn M. (1989). Why are we talking about discourse communities? Or, foundationalism rears its ugly head once more. In Marilyn M. Cooper & Holzman, Michael (Eds.), *Writing as social action* (pp. 202–220). Portsmouth, NH: Boynton/Cook.

Cooper, Marilyn M., & Selfe, Cynthia L. (1990). Computer conferences and learning: Authority, resistance, and internally persuasive discourse. *College English, 52,* 847–869.

Coover, Robert. (1992, June 21). The end of books. *The New York Times Book Review,* pp. 1, 23–25.

Corbett, Edward P.J. (1987). *Classical rhetoric for the modern student* (2nd ed.). New York: Oxford University Press.

Crane, Gregory. (1991). Aristotle's library: Memex as vision and hypertext as reality. In James M. Nyce & Paul Kahn (Eds.), *From memex to hypertext: Vannevar Bush and the mind machine* (pp. 339–352). Boston: Academic Press.

Crary, Karl. (1993). KARL'S FORKING RESPONSE [computer software]. Dallas: University of Texas, Dallas.

DAEDALUS INTERCHANGE [computer software]. (1992). Austin, TX: The Daedalus Group.

Dasenbrock, Reed W. (1988). Becoming aware of the myth of presence. *Journal of Advanced Composition, 8,* 1–11.

de Certeau, Michel. (1984). *The practice of everyday life* (S. Randall, Trans.). Berkeley: University of California Press.

Delany, Paul, & Landow, George P. (Eds.). (1990). *Hypermedia and literary studies.* Cambridge, MA: MIT Press.

Deleuze, Gilles, & Guattari, Félix. (1987). *A thousand plateaus: Capitalism and schizophrenia* (Brian Massumi, Trans.). Minneapolis: University of Minnesota Press.

Demac, Donna A. (1988). Hearts and minds revisited: The information politics of the Reagan administration. In Vincent Mosco & Janet Wasko (Eds.), *The political economy of information* (pp. 125–145). Madison: University of Wisconsin Press.

Derrida, Jacques. (1976). *Of grammatology* (Guyatri Spivak, Trans.). Baltimore: Johns Hopkins University Press. (Original work published 1967)

Derrida, Jacques. (1977). Signature event context. *Glyph, 1,* 172–197.

Derrida, Jacques. (1978). Limited inc: a b c... *Glyph, 2,* 162–254.

Dobrin, David N. (1983). What's technical about technical writing? In Paul V. Anderson, R. John Brockman, & Carolyn R. Miller (Eds.), *New essays in technical and scientific communication: Vol. 2. Research, theory, practice* (pp. 227–250). Farmingdale, NY: Baywood.

Dobrin, David N. (1994). Hoopertext. In Cynthia L. Selfe & Susan Hilligoss (Eds.), *Literacy and computers: The complications of teaching and learning with technology* (pp. 305–315). New York: Modern Language Association.

Dombrowski, Paul M. (1992). Challenger and the social contingency of meaning: Two lessons for the technical communication classroom. *Technical Communication Quarterly, 1*(3), 73–86.

Douglas, Jane Y. (1994). "How do I stop this thing?": Closure and indeterminacy in interactive narratives. In George P. Landow (Ed.), *Hyper/text/theory* (pp. 159–188). Baltimore: Johns Hopkins University Press.

Downing, David B., Harkin, Patricia, & Sosnoski, James J. (1994). Configurations of lore: The changing relations of theory, research, and pedagogy. In D.B Downing (Ed.), *Changing classroom practices; Resources for literary and cultural studies* (pp. 3–34). Urbana, IL: National Council of Teachers of English.

Drucker, Peter F. (1988, January–February). The coming of the new organization. *Harvard Business Review,* 45–53.

Eagleton, Terry. (1991). *Ideology: An introduction.* London: Verso.

Ebert, Teresa L. (1991). The "difference" of postmodern feminism. *College English 53,* 886–904.

Ede, Lisa & Lunsford, Andrea. (1990). *Singular texts/plural authors: Perspectives on collaborative writing.* Carbondale: Southern Illinois University Press.

The 8th annual editors' choice awards. (1993, March). *MacUser,* pp. 91–106.

Eisenstein, Elizabeth L. (1979). *The printing press as an agent of change: Communications and cultural transformations in early-modern Europe* (2 vols.). Cambridge, UK: Cambridge University Press.

Eldred, Janet & Fortune, Ron. (1992). Exploring the implications of metaphors for computer networks and hypermedia. In Gail E. Hawisher & Paul LeBlanc (Eds.), *Re-imagining computers and composition: Teaching and research in the virtual age* (pp. 58–74). Portsmouth, NH: Boynton/Cook.

Ellsworth, Elizabeth. (1989, August). Why doesn't this feel empowering? Working through the repressive myths of critical pedagogy. *Harvard Educational Review, 59,* 297–324.

Ellul, Jacques. (1964). *The technological society* (John Wilkinson, Trans.). New York: Vintage.

English 34 Class. (1991). CONTEXT34 [computer software]. Providence, RI: Brown University.

Faigley, Lester. (1989). Judging writing, judging selves. *College Composition and Communication, 40,* 395–413.

Faigley, Lester. (1992). *Fragments of rationality: Postmodernity and the subject of composition.* Pittsburgh: University of Pittsburgh Press.

Feenberg, Andrew. (1991). *Critical theory of technology.* New York: Oxford University Press.

Fischer, Claude S. (1991). "Touch someone": The telephone industry discovers sociability. In Marcel C. LaFollette & Jeffrey K. Stine (Eds.), *Technology and choice* (pp. 187–116). Chicago: University of Chicago Press.

Fiske, John. (1989). Representations of power: Paradigms and politics. In Lawrence Grossberg, Brenda Dervin, Barbara J. O'Keefe, & Ellen Wartala (Eds.), *Rethinking communication: Vol. 1 Paradigm issues,* (pp. 169–172). Newbury Park, CA: Sage.

Fiske, John. (1992). Cultural studies and the culture of everyday life. In Lawrence Grossberg, Cary Nelson, & Paula Treichler (Eds.), *Cultural studies* (pp. 154–164). New York: Routledge.

Flower, Linda. (1985). *Problem-solving strategies in writing* (2nd ed.). San Diego, CA: Harcourt Brace Jovanovich.

Flower, Linda. (1989). Cognition, context, and theory building. *College Composition and Communication, 40,* 282–311.

Flower, Linda, Hayes, John R., & Swarts, Heidi. (1983). Revising functional documents: The scenario principle. In Paul V. Anderson, R. John Brockman, & Carolyn R. Miller (Eds.), *New essays in technical and scientific communication: Vol. 2. Research, theory, practice* (pp. 41–58). Farmingdale, NY: Baywood.

Forman, Janis. (1990). Leadership dynamics of computer-supported writing groups. *Computers and Composition, 7*(2), 35–46.

Foucault, Michel. (1977). What is an author? In Donald F. Bouchard (Ed.), *Language, counter-memory, practice: Selected essays and interviews* (Donald F. Bouchard & Sherry Simon, Trans.; pp. 113–138). Ithaca, NY: Cornell University Press.

Foucault, Michel. (1979). *Discipline and punish: The birth of the prison* (A. Sheridan, Trans.). New York: Random House.

Foucault, Michel. (1986, Spring). Of other spaces (Jay Miskowiec, Trans.). *Diacritics,*
16, 22–27. (Original work published 1984)

Fowler, H. Ramsey, Aaron, Jane E., & Limburg, Kay. (1992). *The Little, Brown hand-*
book (3rd ed.). Boston: HarperCollins.

FREEHAND. (1994). [Computer program, v. 4.0] Seattle, WA: Aldus.

Freire, Paulo. (1990). *Pedagogy of the oppressed* (Myra B. Ramos, Trans.). New York:
Continuum.

Frisse, Mark E. (1987). Searching for information in a hypertext medical handbook.
Hypertext '87 papers (pp. 57–66). New York: Association for Computing
Machinery.

Gage, John T. (1987). *The shape of reason: Argumentative writing in college.* New
York: Macmillan.

George, Diana. (1989, Spring–Summer). The politics of social construction and the
teaching of writing. *Journal of Teaching Writing, 8,* 1–10.

George, E. Laurie. (1990). Taking women professors seriously: Female authority in
the computerized classroom. *Computers and Composition, 7* [special issue],
46–52.

Gibson, William. (1984). *Neuromancer.* New York: Ace/Berkley.

Giroux, Henry A. (1983). *Theory and resistance in education: A pedagogy for the*
opposition. South Hadley, MA: Bergin & Garvey.

Giroux, Henry A. (1991). Modernism, postmodernism, and feminism: Rethinking the
boundaries of educational discourse. In Henry A. Giroux (Ed.),
Postmodernism, feminism, and cultural politics: Redrawing educational
boundaries (pp. 1–59). Albany: State University of New York Press.

Giroux, Henry. (1992a). *Border crossings: Cultural workers and the politics of edu-*
cation. New York: Routledge.

Giroux, Henry A. (1992b). Resisting difference: Cultural studies and the discourse of
critical pedagogy. In Lawrence Grossberg, Cary Nelson, & Paula Treichler
(Eds.), *Cultural studies* (pp. 199–212). New York: Routledge.

Gramsci, Antonio. (1971). *Selections from the prison notebooks of Antonio Gramsci*
(Q. Hoare & G.N. Smith, Eds. & Trans.). New York: International Publishers.

Grossberg, Lawrence. (1989). The formations of cultural studies: An American in
Birmingham. *Strategies, 2,* 114–48.

Grossberg, Lawrence & Slack, Jennifer D. (1985). An introduction to Stuart Hall's
essay [Introduction to Hall, 1985]. *Critical Studies in Mass Communication,*
2, 87–90.

Grudin, Jonathan. (1990). Groupware and cooperative work: Problems and
prospects. In Brenda Laurel (Ed.), *The art of human–computer interface*
design (pp. 171–186). Reading, MA: Addison-Wesley.

Guyer, Carolyn. (1992, December). *Buzz-daze jazz and the quotidian stream.* Paper
presented at the Annual Conference of the Modern Language Association,
New York.

Guyer, Carolyn & Petry, Martha. (1991). Notes for IZME PASS exposé. *Writing on the*
Edge, 2(2), 82–89.

Hairston, Maxine. (1990). Comment. *College English, 52,* 694–696.

Hairston, Maxine. (1992). Diversity, ideology, and the teaching of writing. *College*
Composition and Communication, 43, 179–193.

Hairston, Maxine. & Ruszkiewicz, John J. (1988). *The Scott, Foresman handbook for writers*. Glenview, IL: Scott, Foresman.

Halasz, Frank G. (1988). Reflections on NOTECARDS: Seven issues for the next generation of hypermedia systems. *Communications of the ACM, 31*, 836–852.

Hall, Stuart. (1983). The problem of ideology: Marxism without guarantees. In Betty Matthews (Ed.), *Marx 100 years on* (pp. 57–85). London: Lawrence & Wishart.

Hall, Stuart. (1985, June). Signification, representation, ideology: Althusser and the post-structuralist debates. *Critical Studies in Mass Communication, 2*, 91–114.

Hall, Stuart. (1989). Ideology and communication theory. In Lawrence Grossberg, Brenda Dervin, Barbara J. O'Keefe, & Ellen Wartala (Eds.), *Rethinking communication: Vol. 1. Paradigm issues* (pp. 40–52). Newbury Park, CA: Sage.

Halpern, Jeanne W., & Liggett, Sarah. (1984). *Computers and composing*. Carbondale: Southern Illinois University Press.

Hamper, Ben. (1992). *Rivethead: Tales from the assembly line*. New York: Warner Books.

Haraway, Donna. (1985, March–April). A manifesto for cyborgs: Science, technology, and socialist feminism in the 1980s. *Socialist Review, 80*, 65–105.

Hardman, Lynda. (1989). Evaluating the usability of the Glasgow Online hypertext. *Hypermedia, 1*(1), 34–63.

Harkin, Patricia & Schilb, John. (Eds.). (1991). *Contending with words: Composition and rhetoric in a postmodern age*. New York: Modern Language Association.

Harkin, Patricia & Sosnoski, James. (1992). The case for hyper-gradesheets: A modest proposal. *College English, 54*, 22–30.

Harpold, Terrence. (1990). Threnody: Psychoanalytic digressions on the subject of hypertexts. In Paul Delany & George P. Landow (Eds.), *Hypermedia and literary studies* (pp. 171–184). Cambridge, MA: MIT Press.

Hawisher, Gail E. (1992). Electronic meetings of the minds: Research, electronic conferences, and composition studies. In Gail E. Hawisher & Paul LeBlanc (Eds.), *Re-imagining computers and composition: Teaching and research in the virtual age* (pp. 81–101). Portsmouth, NH: Boynton/Cook.

Hawisher, Gail E., & Selfe, Cynthia L. (1991). The rhetoric of technology and the electronic writing class. *College Composition and Communication, 42*(1), 55–65.

Hayes, John R. & Flower, Linda S. (1980). Identifying the organization of writing processes. In Lee W. Gregg & Erwin R. Steinberg (Eds.), *Cognitive processes in writing* (pp. 3–30). Hillsdale, NJ: Erlbaum.

Heath, Stephen. (1981). On suture. In Stephen. Heath, *Questions of cinema* (pp. 76–112). Bloomington: Indiana University Press. (Original work published 1977–1978)

Hebdige, Dick. (1979). *Subculture: The meaning of style*. London: Routledge.

Hebdige, Dick. (1988). *Hiding in the light: On images and things*. London: Comedia/Routledge.

Heim, Michael. (1987). *Electric language: A philosophical study of word processing*. New Haven, CT: Yale University Press.

Herndl, Carl G., Fennell, Barbara A., & Miller, Carolyn R. (1991). Understanding failures in organizational discourse: The accident at

Three Mile Island and the Shuttle Challenger Disaster. In Charles Bazerman & James Paradis (Eds.), *Textual dynamics of the professions: Historical and contemporary studies of writing in professional communities* (pp. 279–305). Madison: University of Wisconsin Press.

Hirsch, E.D., Jr. (1987). *Cultural literacy: What every American needs to know.* Boston: Houghton Mifflin.

Hirschhorn, Larry. (1984). *Beyond mechanization: Work and technology in a postindustrial age.* Cambridge, MA: MIT Press.

Hocks, Mary & Clark, Rex. (1992). WRITING ABOUT LITERATURE [computer software]. Urbana: University of Illinois.

Horn, Robert E. (1990). *Mapping hypertext: The analysis, organization, and display of knowledge for the next generation of on-line text and graphics.* Waltham, MA: The Lexington Institute.

Horton, William K. (1990). *Designing and writing online documentation: From help files to hypertext.* New York: Wiley.

Horton, William K. (1991). Is hypertext the best way to document your product? An assay for designers. *Technical Communication, 38,* 20–35.

Huff, C., Sproull, L., & Kiesler, S. (1989). Computer communication and organizational commitment: Tracing the relation in a city government. *Journal of Applied Psychology, 19,* 1371–1391.

HYPERCARD. (1987). [computer software, version 1.25]. Cupertino, CA: Apple Computer.

Irish, Peggy M., & Trigg, Randall H. (1989). Supporting collaboration in hypermedia: Issues and experiences. In Edward Barrett (Ed.), *The society of text: Hypertext, hypermedia, and the social construction of information.* (pp. 93–106). Cambridge, MA: MIT Press.

Jameson, Frederic. (1991). *Postmodernism: Or, the cultural logic of late capitalism.* Durham, NC: Duke University Press.

Jameson, Frederic. (1992). *The geopolitical aesthetic: Cinema and space in the world system.* Bloomington: Indiana University Press.

Janangelo, Joseph. (1991). Technopower and technoppression. *Computers and Composition, 9*(1), 47–64.

Johnson-Eilola, Johndan. (1991a, March). *"Click here... no, here... maybe here":* Anarchy and hypertext. Paper presented at the Conference on College Composition and Communication, Boston. (ERIC ED 331 060.)

Johnson-Eilola, Johndan. (1991b). "Trying to see the garden": Interdisciplinary perspectives on hypertext in composition instruction. *Writing on the Edge, 2*(2), 92–111.

Johnson-Eilola, Johndan. (1992). Structure and text: *Writing space* and STORYSPACE. *Computers and Composition, 9*(2), 95–129.

Johnson-Eilola, Johndan. (1993a). Control and the cyborg: Writing and being written in hypertext. *Journal of Advanced Composition, 13,* 381–400.

Johnson-Eilola, Johndan. (1993b). The politics of post-hierarchical organizations: Questions for technical communication educators. In Dan G. Riordan (Ed.), *Proceedings of the 20th Annual Conference of the Council for Programs in Technical and Scientific Communication* (pp. 83–86). Menomonie, WI: Council of Programs in Technical and Scientific Communication.

Johnson-Eilola, Johndan. (1994a, March). *Accumulation, circulation, associa-tion: Economies of text in online research spaces.* Paper presented at the 1994 Conference on College Composition and Communication, Nashville, TN.

Johnson-Eilola, Johndan. (1994b). An overview of reading and writing in hypertext: Vertigo and euphoria. In Cynthia L. Selfe & Susan Hilligoss (Eds.), *Literacy and computers: The complications of teaching and learning with technology* (pp.195–219). New York: Modern Language Association.

Johnson-Eilola, Johndan. & Selber, Stuart A. (1995, May). *Policing ourselves.* Paper presented at the 1995 Computers and Writing Conference, El Paso, TX.

Johnson-Eilola, Johndan. & Selber, Stuart A. (in press). Automating and informat-ing hypertexts: Exploring relations between corporate structures and com-puter technologies. In Patricia A. Sullivan & Jennie Dautermann (Eds.), *Electronic literacies in the workplace: Technologies of writing.* Urbana, IL: National Council of Teachers of English.

Johnson-Lenz, Peter & Johnson-Lenz, Trudy. (1992). Postmechanistic groupware primitives: Rhythms, boundaries, and containers. In Saul Greenburg (Ed.), *Computer-supported cooperative work and groupware* (pp. 271–293). San Diego, CA: Harcourt Brace Jovanovich.

Joyce, Michael. (1988, November). Siren shapes: Exploratory and constructive hypertexts. *Academic Computing,* 10–14, 37–42.

Joyce, Michael. (1990). AFTERNOON, A STORY [computer software]. Cambridge, MA: Eastgate Software.

Joyce, Michael. (1992, December). *Hypertextual rhythms (The momentary advantage of our awkwardness).* Paper presented at the annual meeting of the Modern Language Association, New York.

Joyce, Michael. (1995). *Of two minds: Hypertext pedagogy and poetics.* Ann Arbor: University of Michigan Press.

Kanter, Rosabeth M. (1989, November–December). The new managerial work. *Harvard Business Review,* 85–92.

Kaplan, Nancy. (1991). Ideology, technology, and the future of writing instruction. In Gail E. Hawisher & Cynthia L. Selfe (Eds.), *Evolving perspectives on comput-ers and composition studies: Questions for the 1990s* (pp. 11–42). Urbana, IL and Houghton, MI: The National Council of Teachers of English and Computers and Composition Press.

Kaplan, Nancy & Moulthrop, Stuart. (1991). Something to imagine: Literature, com-position and interactive fiction. *Computers and Composition,* 9(1), 7–24.

Katz, Stephen B. (1992). The ethic of expediency: Classical rhetoric, technology, and the holocaust. *College English,* 54, 255–275.

Kaufer, David & Neuwirth, Chris. (1992). [Review of the book *Writing space.*] *College Composition and Communication,* 43, 259–261.

Killingsworth, M. Jimmie. (1993). Product and process, literacy and orality: An essay on composition and culture. *College Composition and Communication,* 44 , 26–39.

Knoblauch, C.H. (1990). Literacy and the politics of education. In Andrea Lunsford, Helene Moglen, & James Slevin (Eds.), *The right to literacy* (pp. 74–80) New York: Modern Language Association.

Laclau, Erenesto & Mouffe, Chantal. (1985). *Hegemony and socialist strategy: Towards a radical democratic politics*. London: Verso.

Lai, Patrick & Manber, Udi. (1991). Flying through hypertext. *Hypertext '91 proceedings* (pp. 123–132). New York: Association for Computing Machinery.

Lakoff, George & Johnson, Mark. (1980). *Metaphors we live by*. Chicago: University of Chicago Press.

Landow, George P. (1987). Relationally encoded links and the rhetoric of hypertext. *Hypertext '87 papers* (pp. 331–343). New York: Associaton for Computing Machinery.

Landow, George. (1990). THE DICKENS WEB [computer software]. Cambridge, MA: Eastgate Systems.

Landow, George P. (1992a). Bootstrapping hypertext: Student-created documents, INTERMEDIA, and the social construction of knowledge. In Edward Barrett (Ed.), *Sociomedia* (pp. 195–217). Cambridge, MA: MIT Press.

Landow, George. (1992b). Hypertext, metatext, and the electric canon. In Myron Tuman (Ed.), *Literacy online: The promise (and peril) of reading and writing with computers* (pp. 67–94). Pittsburgh, PA: University of Pittsburgh Press.

Landow, George P. (1992c). *Hypertext: The convergence of contemporary critical theory and technology*. Baltimore: Johns Hopkins University Press.

Landow, George P., & Delany, Paul. (1990). Hypertext, hypermedia, and literary studies: The state of the art. In Paul Delany & George P. Landow (Eds.), *Hypermedia and literary studies* (pp. 3–50). Cambridge, MA: MIT Press.

Landow, George & Lanestedt, Jon. (1992). THE IN MEMORIAM WEB (version 1.1 [1.iv]) [computer software]. Cambridge, MA: Eastgate.

Lanham, Richard. (1993). *The electronic word: Democracy, technology, and the arts*. Chicago: University of Chicago Press.

Lash, Scott & Urry, John. (1987). *The end of organized capitalism*. Green Bay: University of Wisconsin Press.

Lazere, Donald. (1992). Back to basics: A force for oppression or liberation? *College English, 54*, 7–21.

Lefebvre, Henri. (1991). *The production of space* (D. Nicholson-Smith, Trans.). Oxford, UK: Blackwell.

Love, James & Nader, Ralph. (1993, August 24). SEC's EDGAR information system: You paid for it, but don't expect to use it. *MacWEEK*, p. 18.

Lynn, Steven. (1990). A passage into critical theory. *College English, 52*, 258–271.

Lyotard, Jean-François. (1984). *The postmodern condition: A report on knowledge* (Geoff Bennington & Brian Massumi, Trans.). Minneapolis: University of Minnesota Press.

Lyotard, Jean-François. (1988). *The differend: Phrases in dispute* (George Van Den Abbelle, Trans.). Minneapolis: University of Minnesota Press.

Lyotard, Jean-François & Thébaud, Jean-Lope. (1985). *Just gaming* (Wlad Godzich, Trans.). Minneapolis: University of Minnesota Press.

Malcolm, Kathryn C., Poltrock, Steven E., & Schuler, Douglas. (1991). Industrial strength hypermedia: Requirements for a large engineering enterprise. *Hypertext '91 proceedings* (pp. 13–24). New York: Association for Computing Machinery.

Mannheim, Karl. (1936). *Ideology and utopia*. (Louis Wirth & Edward Shils, Trans.). New York: Harvest/HBJ.

Marchionini, Gary. (1988, November). Hypermedia and learning: Freedom and chaos. *Educational Technology,* 8–12.

Marchionini, Gary & Shneiderman, Ben. (1988, January). Finding facts vs. browsing knowledge in hypertext systems. *Computer, 21,* 70–80.

Marcuse, Herbert. (1964). *One-dimensional man.* Boston: Beacon Press.

Marvin, Carolyn. (1988). *When old technologies were new: Thinking about electric communication in the late nineteenth century.* New York: Oxford University Press.

Marx, Karl. (1988). Introduction to a critique of political economy. In C.J. Arthur (Ed.), *The German ideology* (pp. 124–152). New York: International Publishers.

Massumi, Brian. (1992). *A user's guide to capitalism and schizophrenia: Deviations from Deleuze and Guattari.* Cambridge, MA: Swerve/MIT Press.

Mathes, J.C. & Stevenson, Dwight W. (1976). *Designing technical reports: Writing for audiences in organizations.* New York: MacMillan.

Mathes, J.C., & Stevenson, Dwight W. (1991). *Designing technical reports: Writing for audiences in organizations* (2nd ed.). New York: Macmillan.

McAleese, Ray. (1989). Navigation and browsing in hypertext. In Ray McAleese (Ed.), *Hypertext: Theory into practice* (pp. 6–44). Norwood, NJ: Ablex.

McCabe, C. (1992). Preface. In F. Jameson, *The geopolitical aesthetic: Cinema and space in the world system* (pp. ix–xvi). Bloomington: Indiana University Press.

McDaid, John. (1991a). "Breaking frames: Hyper-mass media. In Emily Berk & Joseph Devlin (Eds.), *The hypertext/hypermedia handbook,* (pp. 445–457). New York: McGraw-Hill.

McDaid, John. (1991b). Hypermedia as an ecological context for writing. In Gail E. Hawisher & Cynthia L. Selfe (Eds.), *Evolving perspectives on computers and composition studies: Questions for the 1990s* (pp. 203–223). Urbana, IL: National Council of Teachers of English.

McDaid, John. (1993). UNCLE BUDDY'S PHANTOM FUNHOUSE [computer software]. Cambridge, MA: Eastgate.

McKenzie, Alan T. (1993). The academic online. In George Landow & Paul Delany (Eds.), *The digital word* (pp. 201–216). Cambridge, MA: MIT Press.

McKnight, Cliff, Dillon, Andrew & Richardson, John. (1990). A comparison of linear and hypertext formats in information retrieval. In Ray McAleese & Catherine Green (Eds.), *Hypertext: State of the art* (pp. 10–19). Oxford: Intellect.

McLuhan, Marshall. (1964). *Understanding media: The extensions of man* (2nd ed.). New York: Signet.

McMath, Charles F., Tamaru, Robert S., & Rada, Roy. (1989). A graphical thesaurus-based information retrieval system. *International Journal of Man-Machine Studies, 31,* 121–47.

Meggs, Phillip B. (1991). Post war, post mortem: Made for television. *Print, XLV(V),* 54–63.

Meyrowitz, Norman. (1991). Hypertext—Does it cure cholesterol, too? In J. M. Nyce & P. Kahn (Eds.), *From memex to hypertext: Vannevar Bush and the mind machine* (pp. 287–318). Boston: Academic Press.

MICROSOFT WORD FOR THE MACINTOSH (version 5.1) [computer software]. (1992). Seattle, WA: Microsoft.

Miller, Carolyn R. (1979). A humanistic rationale for technical writing. *College English,40,* 610–617.

Miller, Carolyn R., & Selzer, Jack. (1985). Special topics of argument in engineering reports. In Lee Odell & Dixie Goswami (Eds.), *Writing in nonacademic settings* (pp. 309–342). New York: Guilford.

Monk, Andrew F., Walsh, Paul & Dix, Alan J. (1988). A comparison of hypertext, scrolling and folding as mechanisms for program browsing. In D.M. Jones & R. Winder (Eds.), *People and computers IV* (pp. 421–435). Cambridge, UK: Cambridge University Press.

Mosco, Vincent. (1988). Introduction: Information in the pay-per society. In Vincent Mosco & Janet Wasko (Eds.), *The political economy of information* (pp. 3–26). Madison: University of Wisconsin Press.

Mouffe, Chantal. (1979). Hegemony and ideology in Gramsci. In Chantal Mouffe (Ed.), *Gramsci and marxist theory* (pp. 168–204). London: Routledge.

Moulthrop, Stuart. (1989a). Hypertext and "the hyperreal." *Hypertext '89 proceedings* (pp. 259–267). New York: Association for Computing Machinery.

Moulthrop, Stuart. (1989b). In the zones: Hypertext and the politics of interpretation. *Writing on the Edge, 1(1),* 18–27.

Moulthrop, Stuart. (1990). Reading from the map: Metonymy and metaphor in the fiction of FORKING PATHS. In Paul Delany & George P. Landow (Eds.), *Hypermedia and literary studies* (pp. 119–132). Cambridge, MA: MIT Press.

Moulthrop, Stuart. (1991). VICTORY GARDEN [computer software]. Cambridge, MA: Eastgate.

Moulthrop, Stuart. (1993, December). *No war machine.* Paper presented at the Modern Language Association Conference, New York.

Moulthrop, Stuart & Borges, Jorge L. (1987). FORKING PATHS [Unpublished computer software].

Moulthrop, Stuart & Kaplan, Nancy. (1994). They became what they beheld: The futility of resistance in the space of electronic writing. In Cynthia L. Selfe & Susan Hilligoss (Eds.), *Literacy and computers: The complications of teaching and learning with technology* (pp. 220–237). New York: Modern Language Association.

Mulvihill, Peggy. (1992). STORYSPACE: A deep and welcomed experience. *Computers and Composition, 10(1),* 127–134.

Murray, Donald M. (1984). Teach writing as a process, not a product. In Richard L. Graves (Ed.), *Rhetoric and composition: A sourcebook for teachers and writers* (2nd ed., pp. 89–92. Upper Montclair, NJ: Boynton/Cook. (Original work published 1972)

Myers, Greg. (1991). Stories and styles in two molecular biology review articles. In Charles Bazerman & James Paradis (Eds.), *Textual dynamics of the professions: Historical and contemporary studies of writing in professional communities* (pp. 45–75). Madison: University of Wisconsin Press.

National Commission on Libraries and Information Science. (1982). *Public sector/Private sector interaction in providing information services.* Washington, U.S.: Government Printing Office.

Nelson, Theodor H. (1982). A new home for the mind. *Datamation, 28,* 168–80.

Nelson, Theodor H. (1987a). *Computer lib/Dream machines* (2nd ed.). Redmond, WA: Microsoft Press. (Original work published 1974)

Nelson, Theodor H. (1987b). *Literary machines.* Palo Alto, CA: Project Xanadu.

Nicol, Margaret W., & Darnowski, Christina M. (1989, August). Online access to SEC filings. *Database,* 28–33.

Norman, Donald A. (1988). *The design of everyday things.* New York: Doubleday.

Odell, Lee & Goswami, Dixie. (Eds.). (1985). *Writing in nonacademic settings.* New York: Guilford.

Ohmann, Richard. (1985). Literacy, technology, and monopoly capitalism. *College English, 47,* 675–689.

Ohmann, Richard. (1990). Graduate students, professionals, intellectuals. *College English, 52,* 247–257.

O'Malley, Penelope G. (1993). Information delivery systems: The future is here. *Technical Communication, 40*(4), 619–628.

Ong, Walter J. (1982). *Orality and literacy: The technologizing of the word.* London: Methuen.

PAGEMAKER. (1994). [computer software]. Seattle, WA: Aldus.

Paine, Charles. (1989). Relativism, radical pedagogy, and the ideology of paralysis. *College English, 51,* 557–580.

Paradis, James. (1991). Text and action: The operator's manual in context and in court. In C Bazerman & J. Paradis (Eds.), *Textual dynamics of the professions: Historical and contemporary studies of writing in professional communities* (pp. 256–278). Madison: University of Wisconsin Press.

Paradis, James, Dobrin, David & Miller, Richard. (1985). Writing at Exxon ITD. In Lee Odell & Dixie Goswami (Eds.), *Writing in nonacademic settings* (pp. 281–307). New York: Guilford.

Perelman, C. & Olbrechts-Tyteca, L. (1969). *The new rhetoric: A treatise on argumentation* (John Wilkinson & Purcell Weaver, Trans.). South Bend, IN: University of Notre Dame Press.

Phelps, Louise W. (1988). *Composition as a human science: Contributions to the self-understanding of a discipline.* New York: Oxford University Press.

Phelps, Louise W. (1991). Practical wisdom and the geography of knowledge in composition. *College English, 53,* 863–885.

Porter, James E. (1986). Intertextuality and the discourse community. *Rhetoric Review, 5*(1), 34–47.

Poster, Mark. (1990). *The mode of information: Poststructuralism and social context.* Chicago: University of Chicago Press.

Postman, Neil. (1992). *Technopoly: The surrender of culture to technology.* New York: Knopf.

Pratt, Mary L. (1987). Linguistic utopias. In Nigel Fabb (Ed.), *The linguistics of writing* (pp. 48–66). Manchester, UK: Manchester University Press.

Pratt, Mary L. (1991). Arts of the contact zone. *Profession, 91* 33–40.

Pratt, Mary L. (1992). *Imperial eyes: Travel writing and transculturation.* London: Routledge.

Price, Jonathan & Korman, Henry. (1993). *How to communicate technical information: A handbook of software and hardware documentation.* Redwood City, CA: Benjamin/Cummings.

Jef. (1987). The hype in hypertext: A critique. *Hypertext '87 papers* 325–330). New York: Association for Computing Machinery.

L., & Ellis, Clarence A. (1991). rIBIS: A real-time group hypertext system. In Saul Greenburg (Ed.), *Computer-supported cooperative work and groupware* (pp. 223–241). San Diego, CA: Harcourt Brace Jovanovich.

Robins, Kevin & Webster, Frank. (1988). Cybernetic capitalism: Information, technology, and everyday life. In Vincent Mosco & Janet Wasko (Eds.), *The political economy of information* (pp. 44–75). Madison: University of Wisconsin Press.

Robinson, Peter M.W. (1993). Redefining critical editions. In George Landow & Paul Delany (Eds.), *The digital word* (pp. 271–291). Cambridge, MA: MIT Press.

Ronell, Avital. (1989). *The telephone book: Technology, schizophrenia, electric speech.* Lincoln: University of Nebraska Press.

Rosello, Mireille. (1994). The screener's maps: Michel de Certeau's "Wandersmänner" and Paul Auster's Hypertextual Detective." In George P. Landow (Ed.), *Hyper/text/theory* (pp. 121–158). Baltimore: John Hopkins University Press.

Rosenberg, Martin. (1992). Contingency, liberation, and the seduction of geometry: Hypertext as an avant-garde medium. In Richard Gess (Ed.), *After the book: Writing literature, writing technology* [Special issue]. *Perforations, 3.*

Rubens, Philip. (1991). Reading and employing technical information in hypertext. *Technical Communication, 38,* 36–40.

Ruszkiewicz, John. (1992). Counterstatement. *College Composition and Communication, 43,* 520–521.

Saussure, Ferdinand de. (1959). *Course in general linguistics* (Charles Bally, Albert Sechehaye, & Albert Riedlinger, Eds.; W. Baskin, Trans.). New York: McGraw-Hill.

Schilb, John. (1988). Ideology and composition scholarship. *Journal of Advanced Composition, 8,* 22–29.

Schilb, John. (1991). Cultural studies, postmodernism, and composition. In Patricia Harkin & John Schilb (Eds.), *Contending with words: Composition and rhetoric in a postmodern age* (pp. 173–188). New York: Modern Language Association.

Schiller, Dan. (1988). How to think about information. In Vincent Mosco & Janet Wasko (Eds.), *The political economy of information* (pp. 27–43). Madison: University of Wisconsin Press.

Schiller, Herbert I. & Schiller, Anita R. (1988). Libraries, public access to information, and commerce. In Vincent Mosco & Janet Wasko (Eds.), *The political economy of information* (pp. 146–166). Madison: University of Wisconsin Press.

Scholes, Robert. (1985). *Textual power: Literary theory and the teaching of English.* New Haven, CT: Yale University Press.

Scholes, Robert. (1989). *Protocols of reading.* New Haven, CT: Yale University Press.

Searle, John R. (1977). Reiterating the differences: A reply to Derrida." *Glyph, 1,* 198–208.

Selber, Stuart A. (1995b). Metaphorical perspectives on hypertext. *IEEE Transactions on Professional Communication, 38*(2), 59–67.

Selber, Stuart, McGavin, Dan, Klein, William, & Johnson-Eilola, Johndan. (1995). Issues in hypertext-supported collaborative writing. In A. Duin & C. Hansen (Eds.), *Multidisciplinary research in workplace writing: Challenging the boundaries* (pp. 257–280). Hillsdale, NJ: Erlbaum.

Selfe, Cynthia L. (1992, May). *Politicizing and inhabiting virtual landscapes as discursive spaces.* Paper presented at the Eighth Computers and Writing Conference, Indianapolis, IN.

Selfe, Cynthia L., & Eilola, J. Daniel, Jr. (1988). The tie that binds: Building discourse communities and group cohesion through computer-based conferences. *Collegiate Microcomputer, VI,* 339–348.

Selfe, Cynthia L., & Selfe, Richard J. (1994). The politics of the interface: Power and its exercise in electronic contact zones. *College Composition and Communication, 45,* 480–504.

Selfe, Richard, Selber, Stuart, McGavin, Dan, Johnson-Eilola, Johndan, & Brown, Carol (1992). Online help: Exploring static information or constructing personal and collaborative solutions using hypertext. *SIGDOC '92 proceedings* (pp. 97–102). New York: Association for Computing Machinery.

Shackelford, Douglas E. (1991). *Requirements document for the UNC distributed graph service* (Textlab/Collaboratory Report TR91-051). Chapel Hill: University of North Carolina at Chapel Hill.

Shackelford, Douglas E., Smith, John B., & Smith, F. Donelson. (1993). *The architecture and design of a distributed hypermedia system* (Textlab/Collaboratory Report TR93-013). Chapel Hill: University of North Carolina at Chapel Hill.

Shafer, Dan. (1988). *HyperTalk programming.* Indianapolis, IN: Hayden Books.

Shaiken, Harley. (1986). *Work transformed: Automation and labor in the computer age.* Lexington, MA: Lexington Books.

Shannon, Claude. E., & Weaver, Warren. (1949). *The mathematical theory of communication.* Urbana: University of Illinois Press.

Shor, Ira. (1985). *Critical teaching and everyday life.* Chicago: The University of Chicago Press.

Slack, Jennifer D. (1984). *Communication technologies and society: Conceptions of causality and the politics of technological intervention.* Norwood, NJ: Ablex.

Slack, Jennifer D. (1989). Contextualizing technology. In Lawrence Grossberg, Brenda Dervin, Barbara O'Keefe, & Ellen Wartela (Eds.), *Rethinking communication: Vol. 4. Paradigm exemplars* (pp. 329–345). Newbury Park, CA: Sage.

Slack, Jennifer D. (1992). [Review of the book *The mode of information*]. *Communication Theory, 2,* 173–176.

Slack, Jennifer D., Miller, David J., & Doak, Jeffrey. (1993). The technical communicator as author: Meaning, power, authority. *Journal of Business and Technical Communication, 7*(1), 12–36.

Slatin, John M. (1988). Hypertext and the teaching of writing. In Edward Barrett (Ed.), *Text, context, and hypertext: Writing with and for the computer* (pp. 111–119). Cambridge, MA: MIT Press.

Slatin, John M. (1990). Reading hypertext: Order and coherence in a new medium. *College English, 52,* 870–883.

Smith, Catherine F. (1991). Reconceiving hypertext. In Gail E. Hawisher & Cynthia L. Selfe (Eds.), *Evolving perspectives on computers and composition studies: Questions for the 1990s* (pp. 224–252). Urbana, IL: National Council of Teachers of English.

Smith, Catherine F. (1994). Hypertextual thinking. In Cynthia L. Selfe & Susan Hilligoss (Eds.), *Literacy and computers: The complications of teaching and learning with technology* (pp. 264–281). New York: Modern Language Association.

Smith, John B., & Smith, F. Donelson. (1991). ABC: A hypermedia system for artifact-based collaborations. *Hypertext '91* (pp. 179–192). New York: Association for Computing Machinery.

Smith, John B., Weiss, Stephen F., & Ferguson, Gordon J. (1987). *A hypertext writing environment and its cognitive basis* (Rep. No. TR87-033). Chapel Hill: University of North Carolina at Chapel Hill.

Smith, John B., Weiss, Stephen F., Ferguson, Gordon J., Bolter, Jay D., Lansman, Marcy & Beard, David V. (1986). *WE: A writing environment for professionals* (Rep. No. TR86-025). Chapel Hill: University of North Carolina at Chapel Hill.

Smith, Neil. (1993). Homeless/global: Scaling places. In Jon Bird, Barry Curtis, Tim Putnam, Gworge Robertson, & Lisa Tickner (Eds.), *Mapping the futures: Local cultures, global change* (pp. 87–119). London: Routledge.

Soja, Edward. (1989). *Postmodern geographies: The reassertion of space in critical social theory.* London: Verso.

Spilka, Rachel. (1989). Interacting with multiple readers: A significant component of document design in corporate environments. *Technical Communication, 36,* 368–372.

Spivak, Gayatri C. (1976). Translator's preface. In Jacques Derrida, *Of grammatology* (Gayatri C. Spivak, Trans.; pp. ix–xc). (Original work published 1967)

Sproull, Lee & Kiesler, Sara. (1991). *Connections: New ways of working in the networked organization.* Cambridge, MA: MIT Press.

Stenger, Nicole. (1991). Mind is a leaking rainbow. In Michael Benedikt (Ed.), *Cyberspace: First steps* (pp. 49–58). Cambridge, MA: MIT Press.

STORYSPACE for the Macintosh (version 1.12) [computer software]. (1991). Cambridge, MA: Eastgate.

Sudol, Ronald A. (1991). The accumulative rhetoric of word processing. *College English, 53,* 920–932.

Sullivan, Dale. (1990). Political-ethical implications of defining technical communication as a practice. *Journal of Advanced Composition, 10,* 375–386.

Sullivan, Patricia. (1991a). Collaboration between organizations: Contributions an outsider can make to negotiation and cooperation during composition. *Technical Communication, 38,* 485–492.

Sullivan, Patricia. (1991b). Taking control of the page: Electronic writing and word-publishing. In Gail E. Hawisher & Cynthia L. Selfe (Eds.), *Evolving perspectives on computers and composition studies: Questions for the 1990s* (pp. 43–64). Urbana, IL: National Council of Teachers of English.

Summit, R. (1986). *Information today.* Learned Information, Inc.

Swales, John M. (1990). *Genre analysis: English in academic and research settings* New York: Cambridge University Press.

Swearingen, C. Jan. (1990). Bloomsday: Doomsday book for literacy. In Andrea Lunsford, Helene Moglen, & James Slevin (Eds.), *The right to literacy* (pp 216–224). New York: Modern Language Association.

Takayoshi, Pamela. (1994). Building new networks from old: Women's experiences with electronic communications. *Computers and Composition, 11*(1), 21–36.

Taylor, Mark C., & Saarinen, Esa. (1994). *Imagologies: Media philosophy*. New York: Routledge.

Thompson, Diane F. (1988). Interactive networking: Creating bridges between speech, writing, and composition. *Computers and Composition, 5*(3), 17–27.

Tompkins, Jane. (1988). A short course in poststructuralism. *College English, 50,* 733–747.

Tompkins, Jane. (1990). Pedagogy of the distressed. *College English, 52,* 653–660.

Trigg, Randall H., Suchman, Lucy A. & Halasz, Frank G. (1986). Supporting collaboration in NOTECARDS. In *Proceedings of the conference on computer supported cooperative work.* (pp. 1–10). New York: Association for Computing Machinery.

Trimbur, John. (1989). Consensus and difference in collaborative learning. *College English, 51,* 602–616.

Trimbur, John & Braun, Lundy A. (1992). Laboratory life and the determination of authorship. In Janis Forman (Ed.), *New visions of collaborative writing* (pp. 19–36). Portsmouth, NH: Boynton/Cook.

Tuman, Myron C. (Ed.). (1992a). *Literacy online: The promise (and peril) of reading and writing with computers.* Pittsburgh, PA: University of Pittsburgh Press.

Tuman, Myron C. (1992b). [Review of the book *Writing space.*] *College Composition and Communication, 43,* 261–263.

Tuman, Myron (1992c). *Word perfect: Literacy in the computer age.* Pittsburgh, PA: University of Pittsburgh Press.

Turkle, Sherry & Papert, Seymour. (1990). Epistemological pluralism: Styles and voices within the computer culture. *Signs: Journal of Women in Culture and Society, 16*(11), 128–157.

Ulmer, Gred. (1992). Grammatology (in the stacks of) hypermedia: A simulation. In Myron Tuman (Ed.), *Literacy online: The promise (and peril) of reading and writing with computers* (pp. 139–158). Pittsburgh, PA: University of Pittsburgh Press.

vanLehn, Kurt. (1985). *Theory reform caused by an argumentation tool.* (Rep. No. ISL-11.) Palo Alto, CA: Xerox PARC.

Virbel, Jacques. (1993). Reading and managing texts on the bibliothèque de France station. In George Landow & Paul Delany (Eds.), *The digital word* (pp. 31–51). Cambridge, MA: MIT Press.

Virilio, Paul. (1986). *Speed and politics: An essay on dromology* (Mark Polizzotti, Trans.). New York: Semiotext(e).

Virilio, Paul. (1993). The third interval: A critical transition. In Verena A. Conley (Ed.), *Rethinking technologies* (pp. 3–12). Minneapolis: University of Minnesota Press.

Virilio, Paul & Lotringer, Sylvère. (1983). *Pure war* (Mark Polizzotti, Trans.). New York: Semiotext(e).

Walker, Janet H. (1987). Document examiner: Delivery interface for hypertext documents. *Hypertext '87 papers* (pp. 307–323). New York: Association for Computing Machinery.

Welch, Kathleen E. (1987). Ideology and freshman textbook production: The place of theory in writing pedagogy. *College Composition and Communication, 38,* 269–282.

Raymond. (1983). *Keywords: A vocabulary of culture and society* (2nd ed.). York: Oxford University Press.

ngdon. (1977). *Autonomous technology: Technics-out-of-control as a theme in political thought.* Cambridge, MA: MIT Press.

Winner, Langdon. (1986). *The whale and the reactor: A search for limits in an age of high technology.* Chicago: University of Chicago Press.

Winograd, Terry & Flores, Fernando. (1987). *Understanding computers and cognition: A new foundation for design.* Reading, MA: Addison-Wesley.

Wood, Denis. (1992). *The power of maps.* New York: Guilford.

Woolever, Kristin R. & Loeb, Helen M. (1994). *Writing for the computer industry.* Englewood Cliffs, NJ: Prentice-Hall.

WORDPERFECT FOR THE POWER MACINTOSH (Version 3.0a) [computer software]. (1994). Orem, UT: WordPerfect Corporation.

Wright, Patricia. (1991). Cognitive overheads and prostheses: Some issues in evaluating hypertexts. *Hypertext '91 Proceedings* (pp. 1–12). New York: Association for Computing Machinery.

Wright, Patricia & Lickorish, Ann. (1990). An empirical comparison of two navigation systems for two hypertexts. In Ray McAleese & Catherine Green (Eds.), *Hypertext: State of the art* (pp. 85–93). Oxford: Intellect.

Yankelovich, Nicol, Haan, Bernard J., Meyrowitz, Norman K., & Drucker, Steven M. (1988). INTERMEDIA: The concept and construction of a seamless information environment. *Computer, 21*(1), 81–96.

Yates, Francis. (1966). *The art of memory.* Chicago: University of Chicago Press.

Zuboff, Shoshana. (1988). *In the age of the smart machine: The future of work and power.* New York: Basic Books.

Author Index

A

Aaron, J. E. 247
Ackerman, J. 97, 98, *244*
Allen, J. 69n, *243*
Althusser, L. 43, *243*
Amato, J. 103, 112, 122, *243*
Anderson, K. T. 22, 144, *244*
Anderson, P. V. 235, *243*
Anzaldúa, G. 37, 42, *243*
Aronowitz, S. 126, *243*

B

Bader, G. 22, 144, *244*
Bakhtin, M. M. 193, *243*
Barnett, G. A. 72n, *243*
Barthes, R. 88n, 144, 238, *243*
Bartholomae, D. 98, *243*
Baudrillard, J. 3, 22, 119n, 136, 211, 236, 237, *243*, *244*
Bazerman, C. 22, 97, 113, *244*
Beard, D. V. 101, *257*
Beck, J. R. 144, *244*
Beeman, W. O. 22, 144, *244*
Begeman, M. 190, 215, *245*
Begoray, J. A. 71, 79, *244*
Belsey, C. 22, 136, 148, 153, 205, 238, *244*
Benedikt, M. 122, *244*
Berkenkotter, C. 22, 97, 98, 113, *244*
Berlin, J. A. 17, 141, 142, 147, 177, 185, *244*
Bialostosky, D. H. 22, 205, *244*
Bizzell, P. 112, *244*
Bolter, J. D. 8n, 30, 73, 74n, 88n, 90, 101, 109, 110, 111, 136, 142, 143, 145n, 147, 149, 168, 213, *244*, *257*
Borges, J. L. 116, 123, 163, 169n, *244*, *253*
Brantlinger, P. 154, 177, 178, 180n, 240, *244*
Braun, L. A. 230, *258*

Braverman, H. 78, *244*
Brooke, R. 42, 227, *244*
Brown, C. 230, 233, *256*
Bruffee, K. A. 22, 57, *244*
Burton, R. 56, 118, 119, *245*
Bush, V. 30, 61, 103, 120, 133, 190, *245*

C

Capossela, T. L. 101, *245*
Charney, D. 69, 71, *245*
Clark, R. 126, *249*
Clifford, J. 177, *245*
Cohen, R. 57, *245*
Conklin, J. 79, 190, 215, *245*
Connor, S. 33, *245*
Connors, R. J. 62, *245*
Cook, W. W. 42, *245*
Cooper, M. M. 15, 22, 97, 192, 226n, *245*
Coover, R. 22, 136, *245*
Corbett, E. P. J. 104, 120, *245*
Crane, G. 93, *245*
Crary, K. 165, *245*

D

Darnowski, C. M. 108n, *254*
Dasenbrock, R. W. 142, 147, 157n, 178, *245*
de Certeau, M. 135, 140, 149, 160, 186, *245*
Delaney, P. 30, 88n, 101, 136, 142, 143, 144, 145, 146, 153, 154, 158n, *246*, *251*
Deleuze, G. 49, 56, 70n, 90, 140, 160, 178, 186, 211, 224, 225, *246*
Demac, D. A. 129, 130, *246*
Derrida, J. 13, 22, 105, 148, 156, 158, 160, 178, 204, *246*
Dillon, A. 72, *253*
Dix, A. J. 71, 72, *253*
Doak, J. 64, 69n, 72, 78, 227, *257*
Dobrin, D. 51, *254*
Dobrin, D. N. 51, 63n, 172, *246*

Subject Index

About the Author

Johndan Johnson-Eilola teaches in the undergraduate professional writing major and the graduate rhetoric and composition program at Purdue University. His work on computers and literacy has appeared in *Computers and Composition, Collegiate Microcomputer, The Journal of Advanced Composition, Writing on the Edge, The IEEE Transactions on Professional Communication,* and *Technical Communication,* as well as in several edited collections on composition and technical communication.